THE ULTIMATE

EVERYTHING KIDS'

ACTIVITY BOOK

THE ULTIMATE

EVERYTHING KIDS'

ACTIVITY BOOK

Stretch your brain with fun facts and puzzling activities

Beth L. Blair, Jennifer Ericsson,
Tom Robinson, and Brian Thorton

Avon, Massachusetts

An Everything® Series Book.
Everything® and everything.com® are registered trademarks of F+W Media, Inc.

Contains materials adopted and abridged from *The Everything Kids' States Book*, by Brian Thornton,
© 1997, F+W Media; *The Everything Kids' Word Search Puzzle and Activity Book,* by Beth L. Blair
and Jennifer Ericsson, © 2008, F+W Media; and *The Everything Kids' Science Experiments Book,*
by Tom Robinson, © 2001, F+W Media.

Published by Adams Media, an F+W Media Company
57 Littlefield Street, Avon, MA 02322. U.S.A.
www.adamsmedia.com

ISBN-10: 1-60550-099-2
ISBN-13: 978-1-60550-099-7

Printed in the United States of America.

J   I   H   G   F   E   D   C   B   A

This publication is designed to provide accurate and authoritative information with regard to the subject matter covered. It is sold with the understanding that the publisher is not engaged in rendering legal, accounting, or other professional advice. If legal advice or other expert assistance is required, the services of a competent professional person should be sought.
—From a *Declaration of Principles* jointly adopted by a Committee of the American Bar Association and a Committee of Publishers and Associations

Many of the designations used by manufacturers and sellers to distinguish their products are claimed as trademarks. When those designations appear in this book and Adams Media was aware of a trademark claim, the designations have been printed with initial capital letters.

Cover illustrations by Dana Regan.
Interior illustrations by Kurt Dolber.
Puzzles by Beth L. Blair.

This book is available at quantity discounts for bulk purchases.
For information, please call 1-800-289-0963.

Contents

Introduction

Ready to challenge the world around you? You've come to the right spot!

The Ultimate Everything Kids' Activity Book contains everything you need to stump your sister, puzzle your parents, and train your teacher! Featuring puzzle word searches, fascinating facts about your state (and the other 49 in America!), and fun science experiments, this book will strain your brain—and keep you entertained!

In the first section, you'll become a word sleuth with wacky word searches. You'll find dozens of hidden-word puzzles, plus clever clues that lead to even more challenges. These puzzles are sure to flex your mental muscles. Hunting for hidden treasure is fun!

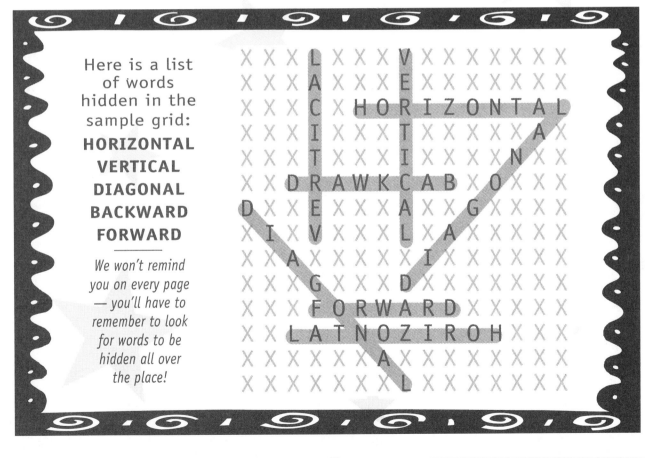

Here is a list of words hidden in the sample grid:

HORIZONTAL
VERTICAL
DIAGONAL
BACKWARD
FORWARD

We won't remind you on every page — you'll have to remember to look for words to be hidden all over the place!

In Part 2, you'll discover the history and landmarks of the 50 states. Filled with fascinating history, geography, and trivia, this information-packed section makes leaning about all 50 states fun. Bursting with 30 puzzles like dot-to-dots, mazes, word searches, rebus puzzles, riddles, and more, you'll take an unforgettable journey across the U.S. of A.!

In Part 3, science has never been so easy—or so much fun! All you need to do is gather a few household items and you can recreate dozens of mind-blowing, kid-tested science experiments. You'll expand your scientific horizons—from biology to chemistry to physics to outer space.

So get your pencil—and your brain—ready. You're going to need both!

Part 1

Wacky Word Searches

Chapter 1

Around the House

Dynamic Duos

There are some foods that we always seem to eat together!

```
X M M I L K K H A M J S
S S T K T X O Q K W X T
P E A N U T B U T T E R
A W J Q D X J R G S J A
G J Q O G W T K E G J W
H E G G S T J E T A G B
E S J T G Q H K Q P D E
T X W B A C A N G P G R
T J K Q G K W X G L X R
I W X L E T T U C E G I
R K J W J Q T Q T S J E
S F R E N C H F R I E S
```

Find one edible item in the upper word search, and then figure out its "companion" food in the lower word search. On the next page, you'll find spaces to write in the mystery foods.

```
X C O O K I E S J J G C
S K R Y J K G H E Y K R
R M E A T B A L L S U E
E G J H C Q E J L Q K A
G H J G H K S K Y H J M
R J H Y H E E H U K S M
U Q B U T T E R J G E G
B Q G Y H C H H S I G H
M A Q K G H C H Q K N Y
A K C K J U H Y K G A H
H Y H O H P H J Y H R Y
G H Q G N K O T A M O T
```

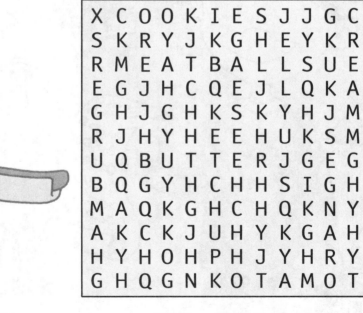

E _ _ _ _ & B _ _ _ _ _

M _ _ _ _ & C _ _ _ _ _ _ _

B _ _ _ _ _ & B _ _ _ _ _ _

A _ _ _ _ _ _ & O _ _ _ _ _ _

P _ _ _ _ _ _ _ _ _ _ & J _ _ _ _ _

S _ _ _ _ _ _ _ _ _ _ & M _ _ _ _ _ _ _ _ _

C _ _ _ _ _ _ & C _ _ _ _ _ _ _

S _ _ _ _ _ _ _ _ _ _ _ _ _ & _ _ _ _ _

L _ _ _ _ _ _ _ & _ _ _ _ _ _

H _ _ _ & C _ _ _ _ _ _

F _ _ _ _ _ _ _ _ _ _ & K _ _ _ _ _ _

H _ _ _ _ _ _ _ _ & H _ _ _ _ _ _ _ _ _

Extra Help: We left you the first letter of each pair and a few pictures to get you started.

Lotsa Laundry

Mom threw a load of white laundry into the washing machine. Oh no! One piece of red clothing got mixed in by mistake. It will turn everything pink! Use a pink marker to highlight all the clothes in the washing machine.

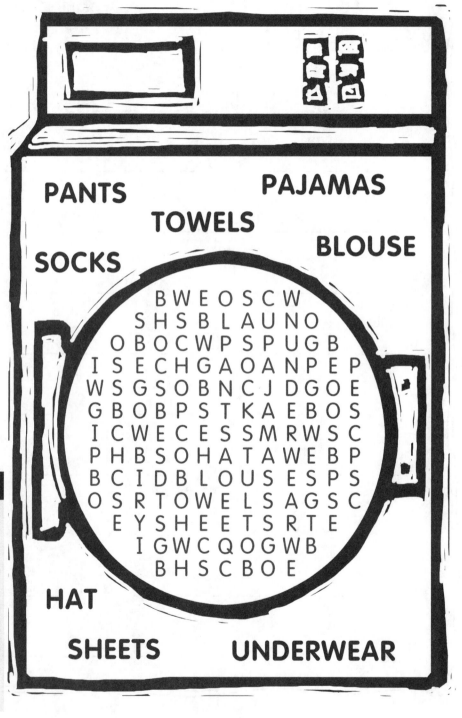

PANTS

PAJAMAS

TOWELS

SOCKS

BLOUSE

```
B W E O S C W
S H S B L A U N O
O B O C W P S P U G B
I S E C H G A O A N P E P
W S G S O B N C J D G O E
G B O B P S T K A E B O S
I C W E C E S S M R W S C
P H B S O H A T A W E B P
B C I D B L O U S E S P S
O S R T O W E L S A G S C
E Y S H E E T S R T E
I G W C Q O G W B
B H S C B O E
```

HAT

SHEETS

UNDERWEAR

Extra Fun:

Now use the marker to highlight the letters in the word L-A-U-N-D-R-Y. Once you have finished, look at the pattern you have made. You will see which piece of clothing turned the laundry pink!

Cutting the Cake

The birthday girl has to cut pieces of cake for all of her guests. Look carefully inside the cake for the twelve people on the list who came to celebrate!

MOTHER UNCLE
FATHER GRANDMA
SISTER GRANDPA
BROTHER FRIEND
COUSIN NEIGHBOR
AUNT CLASSMATE

Added Fun: The letters B-I-R-T-H-D-A-Y G-I-R-L form a small rectangle somewhere in the cake— the birthday girl's name will be inside of it!

C L A S S M A T E O F U T F
E F T S R O B H G I E N O T
G R A N D M A M J F S C F U
R I E S O F U E O J S L A F
A E U H J E O F K T U E T S
N N E O T J B I R T H J H E
D D T F U O L A M Y D E E T
P S I S T E R I G Y A J R O
A U N T F S S B E O F E U F
N I S U O C U E

The birthday girl's name is:

Trail of Toys

The kids in this house sure need to pick up their stuff! First, look at the picture and circle eleven things the kids have been playing with. Then highlight the names of those items in the letter grid. Look carefully: Answers can go backwards and diagonally too!

```
L J A E T A K S E C I
L A T E D D Y B E A R
A C R J U R M A P R O
B K U P E U S L L O D
E S C E A M K L N D B
S O K I T E S O K A O
A I T E N N I O O S X
B N C R A Y O N S B B
```

Bathroom Humor

Find all the items listed below in the grid. Read the remaining letters from left to right and top to bottom to find a funny bathroom joke!

BATHTUB
SHOWER
MIRROR
TOILET
SINK
THERMOMETER
TOOTHBRUSH
LAUNDRY
    BASKET
TISSUES
TOOTHPASTE
WATER
HAIRBRUSH
SOAP
SHAMPOO
COMB
CUP
TOWELS
TOYS
FLOSS
BATHMAT
MEDICINE
    CABINET

```
L W T H O S R O R R I M
A H O T O I L E T T O E
U S Y A P N L W A H H D
N U S Y M K S S T E A I
D R E A L S T H R I C
R B U T H T A B P M R I
Y H S E S S O A A O B N
B T H S P I O T N M R E
A O O T O S H H E E U C
S O W B C L A M T T S A
K T E H U E F A R E H B
E B R O P W A T E R O I
T M M ? R O O B B E R N
D U T O O T H P A S T E
C K Y ! C S E U S S I T
```

Perfect Pets

Eight words are listed below. These are NOT the words you will be looking for in the puzzle. You must think of a rhyming word for each one that might make a perfect pet—then look for these animals in the letter grid!

Extra Fun: After you have found all the pets, read the remaining letters from left to right and top to bottom. You will find the name of one pet for which there is no rhyme!

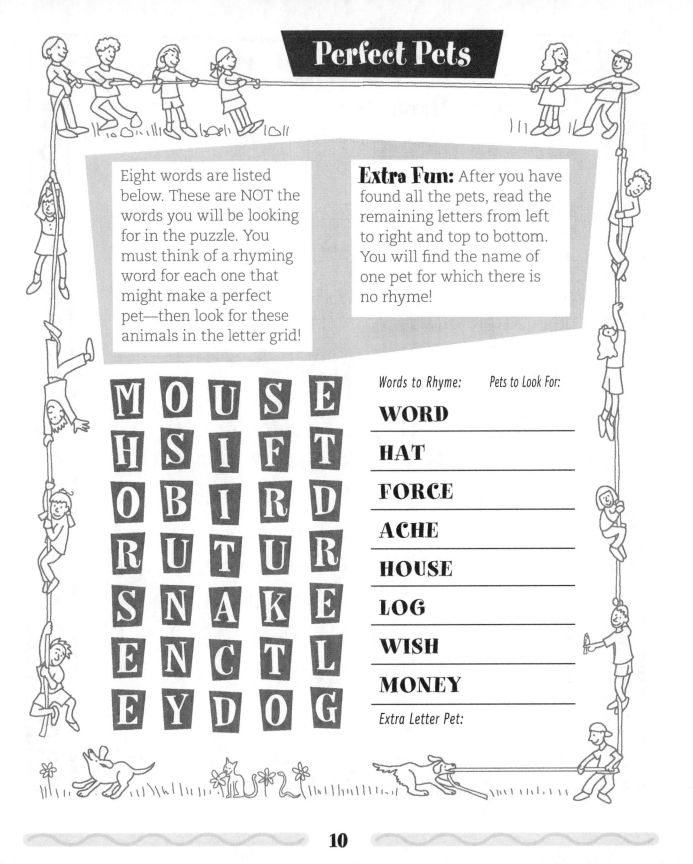

M	O	U	S	E
H	S	I	F	T
O	B	I	R	D
R	U	T	U	R
S	N	A	K	E
E	N	C	T	L
E	Y	D	O	G

Words to Rhyme: *Pets to Look For:*

WORD _____

HAT _____

FORCE _____

ACHE _____

HOUSE _____

LOG _____

WISH _____

MONEY _____

Extra Letter Pet:

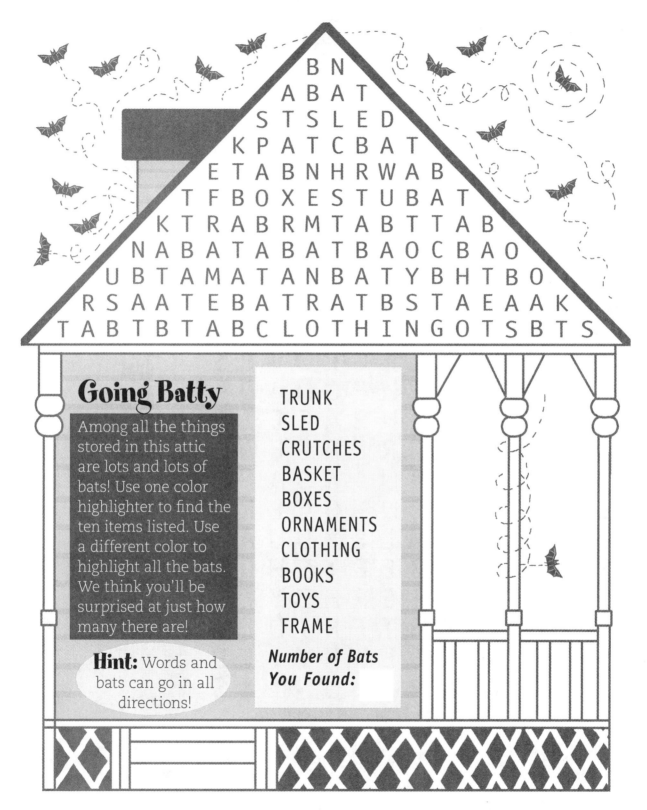

B N
A B A T
S T S L E D
K P A T C B A T
E T A B N H R W A B
T F B O X E S T U B A T
K T R A B R M T A B T T A B
N A B A T A B A T B A O C B A O
U B T A M A T A N B A T Y B H T B O
R S A A T E B A T R A T B S T A E A A K
T A B T B T A B C L O T H I N G O T S B T S

Going Batty

Among all the things stored in this attic are lots and lots of bats! Use one color highlighter to find the ten items listed. Use a different color to highlight all the bats. We think you'll be surprised at just how many there are!

Hint: Words and bats can go in all directions!

TRUNK
SLED
CRUTCHES
BASKET
BOXES
ORNAMENTS
CLOTHING
BOOKS
TOYS
FRAME

Number of Bats You Found:

BROOM PAIL RAG

TRASH BAG

SPONGE

RUBBER GLOVES

More Chores!

Helping around the house seems like endless work. Just when you finish one task, there is something else to do—sort of like this puzzle! You must find a string of words one right after the other. The trick is that the last letter of each word is the first letter of the next one!

We left you the first word of the string, and a jumbled list of all the other words. Put them in order, and good luck with your chores!

```
D R U B B E R G L O V E S
U O N V C E U P O N A D C
S T T R A S H B A G E I R
T M E T H C R E R E E W U
P E E W S O U A W S A P B
A O R I O P N U O C E R S
N N L M A M L E M D U A E
T P A I L B E E T S H G G
O O H N S P E R H B Y E N
B M Y S A H T F R I D E O
N G D O J E E N N Y I L P
I V S E D N E D U S T X S
```

1 vacuum
__ weeds
__ tidy
__ mow
__ polished
__ scrub
__ helps
__ sweep
__ dust
__ brush

Extra Fun: After you've found the entire word string, try to find the names of the eight cleaning supplies you see listed around the page.

MOP SOAP DUSTPAN

Fun for Frank

On a rainy day, Frank likes to read a book, use his computer, or watch TV. Find eight words related to each activity in the three mini word searches. The trick is to figure out which puzzle grid each word is in!

Movie Night

You're having some friends sleep over—which films might you watch? See what's available by matching the two halves of each movie title. Then highlight these films in the letter grid! Careful: Four of the films have titles that are only one word.

Extra Fun: Find six food items kids love to munch on while watching movies!

Bedknobs
Charlotte's
Chicken
Finding
Freaky
Ghost
Happy
Lion
Little
Madagascar
Mary
Pinocchio
Star
Wizard

Poppins
Aladdin
busters
Cars
Feet
Friday
King
Mermaid
Nemo
of Oz
and Broomsticks
Run
Web
Wars

```
G M Y A L I T T L E M E R M A I D L L T I M P E
H A P P Y F E E T I F A V O A R I T E M O V O C
O I E I I R S T H R O E O R I R G I C A R S P H
S N A N L E V P E A R N S C I O Y N O F T H C A
T E L O R A O I D C U C K H E R S P W I T H O R
B Z A C R K O Z M S O S W I Z A R D O F O Z R L
U T D C L Y A Z N A D G E C N N E W I P L D N O
S E D H M F Y A N G E C X K T G F C H I P S A T
T V I I R R I T E A M A O E V I E I S T H I E T
E O N O I I F I N D I N G N E M O G I N S A N E
R L P R I D E A N A D D P R R E J U D I O C E S
S T A R W A R S W M I Y T U H S I R L A D U R W
E N C E O Y L I V I E R A N I C E C R E A M N E
B E D K N O B S A N D B R O O M S T I C K S D B
```

Monday

```
C H I B L Y H
F A I R I C O
S T E E R O S
W S S E A O U
T W Y Z N L Y
E R E Y I I N
D R W R M D N
```

Tuesday

```
I C L O U D Y
S H O W E R S
W I R A N I I
A L W T E Z W
R L E O L Z N
N Y L V E L D
R N Y A I E Y
```

COOL   *BREEZY*   CLOUDY

FAIR

DRY

Five-Day Forecast

Twenty weather words are scattered across these pages. All of them can be found in the small grids. When you have located four words for each day, you will know what the weather will be this week!

BRIGHT

DRIZZLE

CHILLY   HAZY   **HOT**

16

Wednesday

A	C	P	H	Z	Y	L
U	O	O	W	A	R	N
D	Y	U	N	W	E	T
M	I	R	A	I	N	Y
L	G	I	H	N	T	W
D	I	N	T	D	H	S
T	A	G	R	Y	S	A

Thursday

A	B	R	O	W	R	H
U	R	N	D	A	O	T
M	I	L	D	M	I	Y
T	G	W	H	R	N	O
W	H	Y	A	N	R	H
E	T	E	U	M	Y	T
W	S	S	W	A	R	M

Friday

B	O	R	W	R	M	I
R	H	A	Z	Y	S	C
G	U	O	I	K	P	L
T	M	T	T	C	O	D
M	I	R	A	I	U	Y
O	D	M	E	T	N	I
H	T	O	C	S	G	A

HUMID   MILD

SUNNY

RAINY

SHOWERS

STICKY   POURING

WARM   WET   WINDY

Backyard Birds

Listed below are two dozen common backyard birds in alphabetical order. You should be able to find all of them in the feeder. Be careful, though, because four of the bird names have been scrambled. You'll have to figure out which bird to look for before you can find it in the grid!

BLUEBIRD

BLUE JAY

BUNTING

DINRACDAL

CHICKADEE

CROW

FLICKER

GOLDFINCH

GROSBEAK

KAWH

JUNCO

MARTIN

MOURNING DOVE

NUTHATCH

ORIOLE

PHOEBE

BRONI

SPARROW

SWIFT

TITMOUSE

VIREO

WARBLER

REPODWOECK

WREN

Going Buggy

Find all fifteen insects hidden in the grid. Read the remaining letters from left to right and top to bottom to reveal a silly bug joke and its answer!

Remember to look for bugs up, down, sideways, backwards, and diagonally.

ANT
BEE
FLEA
FLY
TICK
GNAT
SPIDER

BEETLE
TERMITE
BUTTERFLY
COCKROACH
DRAGONFLY
FIREFLY
LADYBUG
MOSQUITO

```
W K C I T H Y D O
B E O E E E B G S
B U C Z F Z U R ?
O B K E L B T E C
T A R U Y E T D E
I S O D E E E I T
U T A H E T R P I
Q L C Y C L F S M
S T H A A E L F R
O G N A T N Y T E
M W H A I S T L T
D R A G O N F L Y
E Y L F E R I F !
```

Obstacle Course Opposites

GO   OVER
UP   FIRST
IN   LONG
HIGH   SLOW
PUSH   FORWARD

↺ Look for the OPPOSITE of these words!

Oliver has set up an amazing obstacle course in his yard. Think of the opposite word for the ten words listed. Find the new words in the grid.

Hint: The words can go across the dotted lines!

Great Gardens

Mom and Dad are out working in the yard. Search among the W-E-E-Ds for the nine varieties of plants hidden in each garden.

Hint: Mom loves flowers and Dad is crazy about vegetables.

CARROT   LETTUCE   POTATO   VIOLET

CORN   MARIGOLD   ROSE   ZUCCHINI

CUCUMBER   MUM   TOMATO

DAISY   PANSY   TULIP

EGGPLANT   PEPPER

GERANIUM   PETUNIA

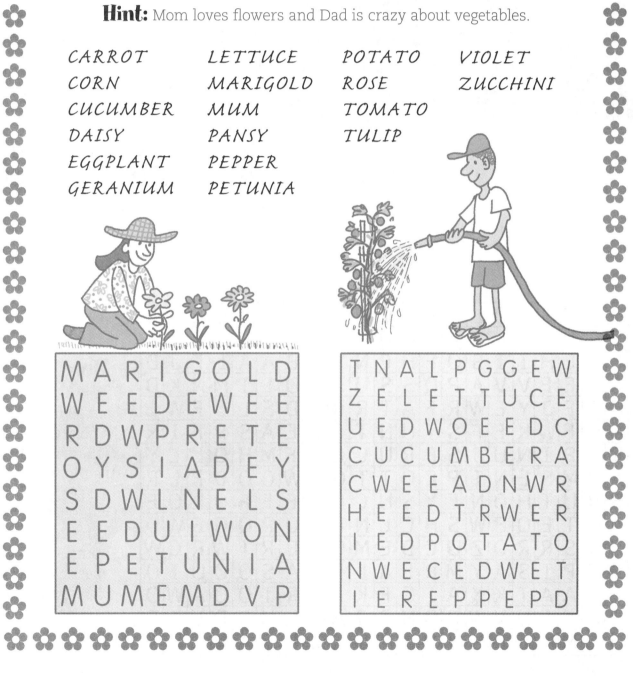

```
M A R I G O L D
W E E D E W E E
R D W P R E T E
O Y S I A D E Y
S D W L N E L S
E E D U I W O N
E P E T U N I A
M U M E M D V P
```

```
T N A L P G G E W
Z E L E T T U C E
U E D W O E E D C
C U C U M B E R A
C W E E A D N W R
H E E D T R W E R
I E D P O T A T O
N W E C E D W E T
I E R E P P E P D
```

Fantastic Fort

Some great forts for kids have been built in trees! In this puzzle, you will look for trees and shrubs, tree parts, and tools used to build a tree fort. Use a light marker to highlight all these words in the letter grid. Then use the same color marker to highlight the extra letter Fs.

ASH	BARK	STUMP	POPLAR
ELM	ROOT	SUMAC	WILLOW
FIR	PINE	SPRUCE	HICKORY
IVY	BEECH	BALSAM	JUNIPER
OAK	LILAC	HAMMER	REDWOOD
SAW	MAPLE	LADDER	SYCAMORE
YEW	NAILS	LAUREL	WISTERIA
BUD	OLIVE	BAMBOO	CRABAPPLE
LEAF	TRUNK	BRANCH	HYDRANGEA
PALM	BIRCH	CHESTNUT	HONEYSUCKLE
TWIG	HOLLY	DOGWOOD	COTTONWOOD

B	A	M	B	O	O	L	I	L	A	C	H	Y	D	R	A	N	G	E	A	L
E	A	L	F	I	L	F	L	M	N	H	K	V	W	X	B	N	G	H	I	A
E	B	E	H	I	I	S	O	F	H	E	N	Y	F	B	A	A	L	F	J	D
C	C	E	F	V	V	A	P	Q	S	S	U	Z	A	U	L	I	M	N	K	D
H	D	F	J	Y	E	W	R	F	A	T	R	B	F	D	S	L	O	F	W	E
C	G	F	W	K	F	F	S	T	U	N	T	C	D	E	A	S	P	F	I	R
R	E	P	I	N	U	J	S	P	R	U	C	E	F	F	M	H	O	L	L	Y
A	Y	M	S	E	N	I	P	C	O	T	T	O	N	W	O	O	D	F	L	R
B	R	U	T	H	O	N	E	Y	S	U	C	K	L	E	F	F	O	L	O	E
A	O	T	E	Q	B	W	S	H	C	L	N	P	E	O	P	Q	G	E	W	D
P	K	S	R	R	O	Z	U	C	D	E	M	O	L	B	R	T	W	R	G	W
P	C	P	I	S	A	Y	M	R	E	A	L	P	P	A	S	O	O	U	I	O
L	I	A	A	T	K	X	A	I	G	F	K	L	A	R	T	O	O	A	W	O
E	H	L	F	U	V	W	C	B	H	I	J	A	M	K	U	R	D	L	T	D
H	A	M	M	E	R	S	Y	C	A	M	O	R	E	B	R	A	N	C	H	F

More Fun

Use a dark colored marker to color in the squares with the remaining letters. You will see that someone has put a silly message on this fort!

Ready to Ride

Before you hop on your bike, see if you can find all fifteen bicycle parts hidden in the wheels.

BRAKE   RIM
CHAIN   SEAT
FRAME   SPOKE
GEAR   TOECLIP
TIRE   WHEEL
LEVER   REFLECTOR
PEDAL   HANDLEBARS
RACK

```
    B R G E                      H T N U
  O M W E O I                  K C R I F O
  T P C H A I N K            H T H O H R I M
O B S T E R K E D B          R A O A T C A E U S
U R E E E R M L L R          B N E I C U M U H B
H A N D L E B A R S          K D C L E V E R A K
S K H A N D L D E K          E L L B L S R A N R
  E I C H A N E N            B I A F P I C D
    E K O P S P                P S E A T K
      W E E L                    N R A B
```

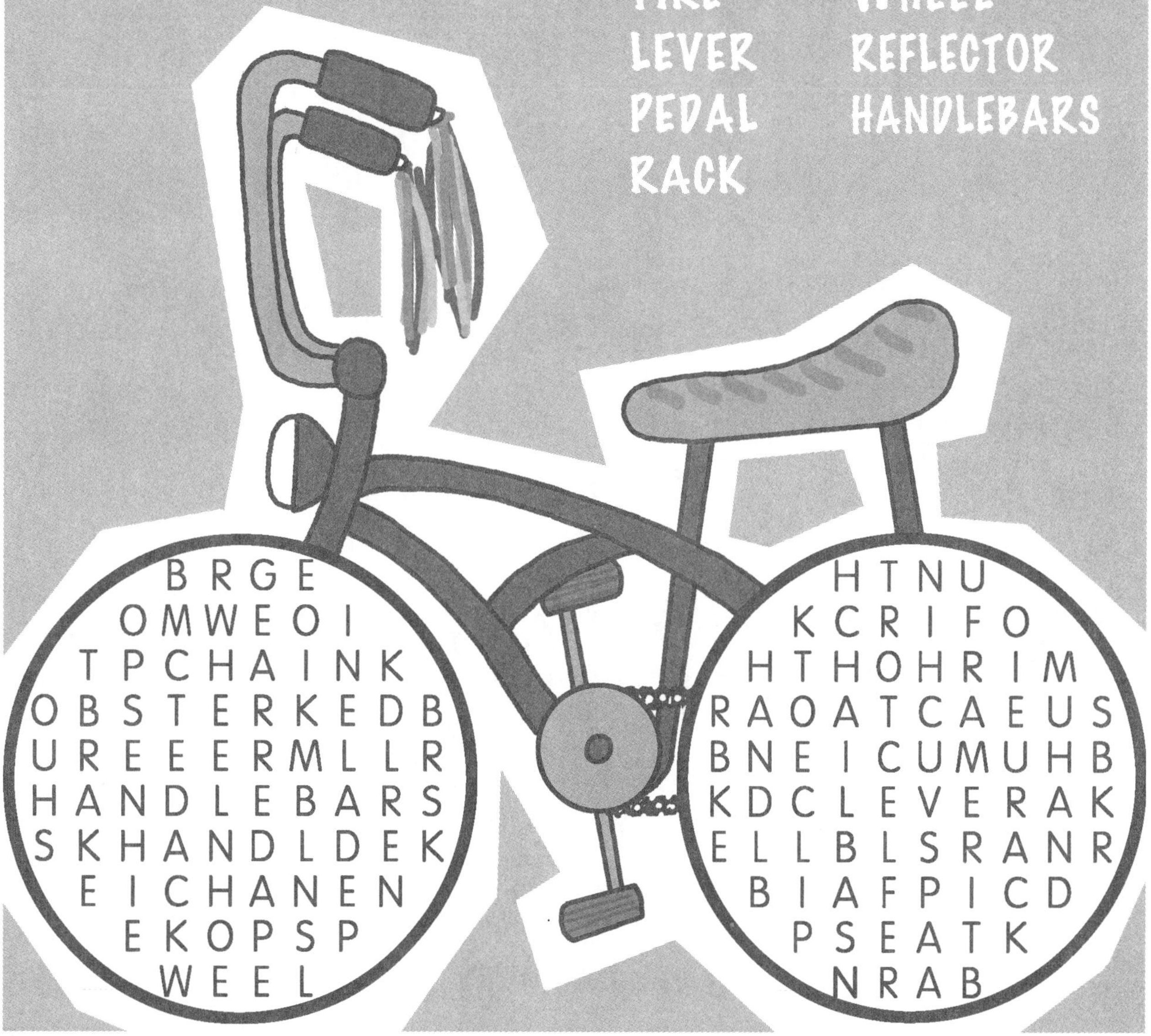

Outdoor Eating

It's time for a barbecue! What items often get cooked on the grill, and what foods do people expect on the picnic table? These items are so familiar that there's no list of words, but here is a hint: There are twenty foods in all.

Don't forget that words can go in all directions, and diagonally too!

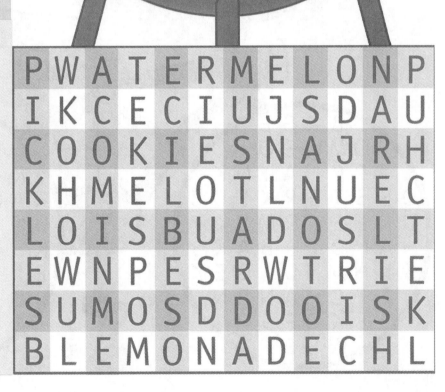

O T A T O P N
H A M B U R G E R
M A O F S H P S K I T
B F S T E A K T C B A
R I G T D P O F I S H
H S N R O C K H I
C R N K G F C

P W A T E R M E L O N P
I K C E C I U J S D A U
C O O K I E S N A J R H
K H M E L O T L N U E C
L O I S B U A D O S L T
E W N P E S R W T R I E
S U M O S D D O O I S K
B L E M O N A D E C H L

Hide & Seek

Use the alphabet-to-number decoder at the bottom of the page to figure out the outdoor hiding spots we've hidden in the grid.

12-7-7-3-10

11-9-4-4

10-6-4-3

8-7-9-2-6

12	7	10	6	4	4	5	8
7	12	7	7	3	10	1	7
1	7	2	9	8	6	3	9
3	1	10	3	3	4	2	2
11	9	4	4	11	3	4	6
5	1	6	5	2	12	7	7
6	3	5	1	9	1	5	4

1=A
2=C
3=D
4=E
5=G
6=H
7=O
8=P
9=R
10=S
11=T
12=W

Driveway Fun

The kids have been having a grand time playing outside. See if you can find all of their toys hidden in the driveway grid.

car   hula hoop
bat   jumprope
bike   balloon
ball   truck
chalk
jacks

```
                    A
                  B A T
                H A I C D
              E U I L K E T
            T T L O L A E L D
          I K R A A S T O R E O
          K R O U H A E T A P Y P T
          E S A B C O N L O N O U R D
          B B U M M E O R B U Y A U N
          A J U M P R O P E R N A C S
          I A L B I K O W T R A N K E
          T C R A B L O C A T C M C H
          A K A P P L L E K G S E I N
          A S I R I A E T S E O R T A
        O C H N I B E S S O T N S N
        S E D A L B R E L L O R
        D S B E E S T W G H
        E B A L L O O N
        O Q L I P A
        U T S K
        K Y
```

pogostick
rollerblades
skateboard

kite   rocket
ramp   bubbles
yoyo   wagon   marbles

The word search grid on the bus:

```
S T O P S I G N N E R D L I H C
A         D     E           D
S         E     F           R
W         N     S           I
O O R W I U T W I E R S S E E S
R M O N N O C A T E P L L O R E R K E A
R W P D E D N R O H E S H O N A A I F R
I W I N D S H I E L D W I P E R S S T A E S
M         S T P O A S I G S N T
          O N F L O O R M A S
```

AISLE, CHILDREN, DOOR, DRIVER, ENGINE, FLOOR, HORN, MIRRORS, SEATS, STOP SIGN, WHEELS, WINDOWS, WINDSHIELD, WIPERS

Hop on the Bus

Every day, the school bus picks up children all around town. Use a yellow marker to highlight these fourteen familiar things you would find on a school bus.

School Stuff

We bet you know your way around a school! Match a word from column 1 with a word from column 2. Find both words together in the grid.

Column 1:

CLASS
PRINCIPAL'S
WATER
LIBRARY
FLAG
CHALK
HALL
BUS

Column 2:

FOUNTAIN
BOARD
ROOM
BOOK
STOP
OFFICE
POLE
WAY

```
P R I N C I P A L S O F F I C E
S A C P L E S C H O L O L Y O L
T B H Q A D R A O B K L A H C I
E C A L S K B R D E X W G I E B
P O T S S U B I F F L G P H I A
B C D E R F R O O L M L O O R R
A R K O O B Y R A R B I L F J Y
S U S T O L I H O M N O E F K B
C L A S M W A T R F O N T O N O
W A T E R F O U N T A I N E X K
```

```
X P U P P Y I P P I P D P A T R I C K G
P R I S C I L L A B C H E F P E N C I L
H P I Z Z A A P P U F F Y H I P A N S Y
I P L A Y P A U L P A R T L P I L L C W
L P X P O M P P         L J K R P E
O A A X E B E A         L I E M I C
M B Y L A G N I         N P S A R N
E E A X M C G L         E O P L A E
N B P O T E D Y P O N C H O R P Q U T D
A E X P A T R I C I A P I N T S E A E U
P O T E P P E N G U I N T Y L L O P U R
I H T R O P H I L L I P P U D D L E V P
G P O S P P P A
P P C E C I I I
A O S P O C N T
T T E H R K O R
I A R O N R L O
E T P N D I P P
N O F E G H E J
C C P P E T T K
E D P A R K E R
E S P A R K R P
L A C S A P M O
P E Y C R E P O
O N N O G N P D
R I P I Q N A L
T H A R S Y N E
S P I E R R E T
```

Plenty of Pals

Pippi knows thirty kids at school whose names all start with the letter P! Can you find all of Pippi's pals in the grid?

Extra Fun:

— Could any of the names be given to either a boy or a girl?

— Which name is hidden twice?

— While you are looking for names in the grid, what else do you notice about this puzzle?

Paige
Palmer
Pamela
Pansy
Parker
Pascal
Patience
Patricia
Patrick
Paul
Paula
Pedro
Peggy
Penny
Pepe
Percy
Persephone
Peter
Phillip
Philomena
Phineas
Phoebe
Phyllis
Pierre
Pippi
Polly
Portia
Prescott
Priscilla
Prudence

Hi, Polly, Peter, and Penelope!

Hi, Pippi!

What's in the Backpack?

You can learn a lot about kids from their backpacks! Find all the words and you will know Stacey and Tracey's favorite subjects—and school supplies!

ART, BINDER, COMPUTER, ENGLISH, ERASER, FOLDER, GYM, HISTORY, LUNCH, MARKER, MATH, MUSIC, PAPER, PEN, PENCIL, READING, RULER, SCIENCE

STACEY

```
Y R O T S I H
K E R A R B A
N P E N C I L
E A A B T N U
P P D R C D N
M E I D T E C
U R N E F R H
S G G Y M H I
H S I L G N E
```

TRACEY

```
R F O L D E R
E R U L E S J
T M U S I C K
U A L P E I R
P R M A R E U
M K M M S N L
O E O A P C E
C R R T Q E R
P E T H M A T
```

Shape Up!

Fifteen words related to shapes are scattered around this page. The trick is to figure out whether they belong in the circle, the triangle, or the square!

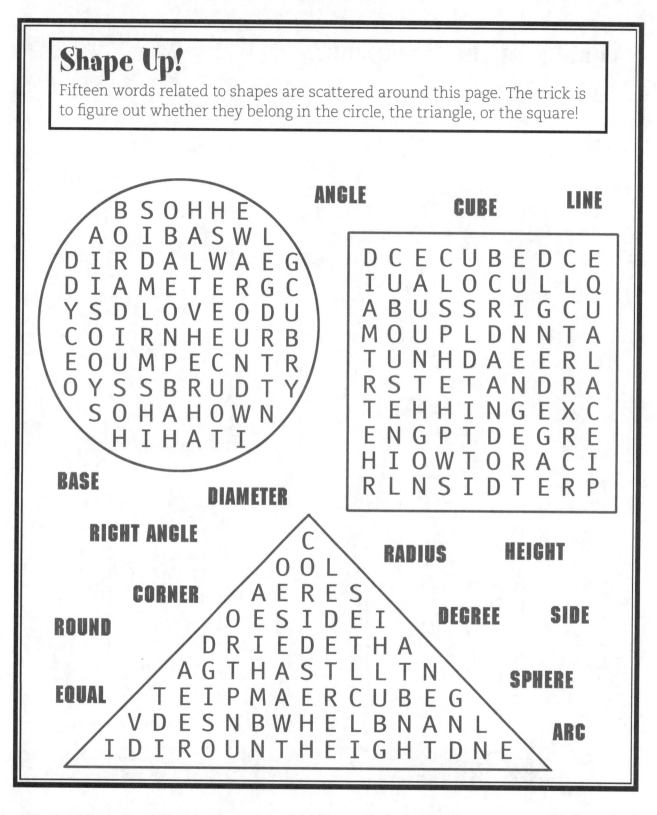

ANGLE   CUBE   LINE

```
B S O H H E
A O I B A S W L
D I R D A L W A E G
D I A M E T E R G C
Y S D L O V E O D U
C O I R N H E U R B
E O U M P E C N T R
O Y S S B R U D T Y
S O H A H O W N
H I H A T I
```

```
D C E C U B E D C E
I U A L O C U L L Q
A B U S S R I G C U
M O U P L D N N T A
T U N H D A E E R L
R S T E T A N D R A
T E H H I N G E X C
E N G P T D E G R E
H I O W T O R A C I
R L N S I D T E R P
```

BASE

DIAMETER

RIGHT ANGLE

RADIUS   HEIGHT

CORNER

DEGREE   SIDE

ROUND

```
C
O O L
A E R E S
O E S I D E I
D R I E D E T H A
A G T H A S T L L T N
T E I P M A E R C U B E G
V D E S N B W H E L B N A N L
I D I R O U N T H E I G H T D N E
```

SPHERE

EQUAL

ARC

You're It!

It's a game of tag at recess! Move quickly through the letters picking up eight "fast" words as you go. Rules: Words follow one after the other in an unbroken line. Move up, down, and sideways, but not diagonally. Words can spell around corners!

1. **CHASE**   2. **SPRINT**   3. **DASH**   4. **RUN**

5. **QUICK**   6. **HUSTLE**   7. **SWIFT**   8. **SPEED**

START

C	S	P	R	I	N	X	L	E	S
H	E	R	I	K	Y	S	T	O	W
A	S	I	N	I	L	U	S	F	I
S	H	S	T	L	K	H	U	T	S
E	R	A	D	O	C	K	P	E	P
S	U	N	Q	U	I	C	K	E	D

END

Got Art?

Follow the directions to see what Maya is painting in art class. Find the six words and fill in their boxes with the colors suggested.

Blue: PAINT, WATER, EASEL, SMOCK

Green: PAINTBRUSH, PAPER

Then fill in the boxes Y, B, and G using this color chart:

Y = YELLOW

B = BLUE

G = GREEN

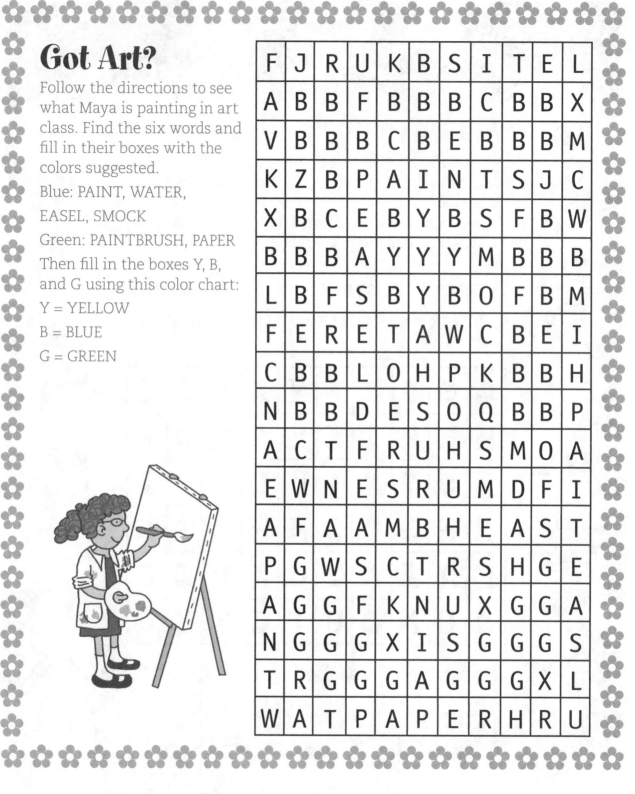

F	J	R	U	K	B	S	I	T	E	L
A	B	B	F	B	B	B	C	B	B	X
V	B	B	B	C	B	E	B	B	B	M
K	Z	B	P	A	I	N	T	S	J	C
X	B	C	E	B	Y	B	S	F	B	W
B	B	B	A	Y	Y	Y	M	B	B	B
L	B	F	S	B	Y	B	O	F	B	M
F	E	R	E	T	A	W	C	B	E	I
C	B	B	L	O	H	P	K	B	B	H
N	B	B	D	E	S	O	Q	B	B	P
A	C	T	F	R	U	H	S	M	O	A
E	W	N	E	S	R	U	M	D	F	I
A	F	A	A	M	B	H	E	A	S	T
P	G	W	S	C	T	R	S	H	G	E
A	G	G	F	K	N	U	X	G	G	A
N	G	G	G	X	I	S	G	G	G	S
T	R	G	G	G	A	G	G	G	X	L
W	A	T	P	A	P	E	R	H	R	U

Janitor's Closet

You never know what Jack the Janitor will have in his closet. Can you find all twenty-five items?

```
T H I S C L D O S E
P B A N D A I D S H
A C L E A N S E R S
P T U X I S I T O I
E T N T A L N L Y L
R F C E U T F P O O
T S H N L R E O P P
O E B S V A C U U M
W V O I F S T A L F
E O X O L H A K S L
L L I N T B N N T A
L G L C O A T D O S
T S I O I G O F O H
R U G R L S S B B L
E E H D E F U A L I
V T T H T I N T G G
I S B P P I W T I H
R U H A M M E R T T
D H L O P T I R H S
W A B T E E D I Y T
E H S O R K I E S C
R G S L C K S O S S
C E T A T U M Y H O
S H A T U B R O O M
```

BANDAIDS
BATTERIES
BOOTS
BROOM
BUCKET
CLEANSERS
COAT
DISINFECTANT
EXTENSION CORD
FLASHLIGHT
GLOVES
HAMMER
HAT
KEYS
LIGHTBULBS
LUNCHBOX
MOP
PAPER TOWELS
PHOTOS
POLISH
RAGS
SCREWDRIVER
TOILET PAPER
TRASHBAGS
VACUUM

Lunch Line

Something weird has happened to the menu in the school cafeteria! Solve the simple first-to-last code, and then find the five food items each student has picked to eat. All items are used at least once, but some are used twice!

Try using a single line of color to highlight each word as you find it!

IZZAP   OUPS

OTDOGH   ALADS

ANDWICHS   RIESF

```
I P U O S T H I
N K T H A E T C
S A N D W I C H
I L I K E K L I
U D D U L O A P
N C H I B O P S
E S M T O C P F
```

```
A I L C O R N
T Z H H E M E
C Z A I L S E
J U I C E B L
O E C K A U P
O S P E A S P
K E U N S E A
```

Detention!

There are many reasons you might have to stay after school for detention. Highlight these thirteen reasons in the grid, and then gather the leftover letters from left to right and top to bottom. Write them in order on the dotted lines to reveal a silly joke and its silly answer!

___ ___ ___ _____

_____ _____?

__ ___ _ _____

_____!

DISRESPECTFUL
FIGHT
HITTING
KICK
LYING
RUDE
SPITTING
STEAL
SWEAR
TARDINESS
THREAT
VANDALISM
VIOLENCE

D I S R E S P E C T F U L
E W T H U Y T G W A S T S
C H E E M D A N A L G N W
N E A T G I E I V Y E N E
E D L E T E R T N I T I A
L O N F I G H T ? N H E R
O H A H I T T I N G D K A
I N E G A T I P V E A C T
V A N D A L I S M T I I T
U T A R D I N E S S D K E

Around Town

Fill in the blanks in each of these sentences about your community. Find each of the places or people in the letter grid on the next page!

1. Visit the _ _ _ _ _ _ _ _ when you need a good book.

2. Call the _ _ _ _ _ _ _ to report a crime!

3. Your dog gets its shots at the _ _ _ .

4. Fill the fridge at the _ _ _ _ _ _ _ _ _ _ _ _ _ _ .

5. On Sunday, you might go to _ _ _ _ _ _ _ with your family.

6. By some stamps and mail a letter at the
   _ _ _ _ _ _ _ _ _ _ _ .

7. Mom will call the _ _ _ _ _ _ _ _ if you feel sick.

8. Pick up a hammer and some nails at the
   _ _ _ _ _ _ _ _ _ _ _ _ _ .

9. The _ _ _ _ is the place to have a savings account.

10. If you need a haircut, visit a _ _ _ _ _ _ _ _ _ _ _ _ .

11. See a matinee at the _ _ _ _ _ _ _ _ _ _ _ _ _ .

12. The _ _ _ _ _ _ _ _ _ _ _ _ _ will respond if
    a building is burning!

40

B F A N K I W I H A I D R E
S I M O V I E T H E A T E R
G R O C E R Y S T O R E H O
R E S S E R D R I A H I C T
O F D R S S R U P O L C E S
D I F H A R D V I N D C S E
A G D R A W I M E N B H S R
E H Y G A L K O R T A U E A
C T E R A N D V Y D N R R W
I E O N A E F I R O T C O D
L R O B R R E T T H I H S R
O S W A R E B H P F I R F A
P O S T O F F I C E U Z Z H
E S O I D I D N L T H A V E

Savings Sum

Ethan has been saving coins. Now he wants to deposit the money at the bank! Find all the PENNIES, NICKELS, DIMES, and QUARTERS in the letter grid, and then add them up to see how much money Ethan has saved. Clue: The piggy bank is really full!

Love Letter

Scott is at the post office to mail a valentine to a special friend. What does the card say? Start at the white letter and read all the way around the edge of the valentine to find the first seven words of a familiar verse. Now look for the remaining six words in the center of the heart!

Extra Fun: See how many "kisses" Scott included on his card!

R _ _ _ _ _

A _ _ _

R _ _.

V _ _ _ _ _ _

A _ _ _

B _ _ _ _.

S _ _ _ _ _

I _

S _ _ _ _ _,

A _ _

S _

A _ _

Y _ _!

In the Bag

What did Mom buy at the grocery store? Look for the sixteen food items in the grocery bags. Which item isn't there? **Hint:** The words are separated into the bags by type of food!

BANANA, BEANS, BREAD,
BUTTER, CARROT, CEREAL,
CHEESE, COOKIES, EGGS,
LETTUCE, MILK, NUTS, PASTA,
PLUM, SOUP, YOGURT

```
B A N A N A I
E C U T T E L
A C O M O O K
N E U I R S B
S L I L R H U
P O P O A E T
M G G K C Y R
```

```
D C E S O O P
Y O G U R T E
A H G D E D S
M E S Y T N E
O I I S T U E
A E L L U S H
B R E K B T C
```

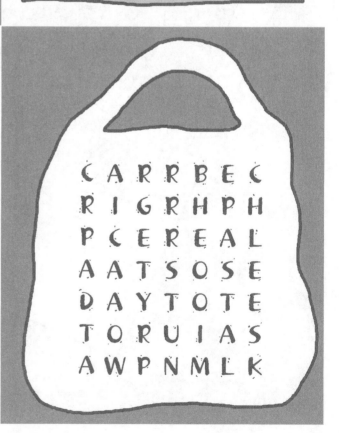

```
C A R R B E C
R I G R H P H
P C E R E A L
A A T S O S E
D A Y T O T E
T O R U I A S
A W P N M L K
```

Snip! Snip!

When your hair gets shaggy, it's time to visit the barber. Let's give these words a haircut! Remove one letter from each to make a new word. The ten new words are the ones you will find in the grid—they are all in different places! Extra Fun: Some of the words can be "trimmed" twice to make two new words.

```
S A H U L E M A
R B A R I A B O
A J K H E R I M
E B N B J S A B
H A I R B A Q L
E L Q F H I L I
B O C R B N I P
```

SHEARS becomes _ _ _ _ _ _ _ and _ _ _ _ _

CHAIR becomes _ _ _ _ _ and _ _ _ _

SINK becomes _ _ _ _ and _ _ _

SNIP becomes _ _ _ _

COMB becomes _ _ _

TRIM becomes _ _ _ _

CLIP becomes _ _ _

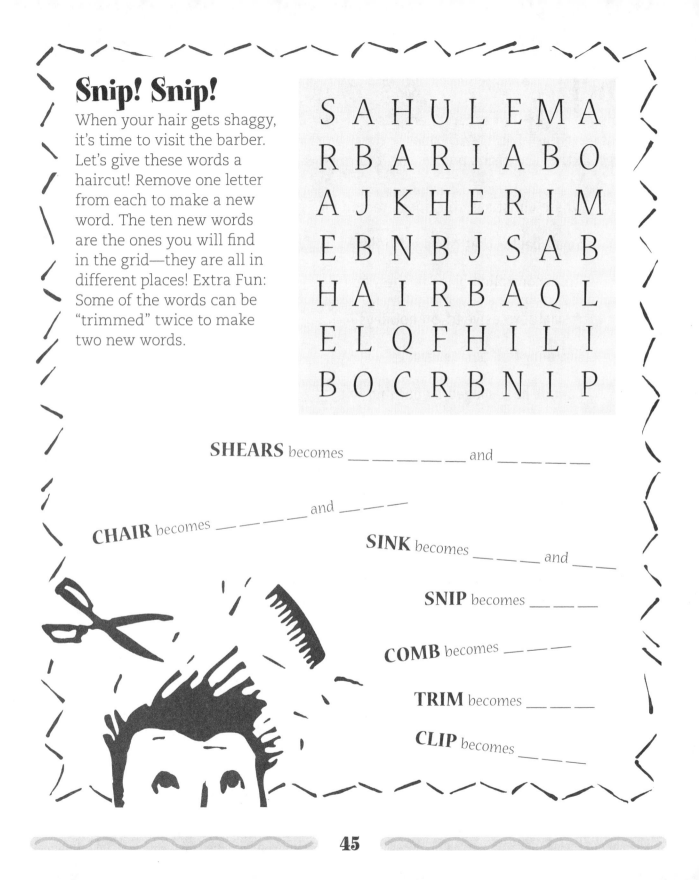

On Fire!

Things sure are hot around here! Use the definitions to figure out all the words that have F-I-R-E in them. Look for these words in the letter grid on the next page. Extra Fun: In the puzzle, the letters F-I-R-E look like a bunch of flames!

Where Christmas stockings are hung = _ _ _ _ _ _ _ _ _

Small beetle that gives off light = _ _ _ _ _ _ _ _

An uncontrolled blaze in the woods = _ _ _ _ _ _ _ _ _

A small explosive lit on holidays = _ _ _ _ _ _ _ _ _ _ _

Building for "pumper trucks" = _ _ _ _ _ _ _ _ _

Cannot be damaged by burning = _ _ _ _ _ _ _ _ _ _

What you burn in a fireplace = _ _ _ _ _ _ _ _

A place where you toast marshmallows = _ _ _ _ _ _ _ _ _

Long red truck with a loud siren = _ _ _ _ _ _ _ _ _ _ _

Explosive noise from an engine = _ _ _ _ _ _ _ _

Device that sprays foam on flames =

_ _ _ _ _ _ _ _ _ _ _ _ _ _

Colorful display on the 4th of July = _ _ _ _ _ _ _ _ _

Person who puts out a burning house =

_ _ _ _ _ _ _ _ _ _ _

Handy Hardware

Search the local hardware store for sixteen items you might need for that next home-improvement project!

HOSE, LAWNMOWER, PAINT, SHOVEL, RAKE, PAIL, NAILS, BROOM, SEEDS, BATTERY, WHEELBARROW, ROPE, SAND, SHADE, SPONGE, DOORKNOB

```
E E D I R E W O M N W A L
U S O P A I B W E A D Y I
S P O N G E R H T I O R A
H L R O S H O V E L V E P
A D K E E B O E K S P T B
D E N T E A M E A O G T A
E S O A D T O L R T O A R
H O B T S P A I N T H B R
W H E E L B A R R O W E O
```

Road Trip

There are always lots of things to pack for a road trip. Look in the little car to find all the items pictured here. Do you think they will all fit?

Helpful Hint: The pictures may bring to mind several different words. For example, you might look for "puppy" when the word we've hidden is "dog." Keep looking until you find the correct word for each picture!

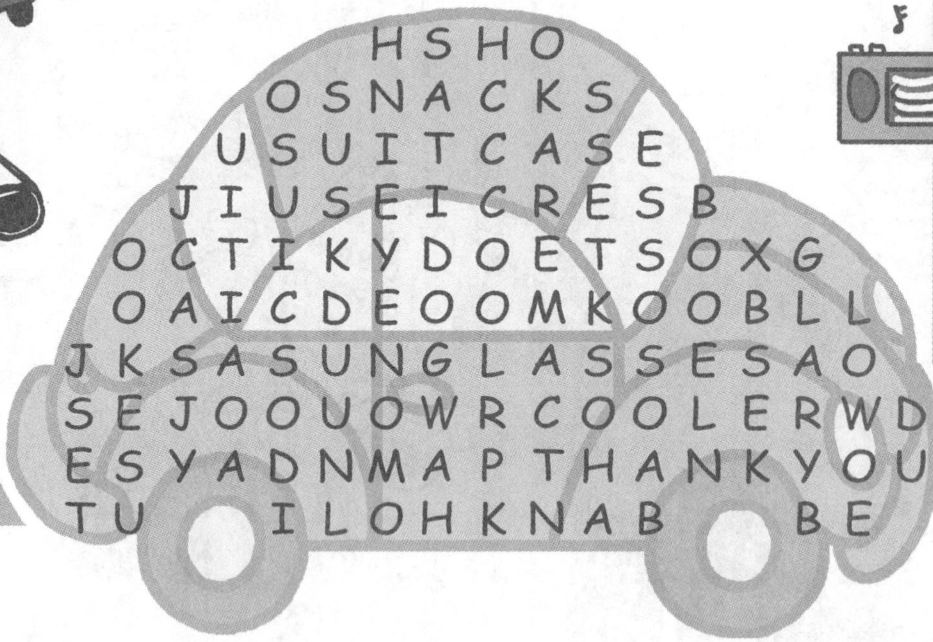

```
      H S H O
    O S N A C K S
  U S U I T C A S E
  J I U S E I C R E S B
O C T I K Y D O E T S O X G
O A I C D E O O M K O O B L L
J K S A S U N G L A S S E S A O
S E J O O U O W R C O O L E R W D
E S Y A D N M A P T H A N K Y O U
T U   I L O H K N A B     B E
```

New Hampshire Holiday

Driving through scenic New Hampshire, you can learn a lot from a map! Find all twenty words listed here, but also look for one other place of interest that is plentiful in this state. How many times do you find it in the grid?

AIRPORT, BORDER, CAMPSITE, CITIES, COVERED BRIDGE, ELEVATION, EXITS, FOREST, GOLF COURSE, HIGHWAY, HOSPITAL, LAKE, MILES, MOUNTAIN, PICNIC AREA, RIVER, ROADS, SKI AREA, TOLL, TOWN

```
X L R T R O P R I A R P A R K H
E L E V A T I O N E E T O W N I
T X V P A R K F R R D E P H T G
I M I L E S S K I A R E A O S H
S E R T E G O L F C O U R S E W
P O R I S P R A P I B D K P R A
M I T D P A R K E N T H E I O Y
A I A P A R K E G C L L O T F G
C O V E R E D B R I D G E A R A
R N I A T N U O M P A R K L N I
```

Motor Messages

On a cross-country trip, you will see lots of silly sayings on license plates. Even the spelling is silly! Figure out the real message on each of these license plates, and then look for it spelled out in the grid.

BCNU	GR82CU	I12BUGU
2DUM2NO	UR1DRFL	W84ME
CRAZ4U	LUV2LAF	ZPDDUDA

```
N L O Z I S L A R O F E M I T E H T R
Y O U A R E W O N D E R F U L T H Z W
G V O O D M E N T O C O M E T O A I H
O E D I W A N T T O B U G Y O U O G O
H T F T H E I R P A R T Y I B E L R L
D O I E B E S E E I N G Y O U V E E E
E L T H I S S I T H E T S E B R A A N
W A I T F O R M E N D O M U O H T T U
A U G H T O T A R E N E G R I N T T B
R G H E W O T O O D U M B T O K N O W
I H R L D L Z Z U P S I H T E K I S C
F M I W O N D E R W O H J E N Z L E H
Z I P P I T Y D O O D A H Y W I L E O
O L L I N N A E N E R I T C O L U Y L
R G O T T O F I C R A Z Y F O R Y O U
E H T O N A T O O R R F I T A R D U T
```

Under the Big Top

Vacation is a great time to see the circus! Find the words hidden in the three rings. When you are done, you will know what act is performing in each place. Careful—one piece of equipment is not used!

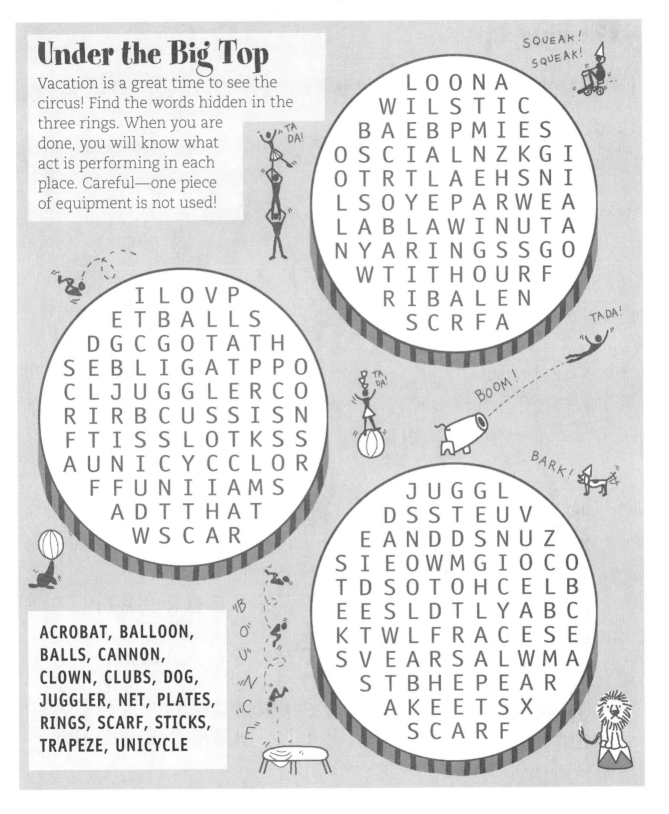

SQUEAK!
SQUEAK!

TA DA!

```
L O O N A
W I L S T I C
B A E B P M I E S
O S C I A L N Z K G I
O T R T L A E H S N I
L S O Y E P A R W E A
L A B L A W I N U T A
N Y A R I N G S S G O
W T I T H O U R F
R I B A L E N
S C R F A
```

TA DA!

BOOM!

TA DA!

BARK!

```
I L O V P
E T B A L L S
D G C G O T A T H
S E B L I G A T P P O
C L J U G G L E R C O
R I R B C U S S I S N
F T I S S L O T K S S
A U N I C Y C C L O R
F F U N I I A M S
A D T T H A T
W S C A R
```

```
J U G G L
D S S T E U V
E A N D D S N U Z
S I E O W M G I O C O
T D S O T O H C E L B
E E S L D T L Y A B C
K T W L F R A C E S E
S V E A R S A L W M A
S T B H E P E A R
A K E E T S X
S C A R F
```

"B
O
U
N
C
E"

ACROBAT, BALLOON, BALLS, CANNON, CLOWN, CLUBS, DOG, JUGGLER, NET, PLATES, RINGS, SCARF, STICKS, TRAPEZE, UNICYCLE

Gearing Up

It is important to take the right equipment if you plan to go camping on your vacation. See if you can find all ten items hiding in the grassy field!

BACKPACK
BINOCULARS
CANTEEN
COOLER
FIRST AID KIT
HIKING BOOTS
LANTERN
MATCHES
SLEEPING BAG
TENT

```
I L B A C K S S T O O B G N I K I H
K A E O O U A E B I N O S E D T O L
B N E T V E I H T H I K N G O C O C
O T P M E P D C I N B A C K P A C K
O E I B E N K T G F O O R B A N L I
S R F I R S T A I D K I T I E T A P
T N N E T I C M K S C A B N M E N P
S R A L U C O N I B C C O O L E R I
B O C K P O C K R A W L O D A N L C
O S L E E P I N G B A G T B O O H K
```

Sunny Seashore

Building at the beach is great fun! Find ten items used to make sandcastles. Then use a dark marker to put a large dot of color over all the letters D-I-G that are not part of the answer words. Connect the dots to make block letters that spell out one more item you really need at the beach!

FUNNEL   PAIL   SHOVEL   SEAWEED

WATER   SHELLS   SAND   RAKE

ROCKS   STICKS

```
I D A E D F G M F D M C D B J
G C F S I B D E U I G E I M D
D I H K G E G J N D I G G C E
E G C C D B I B N I S D I A E
G D L O I G D J E G K B G H W
A C S A W A T E R K P A I L C C L F S A N D O B E
D I L F D I K V D I G U F I D I C I D E M D M O D
G C L H I A F O I C G B E G A T L G E S R I G F I
D I E J G B L H G D I O J I D S H D I H A G D I G
H G H F D K E S D I L H A G K U A G J E K D L D I
I D S L I G F L G F G M M D I C O D I L E I B H G
```

Sail Away

A sailing trip would be a great vacation! Find fifteen parts of a sailboat hidden in the sail.

```
          R
        R I
        I E G
        J K L G
        C E L I
        E A E I N
        D P P L T G
        S A N C H O R
        J Y H U L L D
        A T B I R
        P S T A R B
        A A R Y A I O
        M E B O W R J I
        X A M A P S T E R N
```

ANCHOR, BOOM, BOW, DECK, HULL, JIB, KEEL, MAST, PORT, RIGGING, RUDDER, SHROUD, STARBOARD, STERN, TILLER

What a Zoo!

The zoo animals are on vacation, running loose! In which exhibit does each belong?

TOUCAN

EMU

ANACONDA

WALLABY

LION

SLOTH

RHINOCEROS

GIRAFFE

WOMBAT

```
O H J M Y G A O D
A N A C O N D A N
E S G S I A T H I
N K U I W C I L L
O R A N G U T A N
S T R O N O G L E
M Y S L O T H S E
```
South American Exhibit

```
I T K H M Y O W
N B O R Y A S S
I W O M B A T E
R E K B A L A B
O R A A L X O O
L A B B L L E O
O O U G A N M K
X I R D W C U A
O O R A G N A K
T R A E E A L L
```
Australian Exhibit

```
L F I A R B E Z F S
H L W O N J L G E T
R H I N O C E R O S
O F F O T H P E P H
O N E S N O H I W I
L L J G I R A F F E
U S T S T R N A N G
L E M Y S E T L F W
```
African Exhibit

ORANGUTAN

ZEBRA

KOOKABURRA

ELEPHANT

KANGAROO

JAGUAR

Famous Places

The United States has many interesting and unique places to visit. First see if you can match each of these travel sites to its state. Then find them all in the grid on the next page.

1. Grand Canyon   __ Florida
2. Statue of Liberty   __ Hawaii
3. Graceland   __ New York
4. Mount Rushmore   __ Tennessee
5. Golden Gate Bridge   __ Virginia
6. Everglades   __ Arizona
7. The Capitol   __ California
8. Gateway Arch   __ New Mexico
9. Niagara Falls   __ Washington, DC
10. Carlsbad Caverns   __ New York
11. Hoover Dam   __ N. Carolina
12. Kitty Hawk   __ Missouri
13. Wrigley Field   __ Illinois
14. Pearl Harbor   __ S. Dakota
15. Williamsburg   __ Nevada

```
I H A V G R U B S M A I L L I W E S
N S N R E V A C D A B S L R A C A T
I L W A T S W D N D T H E D T O P A
A S E E H O U N T R U C K S H M E T
G O L D E N G A T E B R I D G E A U
A R O R C I C L N V T A T E R V R E
R E A N A E G E N O T Y T O A B L O
A E L S P E V C H O W A Y T N H H F
F E Y C I A N A L H A W H S D T A L
A S E V T L V R E V E E A A C W R I
L A Y T O N A G O F R T W O A C B B
L W I T L S O N I A N A K K N S O E
S E V E R G L A D E S G T H Y A R R
W H E E R O M H S U R T N U O M N T
W R I G L E Y F I E L D T N N E Y Y
```

Lots of Luggage

If you are vacationing far away, you might take an airplane to get there quickly. Find all the airport words listed in the luggage, then gather the leftover letters from left to right and top to bottom. They will spell out the answer to this funny knock-knock joke.

KNOCK KNOCK
WHO'S THERE?
ALPACA
ALPACA WHO?

```
D R A O B Y A
L U G G A G E
A L P W A C A
V T N H E T T
I U T F H R E
R P U G L N K
R N I K A Y C
A L Y L O U I
F P P A O C T
L E V A R T K
```

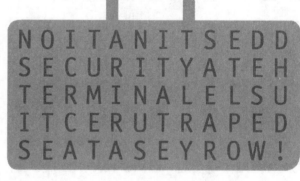

```
N O I T A N I T S E D D
S E C U R I T Y A T E H
T E R M I N A L E L S U
I T C E R U T R A P E D
S E A T A S E Y R O W !
```

ARRIVAL, BOARD, DELAY, DEPARTURE, DESTINATION, FLIGHT, FLY, LUGGAGE, PILOT, PLANE, ROW, RUNWAY, SEAT, SECURITY, TERMINAL, TICKET, TRAVEL

Chapter 6

Animal Friends

Pets at the Vet

These animals are done at the vet. See how quickly you can get them ready to go home! What kind of traveling case is the best for each one? Hint: There are three animals in each carrier.

GERBIL

CANARY

RABBIT

DOG

```
O D S F
H O T O I T
C P H I N C
L O A C Y C A S
I E R N S H C R
T E E K A R A P

E L S O S R T L
Z W A I A F Y E
A H K F I R N T
S N E A K E S E
```

```
P A R A K S E E T S T
I T A R A N T U L A I
T H I A N A K T H T S
A B B I T K A S P I D
H A R D S E T P A R T
I S F D R A Z I L E L
```

MICE

LIZARD

CAT

SNAKE

TARANTULA

HAMSTER

FINCH

PARAKEET

```
    I Z M I        H A L M S T
  T D O G S A      S S I M Y D O
  S P I C D E      P Z A K E E I
  S H E W A A G    O D R G R O D
  C R A B B I T    A R S I E R P
                   D
```

```
C A N A R L Y F I C H
A B E C D I E H K I I
F I C H N B F E
H K I I G R J
H A M S T E R
R L M Q O G P
```

Tall Tale

Giraffes are the tallest animals in the world. Find the six synonyms for the word "tall" hiding in the giraffe's neck. Then write the remaining letters from left to right and top to bottom on the dotted lines. When you are done, you will have the silly answer to the riddle!

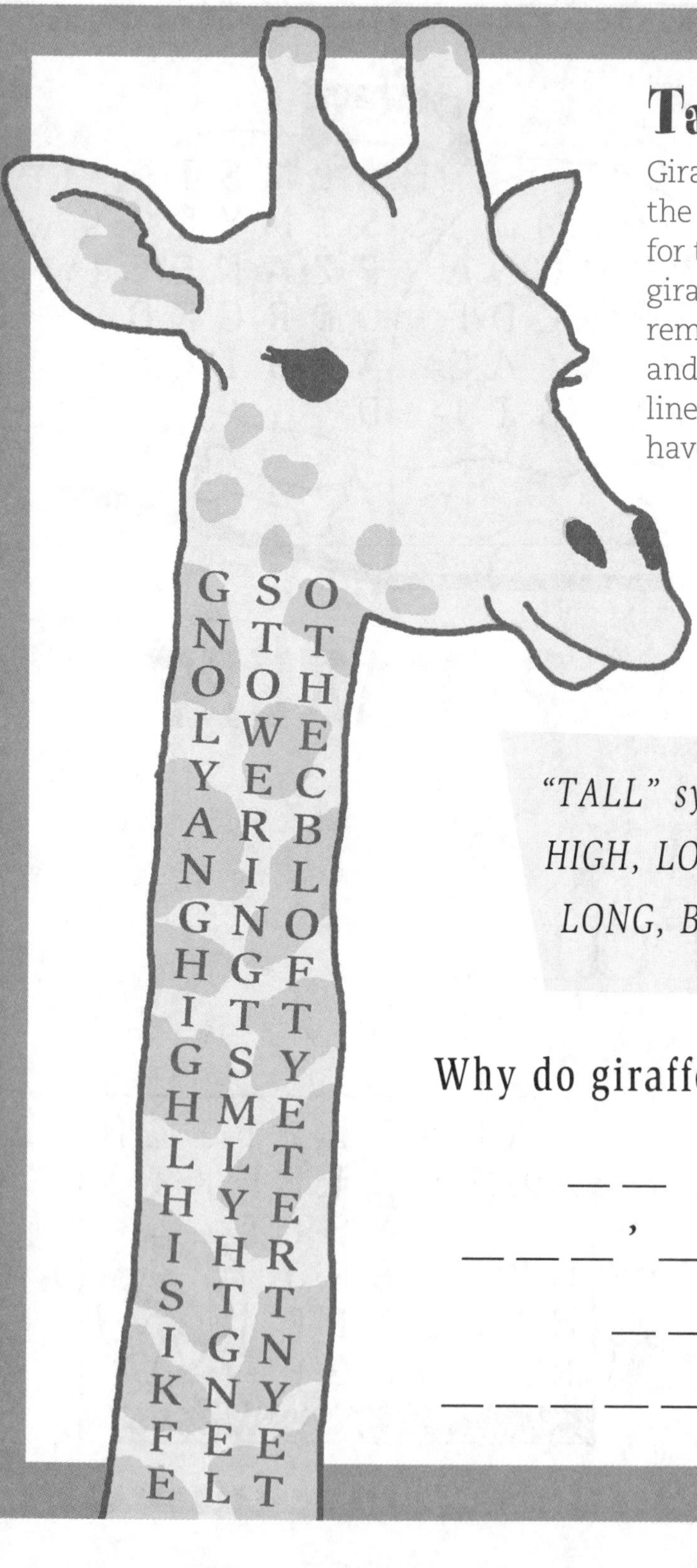

G S O
N T T
O O H
L W E
Y E C
A R B
N I L
G N O
H G F
I T T
G S Y
H M E
L L T
H L E
I Y R
S H T
I T N
K G Y
F N E
E E T
  L

"TALL" synonyms to find:
HIGH, LOFTY, LENGTHY,
LONG, BIG, TOWERING

Why do giraffes have long necks?

__ __   __ __ __ __

__ __ __ , __   __ __ __ __ __

__ __ __ __

__ __ __ __ __ __   __ __ __ __ !

Farm Fun

Each of the ten words rhymes with the name of an animal commonly found on a farm. Figure out each animal name and find it hidden in the barn.

NOW = _ _ _

WEEP = _ _ _ _ _ _

DIG = _ _ _

HAT = _ _ _ _

COARSE = _ _ _ _ _ _

STUCK = _ _ _ _ _

NICE = _ _ _ _ _

FLICK = _ _ _ _ _ _

JUICE = _ _ _ _ _ _

BOAT = _ _ _ _ _

Ocean Alive

Where would ocean animals be without water to live in? Using the letters W-A-T-E-R, complete the twelve animal names, then find them all beneath the waves.

CR_B   SH_IMP   S _ _ HO _ S _

_H_L_   SH _ _ K   LOBS_ _ _

_U_ _L_   _ _ L   J_ _LLYFISH

S_ _L   CL_M   OC_OPUS

B A R C O E L T R U T

H S E A H O R S E W C

A E T N O C T O P U S

L I S S C E O M M P H

L A B E I M L N I W A

H E O A A N I A R B R

J E L L Y F I S H A K

S I C C A L L Y S W P

Holed Up

When the cold weather comes, many animals hole up in burrows, caves, tree trunks, or deep mud to hibernate (sleep) until the warm weather returns. These twelve animals would never hibernate together in the wild, but in this puzzle they are quite cozy together!

woodchuck

chipmunk

bat

bear

frog

turtle

squirrel

skunk

snake

ladybug

mouse

raccoon

```
      W O O D C H
    I Q U H I T W A
  Q W S I S Q U I R S
  E W O O D C H U C K N T
L F L M U N H K A U N A U C
I B A T M S I T U B U K R O
D E D O O P M A E K O T O
Y C Y R U R M T F A S Q L L
B A B R S Q U I R R E L E A
G U U L E U N O O C C A R G
S G S N A K E G I C E A
  T B E R H E M O O S
  N I T B O T W O
    U L D B E N
```

Man's Best Friend

Choosing the right dog for your family can be quite a task. There are so many breeds to choose from! Use a highlighter to find all the dogs hidden in the grid on the following page.

AKITA	DALMATION	PEKINGESE
BASSET HOUND	DOBERMAN PINSCHER	POODLE
BICHON FRISE	GERMAN SHEPHERD	PUG
BOXER	GOLDEN RETRIEVER	ROTTWEILER
BULLDOG	GREAT DANE	SAINT BERNARD
CHIHUAHUA	GREYHOUND	SAMOYED
COCKER SPANIEL	IRISH SETTER	SHIH TZU
COLLIE	LABRADOR RETRIEVER	WHIPPET
DACHSUND	LHASA APSO	YORKSHIRE TERRIER

Which leash goes to which dog?

Extra Fun: Use a dark colored marker to make a big polka dot of color over each letter X. Connect the dots to create a puppy portrait. Maybe this is the dog for you!

```
I R R E H C S N I P N A M R E B O D E
G S H I H T Z U A E N A D T A E R G L
R Y G E R M A N S H E P H E R D L L H
E O L X X P E K I N G E S E X X B A A
Y R Y X M X X A T I K A X X M X A B S
H K I X S B Y X X X X R I O X R R A
O S S X D A L M A T I O N R I X K A A
U H E D X S O X G I H X O I X P L D P
N I V X I S X O X G X O X S W X Y O S
D R X N B E X X X F X X X H H A X R O
A E X R O T T W E I L E R S I E X R D
E T X H X H S O O X U N D E P H X E R
S E X R E O I O X H X E A T P V X T A
I R X E R U N F I X T D H T E A X R N
R R B X I N G B O X N W L E T X O I R
F I F I X D C E X U X C R R X E M E E
N E E H A X X X S P A X X X M S H V B
O R I A P E D H X U X H O T T O H E T
H D L O G B C I X G X E L D O O P R N
C S L C U A I T U X O B U L L D O G I
I G O L D E N R E T R I E V E R N E A
B E C H I H U A H U A T D E Y O M A S
O C O C K E R S P A N I E L P A Y D A
```

Cold Creatures

Break the snowflake code to find the names of ten arctic animals. Then find where they are hiding in the snow bank!

❋=A   ❋=E   ❋=I   ✳=O   ❄=U

C✳R❋B✳❋   P✳L❋R B❄❋R

H✳RP S❋AL   PT❋RM❋G❋N

L❄MM❋NG   SN✳WY ✳WL

M✳SK✳X   B❋L❄GA WH✳L❋

W✳LR❄S   ❋RCT❋C F✳X

```
T A R M                 B E
P S E E L S T I S R A I N A
R O U T P T A R M I G A N S R
A G C A R I B O U O N C E A G C
B R N N I T H I S N K S T H A T T
F E C I W I L L K N E U V E R S T I
W O L T M P O P O L A R B E A R L A C
H Y U I M E A X R M L W O Y W O N S F
A S G N E K O I S A L A E S P R A H O
L E B E L U G A W H A L E F I X I N X
```

Desert Dwellers

Many varieties of snakes live in the desert. Some are poisonous; some are not! Find the seven species curled up together in this grid. Here's the tricky part: The names are not always spelled in a straight line! You can start at the first letter of a name and move up, down, around a corner, and side to side—but not diagonally. One has been done for you.

RATTLESNAKE   KINGSNAKE

GOPHER SNAKE   BANDED SAND SNAKE   GLOSSY SNAKE ✓

CORAL SNAKE   DESERT WORM SNAKE

D M H O R A B O N D

E R A C H L A L A X

S O T G K I N G S R

E W T L E Y D E D E

R T E O S S G O P H

Animals in Danger

All over the world, thousands of animal species are in danger of becoming extinct. Use a marker to highlight the twenty endangered animals. Read the extra letters from left to right and top to bottom to discover some good news about one very familiar animal!

ANGEL SHARK
BLUE WHALE
CHEETAH
CORALS
ELEPHANT

GAZELLE
GIANT PANDA
GORILLA
MANATEE
MANTA RAY

OKAPI
PIKAS
POLAR BEAR
RHINOCEROS
TIGER

ATLANTIC SALMON
GREEN SEA TURTLE
HIPPOPOTAMUS
MONARCH BUTTERFLY
SNOW LEOPARD

```
D R A P O E L W O N S E F E O R U
H R I D E C A D G A Z E L L E H E
I S P A F T E R G I T T W T A I S
P R A E B R A L O P D A E R C N L
P A K R E D E P R N D N B U A O N
O N O M L A S C I T N A L T A C M
P G E R E L H D L K T M U A H E A
O E A M A E E R L R A I E E C R N
T A N R E B E A A L D S W S E O T
A A O T G G L E I S N O H N L S A
M C A G I A N T P A N D A E O N R
U H G T E R T N A H P E L E I N A
S M O N A R C H B U T T E R F L Y
D A N G E L S H A R K A N G G E R
```

Chapter 7

Hobbies

Cool Car Collection

Christopher loves to collect cars, wherever they are! The definitions below suggest words that all contain the letters C-A-R. Look for these words in the puzzle grid on the next page. Extra Fun: In the word search, the letters C-A-R show up as a small picture of a car instead of the letters themselves!

Short, hollow pasta = __ __ __ __ __ __ __ __

Skinny cloth worn around the neck = __ __ __ __ __

A meat eater = __ __ __ __ __ __ __ __ __

One-sided letter sent
   with no envelope = __ __ __ __ __ __ __ __

Orange root vegetable = __ __ __ __ __ __

An animated film = __ __ __ __ __ __ __

Bright red color = __ __ __ __ __ __ __

To throw away = __ __ __ __ __ __ __

Bright red bird = __ __ __ __ __ __ __ __

Fake person made out of straw
   = __ __ __ __ __ __ __ __ __

To slice meat = __ __ __ __ __

Circular, sideways handstand
   = __ __ __ __ __ __ __ __ __

A rug = __ __ __ __ __ __ __

A Christmas song = __ __ __ __ __ __

ZOOM!

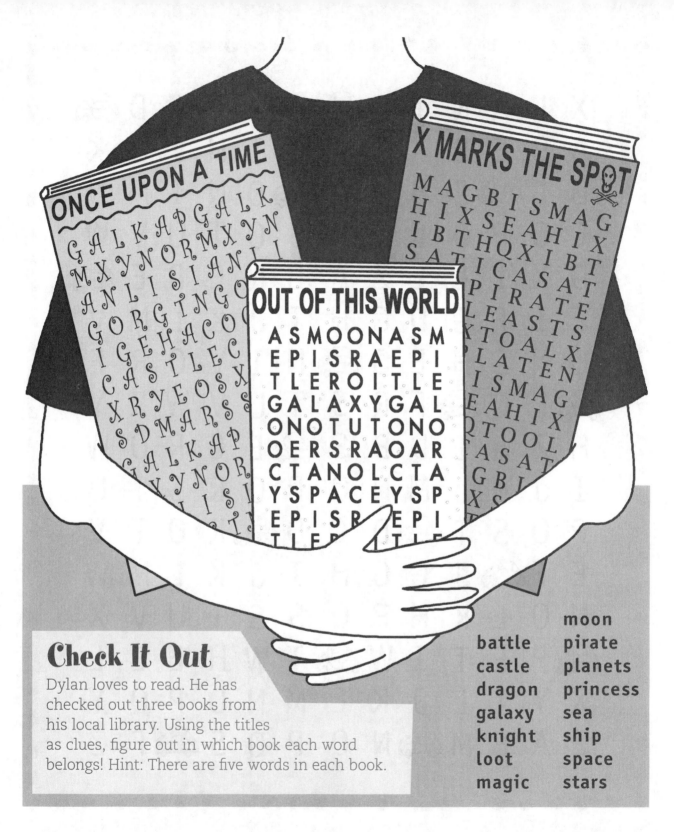

ONCE UPON A TIME

GALKAPGALK
MXYNORMXYN
ANLISIANLI
GORGINGORG
IGEHACOOTC
CASTLECASTLEC
XRYEOSX
SDMARS
GALKAP
XYNOR

X MARKS THE SPOT

MAGBISMAG
HIXSEAHIX
IBTHQXIBT
SATICASAT
PIRATE
LEASTS
XTOALX
PLATEN
ISMAG
EAHIX
QTOOL
CASAT
GBI
S

OUT OF THIS WORLD

ASMOONASM
EPISRAEPI
TLEROITLE
GALAXYGAL
ONOTUTONO
OERSRAOAR
CTANOLCTA
YSPACEYSP
EPISR EPI
TIER ITLE

Check It Out

Dylan loves to read. He has checked out three books from his local library. Using the titles as clues, figure out in which book each word belongs! Hint: There are five words in each book.

battle   moon
castle   pirate
dragon   planets
galaxy   princess
knight   sea
loot   ship
magic   space
   stars

Origami Animals

Take a square of paper, fold it in specific ways, and you can create all kinds of different shapes. This art form is called origami! To see some of the animals that can be made by folding a square of paper, follow these directions:

- The animal names form one long chain.
- Start by finding the word BEAR.
- The last letter of BEAR will be the first letter of the next animal.

Continue until you find all the hidden animals. Remember, the last letter of each animal is the first letter of the next animal.

Helpful Hint: The animals in the list are not in order!

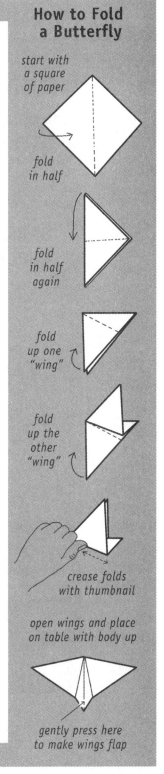

How to Fold a Butterfly

start with a square of paper

fold in half

fold in half again

fold up one "wing"

fold up the other "wing"

crease folds with thumbnail

open wings and place on table with body up

gently press here to make wings flap

BEAR
DOG
TURTLE
TOAD
ELEPHANT
RABBIT
GIRAFFE

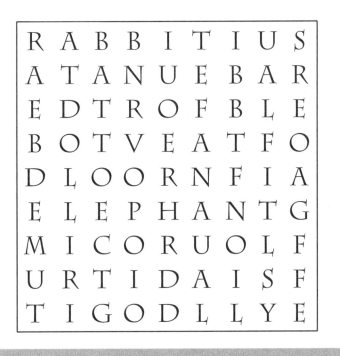

R A B B I T I U S
A T A N U E B A R
E D T R O F B L E
B O T V E A T F O
D L O O R N F I A
E L E P H A N T G
M I C O R U O L F
U R T I D A I S F
T I G O D L L Y E

Delicious Desserts

Brian's hobby is baking. Find the eight types of goodies that he is baking today!

BARS, BROWNIES, CAKES, COOKIES, CUPCAKES, PIES, SQUARES, TARTS

```
N H O N E Y P I S T A C H I H
O P U C U P C A K E S M P K I
R A S P O B E R R Y R R H U B
S E I N W O R B A S T A E V B
C H O C O L K S E K A C U L A
T T E R S C O I T C H A L Q R
C A R R O T P B E U T T E R S
E A M E O T A R T S S E W A T
U C I N N A M O N N U T M E G
```

Aspiring Artist

Annie loves to paint and draw. Can you find her art supplies hidden in the canvas?

Extra Fun: Try highlighting the words in different colors!

ACRYLICS, BRUSH, CANVAS, CHARCOAL, CRAYON, DRAW, EASEL, FIGURE, INK, MARKER, OILS, PAINT, PALETTE, PAPER, PASTEL, PEN, PENCIL, SKETCH, SMOCK, STUDIO, TURPENTINE, WASH, WATERCOLOR

Zap! Pow!

Lots of kids collect comic books. Not only are they great to read, it's also fun to own ones that are hard to find! Speaking of hard to find, can you spot all the superheroes hiding in the grid?

Avengers

Batman

Captain America

Fantastic Four

Flash

Green Lantern

Ninja Turtles

Robin

Spiderman

Superman

Transformers

Wonder Woman

X-Men

```
N I W T O I M E A R G O T O
F A N T A S T I C F O U R N
M L I O C S H B W O N D A R
E N N T A U F A M E T M N E
D I J S P P L T E N O O S T
O F A T H E A X A W R P F N
P S T A A R S M R Y I O O A
Y R U F I M T E V D O R R L
I E R T N A D N E C A O M N
T G T O B N O R N W A B E E
L N L I O T M T N I B O R E
L E E W L A U F L A S H S R
U V S L N U A N D R I C H G
C A P T A I N A M E R I C A
```

Darling Dolls

Donna has a large collection of dolls that she has made. Her hobby is to decorate each doll to match the name it has been given! Can you find all of Donna's dolls?

```
C R Y E O B U N C
H D A I S Y H I A
E I P T R O B I N
R K E N N U R O D
R O N O N A T K Y
Y O N N T S H L I
C R Y S T A L S T
O B U N Y O S O M
C A N D H E D Y I
```

HOLLY	**CHERRY**
CRYSTAL	**DOT**
BROOK	**DAISY**
ROBIN	**PENNY**
BUNNY	**ROSE**
CANDY	**STAR**

Extra Fun: Pick your favorite name from the list and decorate this doll to match. Add hair, a hat, an apron, shoes—whatever you like!

Stitching Time

If quilting is your hobby, you will need a lot of supplies. See if you can find all of the sewing items hidden in this quilt!

```
I W O T H I M B L E U
L D E L D E E N L O V
P O T S M A K E A Q G
P I N C U S H I O N S
A U N I L T S O I M R
T E T S I M E T J U E
T S E S F O T R M E L
E A N O D A I W O Q U
R C I R B A F U S E R
N A L S E T H R E A D
```

THIMBLE, NEEDLE, FABRIC, THREAD, PATTERN, SCISSORS, RULER, PINS, BATTING, PINCUSHION

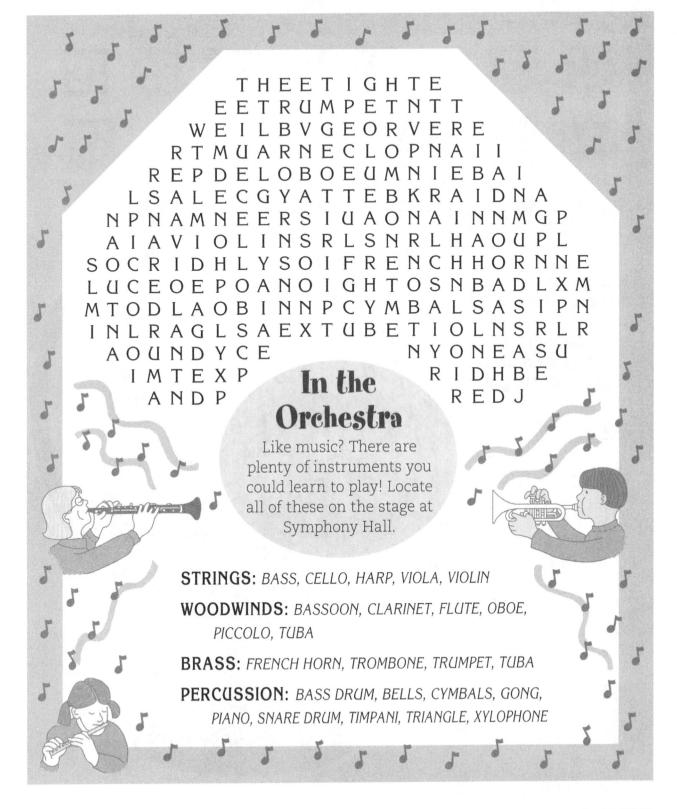

```
T H E E T I G H T E
E E T R U M P E T N T T
W E I L B V G E O R V E R E
R T M U A R N E C L O P N A I I
R E P D E L O B O E U M N I E B A I
L S A L E C G Y A T T E B K R A I D N A
N P N A M N E E R S I U A O N A I N N M G P
A I A V I O L I N S R L S N R L H A O U P L
S O C R I D H L Y S O I F R E N C H H O R N N E
L U C E O E P O A N O I G H T O S N B A D L X M
M T O D L A O B I N N P C Y M B A L S A S I P N
I N L R A G L S A E X T U B E T I O L N S R L R
A O U N D Y C E           N Y O N E A S U
  I M T E X P              R I D H B E
    A N D P                R E D J
```

In the Orchestra

Like music? There are plenty of instruments you could learn to play! Locate all of these on the stage at Symphony Hall.

STRINGS: *BASS, CELLO, HARP, VIOLA, VIOLIN*

WOODWINDS: *BASSOON, CLARINET, FLUTE, OBOE, PICCOLO, TUBA*

BRASS: *FRENCH HORN, TROMBONE, TRUMPET, TUBA*

PERCUSSION: *BASS DRUM, BELLS, CYMBALS, GONG, PIANO, SNARE DRUM, TIMPANI, TRIANGLE, XYLOPHONE*

Saving Stamps

Collecting stamps from all over the world is a very popular hobby. Each stamp contains two letters missing from the countries listed. Fill in the blanks correctly, then find the hidden countries on the globe.

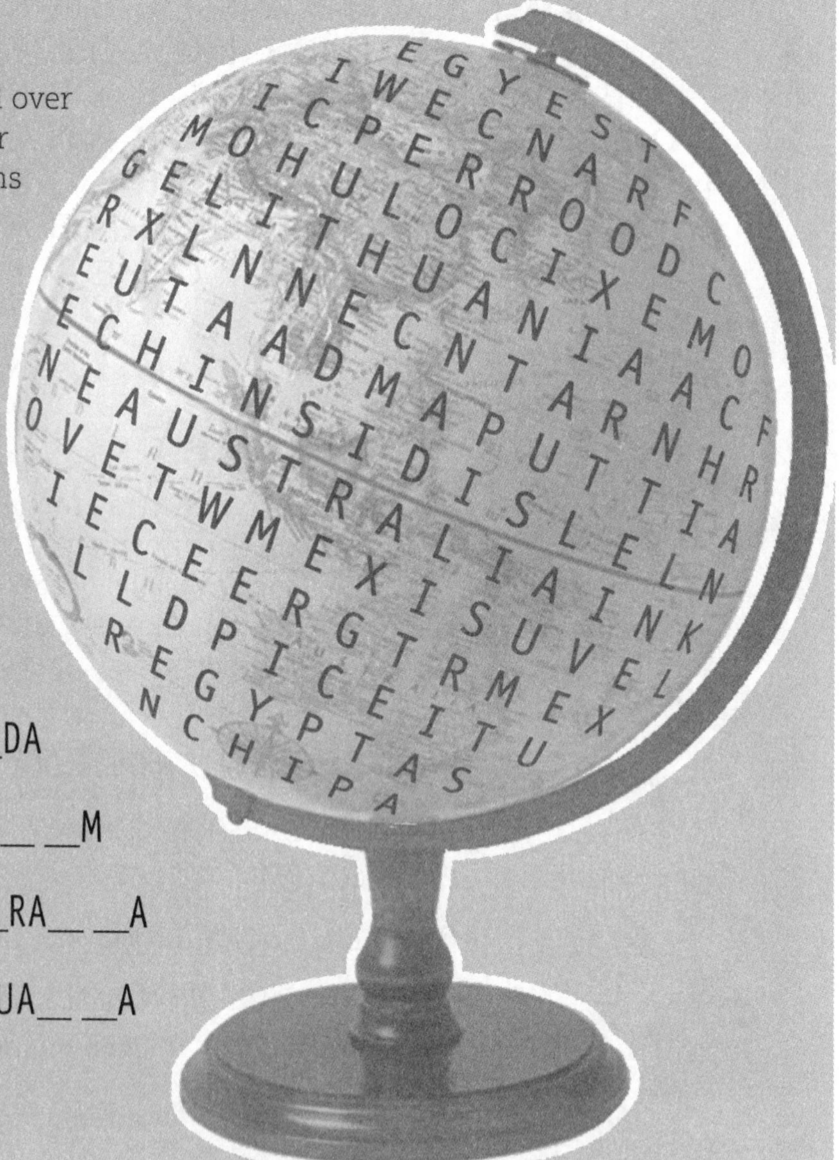

ME__ __CO

EG__ __T

P__ __U

C__ __NA   CA__ __DA

FR__ __CE   V__ __T__ __M

IN__ __A   AU__ __RA__ __A

SW__ __EN   LI__ __UA__ __A

GR__ __CE

Having a Ball

All of these words are specific to basketball, tennis, or golf. Do you know which ones belong together in each ball?

```
      S T D U N
    A B O U N Z E
  S D O O W E F R O
  N E P A K B U L C N I
L U H A N D I C A P C N V
A T O R O E M I G B E T I
J E L G R E E N S O K H F
U S E Y I P U T T G F E T
M Q S T R O K E I E I R S
  F P E I D D A C Y A N
  B I R D I E K D H
  A D T O P L A
    Y W H O E
```

GOLF BALL

Extra Fun:

Instead of circling the answers, use a magic marker to highlight each word with a single line of color!

ACE	**DEFENSE**	**HANDICAP**
ADVANTAGE	**DEUCE**	**HOLES**
BASKET	**DRIBBLE**	**IRON**
BIRDIE	**DUNK**	**JUMP**
BOGEY	**FAULT**	**LOVE**
BOUNCE	**FLAGSTICK**	**MATCH**
CADDIE	**FOUL**	**NET**
CLUB	**GREEN**	**OFFENSE**
COURT	**GUARD**	**PAR**

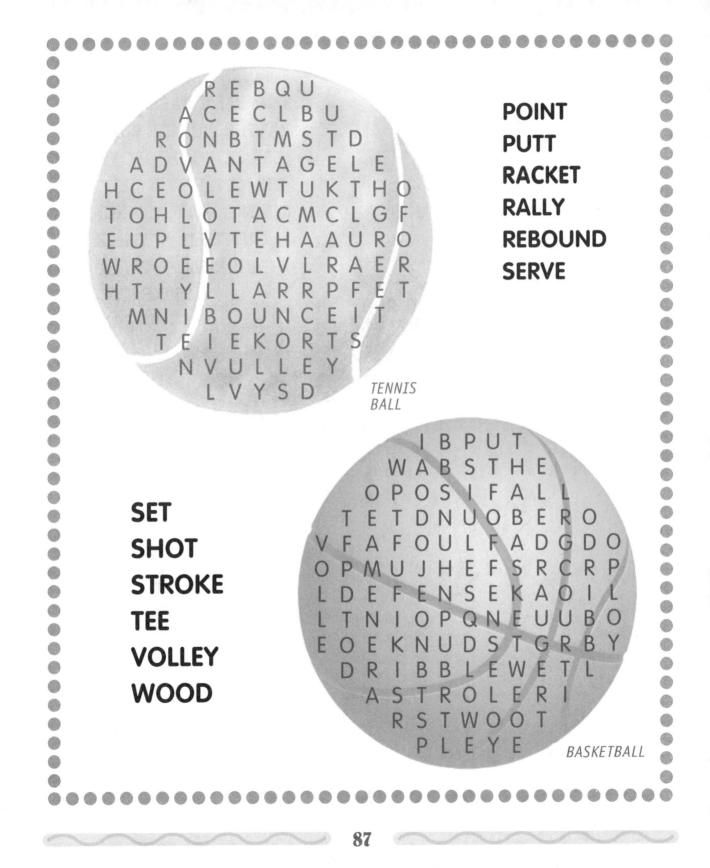

```
        R E B Q U
        A C E C L B U
        R O N B T M S T D
        A D V A N T A G E L E
    H C E O L E W T U K T H O
    T O H L O T A C M C L G F
    E U P L V T E H A A U R O
    W R O E E O L V L R A E R
    H T I Y L L A R R P F E T
    M N I B O U N C E I T
        T E I E K O R T S
        N V U L L E Y
        L V Y S D
```

TENNIS BALL

POINT

PUTT

RACKET

RALLY

REBOUND

SERVE

SET

SHOT

STROKE

TEE

VOLLEY

WOOD

```
        I B P U T
        W A B S T H E
        O P O S I F A L L
    T E T D N U O B E R O
    V F A F O U L F A D G D O
    O P M U J H E F S R C R P
    L D E F E N S E K A O I L
    L T N I O P Q N E U U B O
    E O E K N U D S T G R B Y
    D R I B B L E W E T L
    A S T R O L E R I
    R S T W O O T
    P L E Y E
```

BASKETBALL

Take Me Out to the Ballgame

Find all these baseball terms in the diamond. When you are finished, read the remaining letters from left to right and top to bottom to enjoy a funny joke!

BALK, BALL, BASE, BATTER, BENCH, BUNT, ERROR, FOUL, GLOVE, HELMET, HIT, INFIELD, INNING, MITT, MOUND, OUTFIELD, PITCHER, RUN, SLIDE, STEAL, STRIKE, TAG, TEAM, UMPIRE

```
                W H
              Y D I D
            T R H E B A
          S E E S T E A L
        B H A L G L O V E L
      P C L A Y E R I B L I N
    K T H I T M S E N D Y E L A
  S I H T E E O U T F I E L D S A
L P L D A I A U Y B I ? B E C A N U
B A L K E N M N S E E S A B E U H E
  N E E R N D D E N L U O F R D T
    S T R I K E B C D L A T R E
      T O N T R T H L I A E M
        R G N I G A P G T L
          R H P B U N T E
            A M C T A H
              U I B C
                E !
```

Hit the Slopes

Snowflakes have covered some of the letters in this puzzle. Break the snow code before you find the words on the downhill-ski race course!

G=❄ I=❄
M=❄ O=✳
R=❄

B❄ND❄N❄S
B✳✳T
C✳U❄SE
D❄✳P
F❄N❄SH
FLA❄
_____
STA❄T❄N❄
❄ATE
_____
❄✳✳UL
P✳LES
❄UN
SK❄S
SLAL✳❄
T❄❄E

S I F I N I S H
L E L X P E T C
A T A O M O A G
L O G S O I R I
O N G B G T T S
M E S W U I I N
T P E D L K N S
C O U R S E G T
R L I O N N G H
N E S P I O A W
U S L D O T T S
R A N N D I E L
O I T S M O F B
B E A E T I O L

89

Swim Meet

Dive into this puzzle and race to see how quickly you can find all the swimming words hidden in the pool!

```
E I F I W R E K O R T S T S A E R B T
K T O G F L I P T U R N F O S W I M M
O H I L R N G I T W T S A E E T O U Y
R A O L E B E N R E K P S U R F A C E
T T O N E D A E T C R P T M D A W L L
S M E K S W L F O A A R M I O U H T D
K Y I N T A H L E L M N V N I T I M E
C K E R Y T B N O H A E N D M Y S F M
A R I E L E N D T O M W T O U L T D B
B U T T E R F L Y E P T H E N A L E R
I S S H M E T S O G L O N E R T E O K
```

BACKSTROKE, BLOCKS, BREASTSTROKE, BUTTERFLY, DIVE, FAST, FLIP TURN, FREESTYLE, LANE, LAP, MARK, MEDLEY, METER, POOL, RELAY, SURFACE, TIME, WATER, WHISTLE

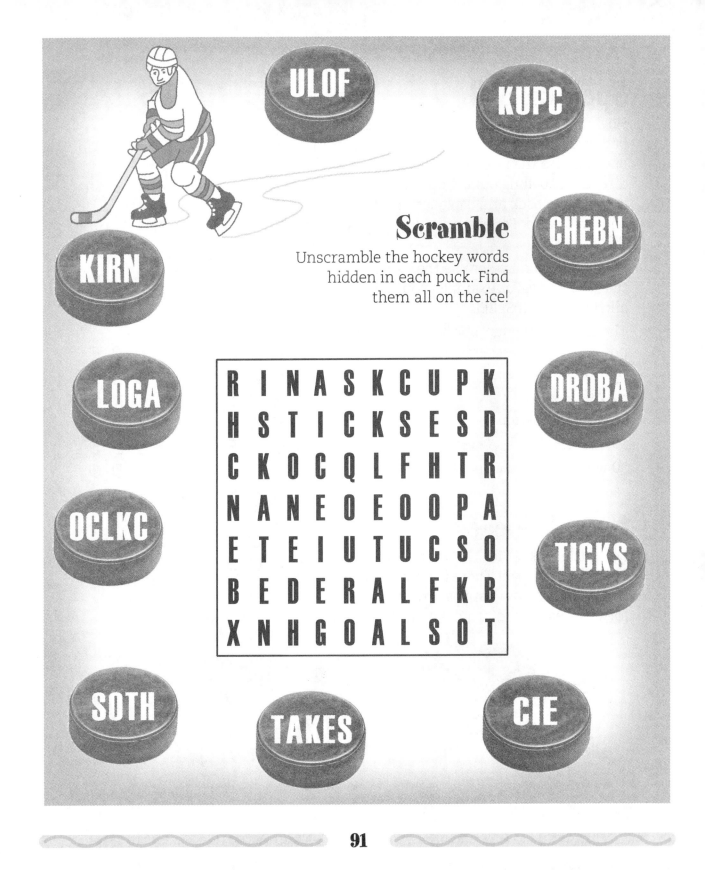

ULOF

KUPC

KIRN

CHEBN

Scramble

Unscramble the hockey words hidden in each puck. Find them all on the ice!

LOGA

DROBA

OCLKC

TICKS

SOTH

TAKES

CIE

```
R I N A S K C U P K
H S T I C K S E S D
C K O C Q L F H T R
N A N E O E O O P A
E T E I U T U C S O
B E D E R A L F K B
X N H G O A L S O T
```

Spelling Ball

How many words can you find in this soccer ball grid? Start at any letter, then move from one space to the next touching space in any direction, spelling out a word as you go. You may double back and use a letter more than once in a word. For example, you may spell the word EVE.

However, you may not use the same letter twice in a row. For example, you are not allowed to spell SLEEP.

The ten-letter bonus word completes this phrase: Playing soccer is much more fun than watching _____!

SCORE:

10 words = Starter

20 words = Pro

30 words = World Cup

Secret Soccer

Be on the lookout for the word SOCCER hiding in this grid! There is only one time where all six letters appear correctly. Look forward, backward, up, down, and diagonally.

```
S R O S O S O C C E
O O R O S O C C E S
C E C C O C C O R O
C S O C E C E S O C
R O S E R E R O S S
S S O C C O S E O O
O C C S O C E C C C
C E R O C O C C C E
C O O C S E O O S E
E C O S R O C C O S
```

92

Floor Exercise

This gymnast has just finished her floor routine. Look for the circular patterns she made on the floor mat! The first letter of each word has been marked with a dot. One has been done for you.

✓ACROBATICS
MOVEMENT
SOMERSAULT
CARTWHEEL
HANDSTAND
ARTISTRY
TUMBLING
DANCE
TURN
JUMP

```
J X Q P X F T· K Q J X O A· K P F
F I M· X J N X U K Q P Y X R Q P
K T F O Q X R S K J R X F X T O
N P X I V K F X S· F T K I X J
I E X E K J Q P T X O V S V Q K
X I M I X I E L X J V M F X J I
O J· K X I E Q U C· P X E K K A Q
P F U X H I X I A X R I J X X J
Q M Q K I W K R I S X Q I R O X
X A T· S X Q T V D X T X C Q P B
K G F U P X K N X F V A· Q F X A
N Q X O M Q J A O X N V S X P T
X I P B Q A X O H· D· I K X C I X
F O L O K P O J E Q A X J Q X P
X K J A F O X O X C N O A P K J
Q X O K Q P O J O K P J Q X O P
```

Fully Equipped

Like sports? There are plenty to choose from! Figure out each picture and letter puzzle below to come up with the names of twelve different sport activities. Then find all the names in the grid on the next page!

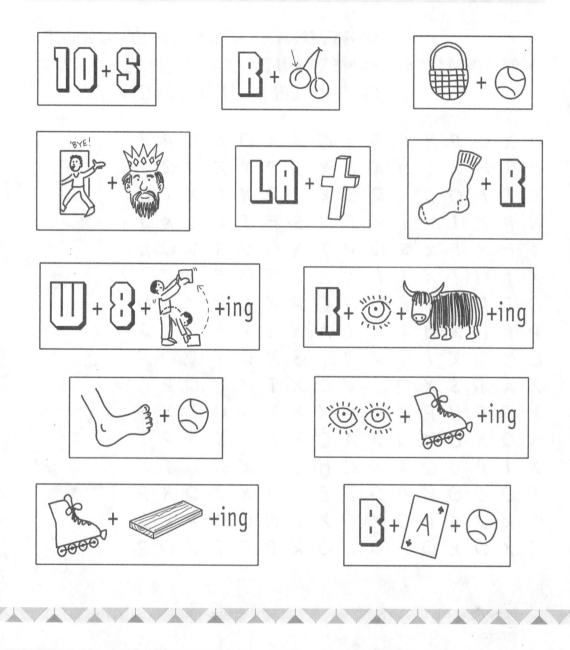

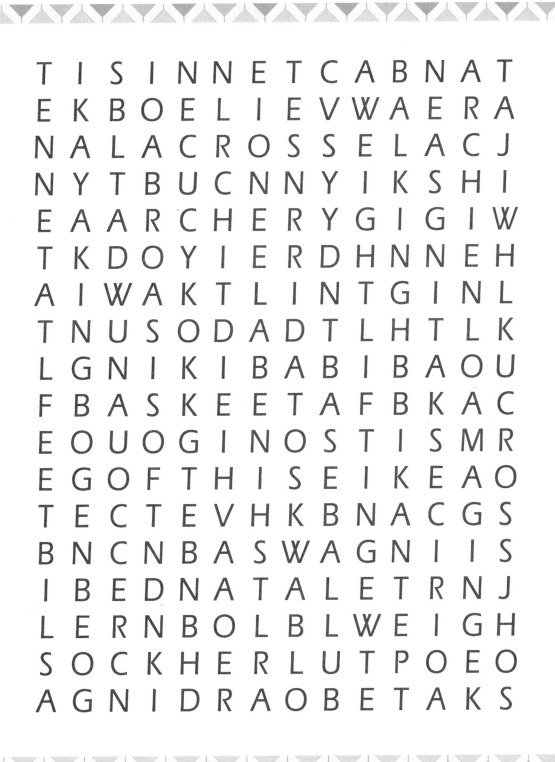

```
T I S I N N E T C A B N A T
E K B O E L I E V W A E R A
N A L A C R O S S E L A C J
N Y T B U C N N Y I K S H I
E A A R C H E R Y G I G I W
T K D O Y I E R D H N N E H
A I W A K T L I N T G I N L
T N U S O D A D T L H T L K
L G N I K I B A B I B A O U
F B A S K E E T A F B K A C
E O U O G I N O S T I S M R
E G O F T H I S E I K E A O
T E C T E V H K B N A C G S
B N C N B A S W A G N I I S
I B E D N A T A L E T R N J
L E R N B O L B L W E I G H
S O C K H E R L U T P O E O
A G N I D R A O B E T A K S
```

Extreme Sports

X sports are action packed and very exciting! These sports often showcase the skills and spectacular tricks of individuals.

```
M X N G N I B M I L C E C I
D T I M X e T o o J R X U M
e G S P S K A T e B o A R D
N O N V O R X O T M C H H e
e R O I X X D C O X K G A N
R X W S F e X R H B C O N e
O T B X X R I O S I L I G R
T e O D I C U S O K I U L O
X X A O U S I S D I M O I T
T W R A N T X T O N B G D X
O T D X O C e A N G I C e T
G N I P M U J e e G N U B O
C X S K Y D I V I N G L A C
```

ICE CLIMBING   SKATEBOARD   SURFING   ROCK CLIMBING

SKYDIVING   BMX BIKING   MOTOCROSS   BUNGEE JUMPING

SNOWBOARD   HANGLIDE

Chapter 9

Imagine That!

Beautiful Ballerina

Emmie dreams that one day she will be a ballerina! Can you find the ten ballet words hidden in the tutu?

```
É U
S T Q J R W I A
L O E U I T T É J O
E T T E U O R I P E S Q
É O L A J É M P T W U A E
T S J R B A M S E Q E É C L
E I A P O I N T E S U I O E U
L E O T A R D E O Q E S L I T E K
O B U A R A B E S Q U E P R T O P
I T I O N S M U S M L R U É S O
É O R I P U I E L A T Q P I
N T S É Q N I B Q É I O
P O S I T I O N S
Q S Y
```

ARABESQUE   PLIÉ
LEOTARD   MUSIC
MIRROR   BARRE
PIROUETTE   JETÉ
POSITIONS   POINTE

Funny Fairy

To find the silly answer to the riddle, use a dark marker to blot out the six fairy words. Collect the remaining letters from left to right and top to bottom.

F E M A L E
S T A I N D
F K G E R U
L W I N G S
Y B C E L T
S M A L L

DUST
FEMALE
FLY
MAGIC
SMALL
WINGS

What do you call a fairy who never takes a bath?

_ _ _ _ _ _ _ _ _ _ _ !

Knight Night

Homophones are words that sound the same but are spelled differently. Words in this puzzle come in pairs—words from the list are in the knight on the right page. Find the homophones on this page!

S E L L F R U P
F N F Y L R M L
H A O I O O A A
R T T S W U I N
W H A L E T D E
H A I T R E E S
S T L U C R K U
E P A L O L O V
I D E W I T C H
Z R E G R O W N
E H E E R I H E
A B E A R P T D
S H I E W A A E
N I G H T W S L
O V H E D S O B
Y W T O K I G N

ATE
BARE
CELL
DEAR
EWE
FLOUR
GROAN
KNIGHT

KNOWS
MADE
ONE
PAUSE
PLAIN
RIGHT

ROOT
SEAS
TALE
WAIL
WAR
WHICH

Remember: Look for these words on this page. Look for their homophones on the other page!

```
O O N C E U E P
K N I G H T W O
N E A T A I E M
T E T H E M R F
P A U S E A E L
W A L S A D B O
C E A E U E T U
I E F U L R P R
R G L W H I C H
K R I L N G C E
N O I S S H W H
O A D O H T A D
W N E P L A I N
S E A S S H W O
R T R O O T A A
N D S C B A R E
```

Presto Chango

Here's your chance to be a real magician!
Change the underlined letter in each word
to form a new word related to magic tricks.
Find these new words in the magician's hat.
Hint: The pictures on this page are clues!

change WIND to W__ND

change FUNNY to __UNNY

change SLOWER to __LOWER

change STIR to ST__R

change CAT to __AT

change RIPE to R__PE

change SCARE to SCAR__

change CARTS to CAR__S

```
S F L E W A N
C W P Q T H S
A O U A U S T
R E H H I D A
F L O W E R R
H R I A S A Q
B U N N Y C U
Q W A D L S I
```

Unusual Unicorn

This unicorn is amazed at all the words that have the letters U-N-I. Figure out each word by using the definitions, then find them all in the grid.

Special clothes that identifies a team = U N I _ _ _ _

All of outer space and everything in it = U N I _ _ _ _ _

All the people in your city or town = _ _ _ _ U N I _ _

Imaginary animal with one horn = U N I _ _ _ _

Gathering of old classmates = _ _ U N I _ _

Long shirt that hangs to the knees = _ U N I _

One-wheeled bike = U N I _ _ _ _ _

Common summer plant with trumpet-shaped

flowers = _ _ _ U N I _

To join together = U N I _ _

Only one of its kind = U N I _ _ _

U I U D E O C O M M U N I T Y T H
I N N T K U T H A N K I T D U O R
U D I S T P U N I Q U E I W Q I E
P N F V L I G C E E L C Y C I N U
U T O T E H O W O R D I I M N U N
N I R Z E R I P E T U N I A U T I
S W M A N Y S T O O U H A R Z O O
Q U I Z P I D E Y T D O Q U I L N

Pirate Booty

Can you find this pirate's buried treasure? You'll have to dig around fer the seven precious gems and metals because he'll not be giving you a list—AAARRRR!

1. _____

2. _____

3. _____

4. _____

5. _____

6. _____

7. _____

```
B O N E S G M A
R G P I C O L A
E M E R A L D S
V B A O F D M A
L O R P M O S P
I T L R U E M P
S T S T I S E H
Y L K B S C H I
D E U A D M A R
N R S K U L L E
D I A M O N D S
X W A R N I N G
```

Marvelous Mermaids

Want to learn a bit about mermaids? Fit each word into its proper place in the paragraph. Then find each word in the giant clamshell!

ENCHANT, LEGEND, LOVELY, OCEAN, SING, SWIM, TAIL, UNDERWATER

Mermaids are _____ fish-women that live _____ in the _____. They have a _____ instead of legs, and can _____ really fast.

_____ says that mermaids can _____ sailors when they _____.

```
J K C O M A E K I
C I N G B U I R D O L
A O C E A N S Y D N U
M S A N O D V L G O S
E A H C L E G E N D T
R L D H S R E V I T H
M A I A Y W L O S E A
J V O N T A I L I C Y
C A T C T L M E A
Q U E S R
I M R E R
E O Y
```

Ask an Alien

Imagine talking with a creature from another planet! Fit the letters A-L-I-E-N into the missing spaces to create some outer space sentences!

Extra Fun: How many UFOs can you find in this puzzle?

"Take me to your L__ __D__R!"

"Which one of the P__ __N__TS do you live on?"

"What fuel do you use in your SP__C__SH__P?"

"There are billions of ST__RS in just one galaxy!"

"What kind of T__CH__O__OGY did you use to build your spaceship?"

"The U__ __V__RS__ is full of stars and galaxies!"

"What are those strange, flashing __IGHTS?"

Greetings, Earthling!

WOW!

```
        T I S T
    W H A U F O H A T U
    S P A C E S H I P W F E
  I R L D L I G U H T I O N T
  E U S A K T E C H N O L O G Y Y
  I F S N I T U F O A I B I R D A
P   O L E A L N E N U I V T S S   P U E
U N I D E N T K F I E D F L Y E N S O B F E C T
O M A N I T I S S V E G R O Y V E R Y H A O R T T O
R U F O I T E O W I T H A U T A U S I N G A N Y
O U S S R O F S A O U R T F T S T L E A D E R O
O U S U T C O R F M E S O U T W H X E R
    O I M I S S O R O S I U F O E I O
      H O N O I O E O H O S
```

Custom Castles

A castle is an enormous building with many parts. See if you can find all the castle words hidden in the castle wall!

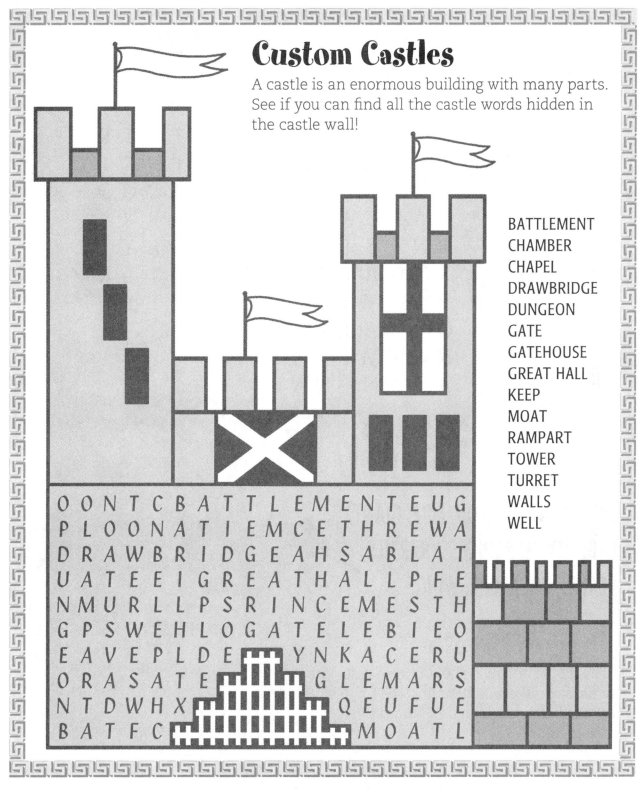

BATTLEMENT
CHAMBER
CHAPEL
DRAWBRIDGE
DUNGEON
GATE
GATEHOUSE
GREAT HALL
KEEP
MOAT
RAMPART
TOWER
TURRET
WALLS
WELL

O O N T C B A T T L E M E N T E U G
P L O O N A T I E M C E T H R E W A
D R A W B R I D G E A H S A B L A T
U A T E E I G R E A T H A L L P F E
N M U R L L P S R I N C E M E S T H
G P S W E H L O G A T E L E B I E O
E A V E P L D E Y N K A C E R U
O R A S A T E G L E M A R S
N T D W H X Q E U F U E
B A T F C M O A T L

```
S O N S C E U P T O W N A T I
S O M C E T F I R E H I E T R
E S A A L L W A E S A F N R I
C E R L C A E D A R A A O G O
N G N E W I W H S U I L P R S
I N I S I R N S U G O G L Y
R T W A E S A V R C E I T A R
P I A V N H E R E P T I L E
O L A A T E H I J
N C Y M Y T H S
A Y A N D D A G
```

CAVE, CLAWS, COLOR, FIRE, GIANT, LAIR, MYTH, PRINCESS, REPTILE, SCALES, TREASURE, WINGS

Dragon Breath

This brave knight is about to do battle with a fierce dragon. Can you find the hidden words before the dragon's flames burn the knight?

Look Again!

Thought you were done hunting for things? Not so fast! See if you can spot each of these picture pieces somewhere in this book. Write the name of the puzzle each piece is from in the space under each box. Hint: There is only one piece from each chapter!

1.

2.

3.

4.

5.

6.

7.

crease folds with thumbnail

8.

9.

Puzzle Answers

<u>E</u> <u>GGS</u> & B <u>ACON</u>

M <u>ILK</u> & C <u>OOKIES</u>

B <u>READ</u> & B <u>UTTER</u>

A <u>PPLES</u> & O <u>RANGES</u>

P <u>EANUT</u> <u>BUTTER</u> & J <u>ELLY</u>

S <u>PAGHETTI</u> & M <u>EATBALLS</u>

C <u>HEESE</u> & C <u>RACKERS</u>

S <u>TRAWBERRIES</u> & C <u>REAM</u>

L <u>ETTUCE</u> & T <u>OMATO</u>

H <u>AM</u> & C <u>HEESE</u>

F <u>RENCH</u> <u>FRIES</u> & K <u>ETCHUP</u>

H <u>OT</u> <u>DOGS</u> & H <u>AMBURGERS</u>

Dynamic Duos • Pages 4–5

The EVERYTHING KIDS' Word Search Puzzle and Activity Book

Lotsa Laundry • Page 6

```
    B W E O S C W
  S H S B L A U N O
O B O C W P S P U G B
I S E C H G A O A N P E P
W S G S O B N C J D G O E
G B O B P S T K A E B O S
I C W E C E S S M R W S C
P H B S O H A T A W E B P
B C I D B L O U S E S P S
O S R T O W E L S A G S C
  E Y S H E E T S R T E
    I G W C Q O G W B
      B H S C B O E
```

A sock!

Cutting the Cake • Page 7

```
C L A S S M A T E O F U T F
E F T S R O B H G I E N O T
G R A N D M A M J F S C F U
R I E S O F U E O J S L A F
A E U H J E O F K T U E T S
N N E O T J B I R T H J H E
D D T F U O L A M Y D E E T
P S I S T E R I G Y A J R O
A U N T F S S B E O F E U F
  N I S U O C U E
```

The birthday girl's name is: <u>Amy</u>

Trail of Toys • Page 8

```
L J A E T A K S E C I
L A T E D D Y B E A R
A C R J U R M A P R O
B K U P E U S L L O D
E S C E A M K L N D B
S O K I T E S O K A O
A I T E N N I O O S X
B N C R A Y O N S B B
```

Puzzle Answers

Bathroom Humor • Page 9

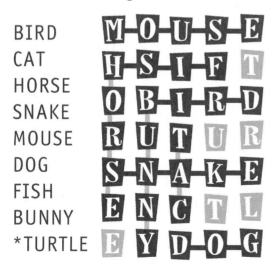

The extra letters read: Who always steals the soap in the bathroom? Robber Ducky!

Going Batty • Page 11

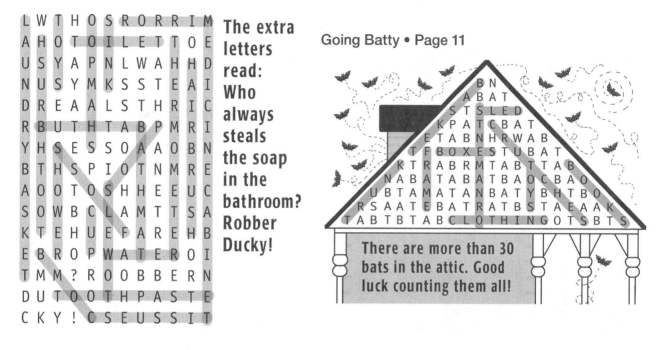

There are more than 30 bats in the attic. Good luck counting them all!

Perfect Pets • Page 10

BIRD
CAT
HORSE
SNAKE
MOUSE
DOG
FISH
BUNNY
*TURTLE

More Chores! • Page 12

Fun for Frank • Page 13

Movie Night • Page 14

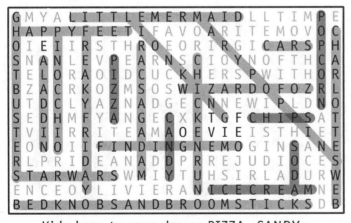

Kids love to munch on: PIZZA, CANDY,
SODA, ICE CREAM, CHIPS and POPCORN.

Five-Day Forecast • Pages 16–17

Monday

```
C H I B L Y H
F A I R I C O
S T E E R O S
W S S E A O U
T W Y Z N L Y
E R E Y I I N
D R W R M D N
```

Tuesday

```
I C L O U D Y
S H O W E R S
W I R A N I I
A L W T E Z W
R L E O L Z N
N Y L V E L D
R N Y A I E Y
```

Wednesday

```
A C P H Z Y L
U O O W A R N
D Y U N W E T
M I R A I N Y
L G I H N T W
D I N T D H S
T A G R Y S A
```

Thursday

```
A B R O W R H
U R N D A O T
M I L D M I Y
T G W H R N O
W H Y A N R H
E T E U M Y T
W S S W A R M
```

Friday

```
B O R W R M I
R H A Z Y S C
G U O I K P L
T M T T C O D
M I R A I U Y
O D M E T N I
H T O C S G A
```

Puzzle Answers

Backyard Birds • Page 18

The four birds with names that were scrambled are:

CARDINAL

HAWK

ROBIN

WOODPECKER

```
B T K H W R E N G E
L R W E O O A R R E
U A A L O O R H O K
E T H O D F B C S K
B E I R P D Z T B C
I I D N E M Y A E I
R B A A C C K H A L
D Y A R K D T T K F
O D A W E C Y U I H
A E C A R D I N A L
V B E R N T S H E G
E E N B V J U N C O
E O R L Y M A M N L
Y H B E E C A O U D
S P A R R O W U S F
E I H A R V E R T I
P S W I F T U N E N
B T O F R E S I S C
O L H S E N N N U H
E B U N T I N G O N
R E D E B T I D M F
I T H O J R E O T I
V E R E D A E V I R
S O O P U M Y E T S
```

Going Buggy • Page 19

```
W K C I T H Y D O
B E O E E E B G S
B U C Z F Z U R ?
O B K E L B T E C
T A R U Y E T D E
I S O D E E E I T
U T A H E T R P I
Q L C Y C L F S M
S T H A A E L F R
O G N A T N Y T E
M W H A I S T L T
D R A G O N F L Y
E Y L F E R I F !
```

Extra letters spell:

Why do bees buzz? Because they can't whistle!

Obstacle Course Opposites • Page 20

```
T H P E B O P
S O O F A S T
A I T U C E R
L F O D O N O
L O W W A S H
U N O E R S
P I T E D L
      D   S
```

Great Gardens • Page 21

```
M A R I G O L D
W E E D E W E E
R D W P R E T E
O Y S I A D E Y
S D W L N E L S
E E D U I W O N
E P E T U N I A
M U M E M D V P
```

```
T N A L P G G E W
Z E L E T T U C E
U E D W O E E D C
C U C U M B E R A
C W E E A D N W R
H E E D T R W E R
I E D P O T A T O
N W E C E D W E T
I E R E P P E P D
```

The EVERYTHING KIDS' Word Search Puzzle and Activity Book

Fantastic Fort • Page 22

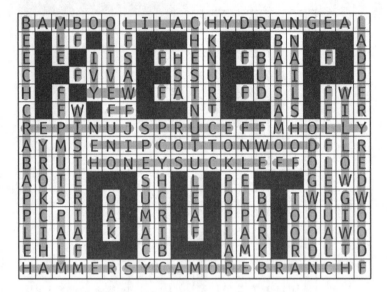

```
B A M B O O L I L A C H Y D R A N G E A L
E   L F   L F     H K       B N       A A
E   E   I I S   F H E N   F B A A   F D D
C   F     V V A     S S   U     L I   D
H   F   Y E W     F A T R   F D S L   F W E
C   F W   F F         N T     A S   F I R
R E P I N U J S P R U C E F F M H O L L Y
A Y M S E N I P C O T T O N W O O D F L R
B R U T H O N E Y S U C K L E F F O L O E
A O T E     S H   L   P E     G E W D
P K S R     O   U C   E   O L B   T W R G W
P C P I     A   M R I   L   P P A   O O U I O
L I A A     K   A I L   F   L A R   O O A W O
E H L F         C B     M     A M K   R D L T D
H A M M E R S Y C A M O R E B R A N C H F
```

Ready to Ride • Page 23

Outdoor Eating • Page 24

Hide & Seek • Page 25

12-7-7-3-10	**WOODS**	
11-9-4-4	**TREE**	
10-6-4-3	**SHED**	
8-7-9-2-6	**PORCH**	

12	7	10	6	4	4	5	8
7	12	7	7	3	10	1	7
1	7	2	9	8	6	3	9
3	1	10	3	3	4	2	2
11	9	4	4	11	3	4	6
5	1	6	5	2	12	7	7
6	3	5	1	9	1	5	4

Puzzle Answers

Driveway Fun • Page 26

School Stuff • Page 29

Plenty of Pals • Page 30

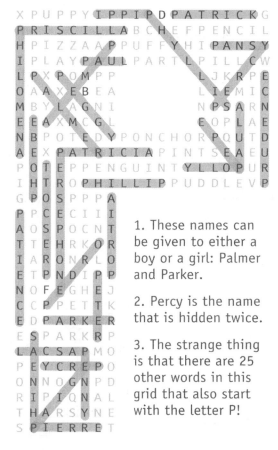

1. These names can be given to either a boy or a girl: Palmer and Parker.

2. Percy is the name that is hidden twice.

3. The strange thing is that there are 25 other words in this grid that also start with the letter P!

Hop on the Bus • Page 28

The EVERYTHING KIDS' Word Search Puzzle and Activity Book

What's in the Backpack? • Page 31

You're It! • Page 33

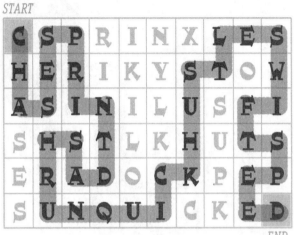

Shape Up! • Page 32

Got Art? • Page 34

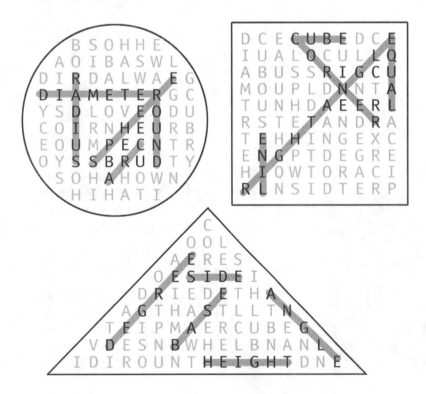

Puzzle Answers

Janitor's Closet • Page 35

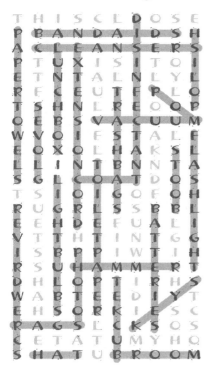

Lunch Line • Pages 36–37

Detention! • Page 38

The extra letters spell:
Why was the magnet
given detention? He had
a negative attitude!

Around Town • Pages 40–41

1. LIBRARY
2. POLICE
3. VET
4. GROCERY STORE
5. CHURCH
6. POST OFFICE
7. DOCTOR
8. HARDWARE STORE
9. BANK
10. HAIRDRESSER
11. MOVIE THEATER
12. FIREFIGHTERS

Savings Sum • Page 42

There are 4 pennies, 3 nickels, 6 dimes, and 7 quarters for a total of $2.54.

Love Letter • Page 43

Roses are red,
Violets are blue,
Sugar is sweet,
and so are you!

In the Bag • Page 44

The one food item not in the bags? Cookies. Darn!

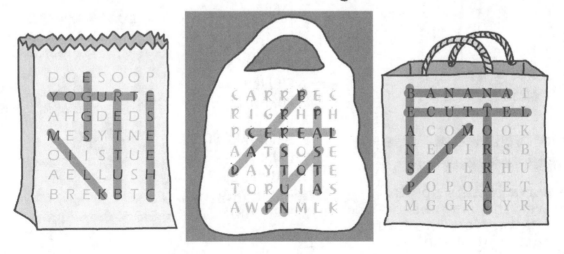

Puzzle Answers

Snip! Snip! • Page 45

Words to search for:

HEARS
EARS
HAIR
AIR
INK
IN
COB
RIM
LIP
PIN

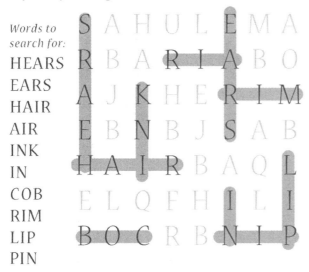

On Fire! • Pages 46–47

FIREPLACE
FIREFLY
WILDFIRE
FIRECRACKER
FIREHOUSE
FIREPROOF
FIREWOOD
CAMPFIRE
FIRE ENGINE
BACKFIRE
FIRE EXTINGUISHER
FIREWORKS
FIREFIGHTER

Handy Hardware • Page 48

121

Road Trip • Page 50

```
        H S H O
      O S N A C K S
      U S U I T C A S E
    J I U S E I C R E S B
  O C T I K Y D O E T S O X G
  O A I C D E O O M K O O B L L
J K S A S U N G L A S S E S A O
S E J O O U O W R C O O L E R W D
E S Y A D N M A P T H A N K Y O U
T U   I L O H K N A B   B E
```

Words to look for: BOOK, CAMERA, COOLER, DOG, JACKET, MAP, MONEY, MUSIC, SNACKS, SUITCASE, SUNGLASSES

New Hampshire Holiday • Page 51

```
X L R T R O P R I A R P A R K H
E L E V A T I O N E E T O W N I
T X V P A R K F R R D E P H T G
I M I L E S S K I A R E A O S H
S E R T E G O L F C O U R S E W
P O R I S P R A P I B D K P R A
M I T D P A R K E N T H E I O Y
A I A P A R K E G C L L O T F G
C O V E R E D B R I D G E A R A
R N I A T N U O M P A R K L N I
```

Under the Big Top • Page 53

```
    L O O N A
    W I L S T I C
  B A E B P M I E S
  O S C I A L N Z K G I
  O T R T L A E H S N I
  L S O Y E P A R W E A
  L A B L A W I N U T A
  N Y A R I N G S S G O
  W I I T H O U R F
    R I B A L E N
    S C R F A
```

```
      I L O V P
    E T B A L S
    D G C G O T A T H
    S E B I I G A T P P O
    C L J U G G L E R C O
    R I R B C U S S I S N
    F T I S S L O T K S S
    A U N I C Y C L O R
    F F U N I I A M S
      A D T T H A T
      W S C A R
```

```
      J U G G L
    D S S T E U V
  E A N D D S N U Z
  S I E O W M G I O C O
  T D S O T O H C E L B
  E E S L D T L Y A B C
  K T W L F R A C E S E
  S V E A R S A L W M A
  S T B H E P E A R
  A K E E T S X
    S C A R F
```

Motor Messages • Page 52

```
N L O Z I S L A R O F E M I T E H T R
Y O U A R E W O N D E R F U L T H Z W
G V O O D M E N T O C O M E T O A I H
O E D I W A N T T O B U G Y O U O G O
H T F T H E I R P A R T Y I B E L R L
D O I E B E S E E I N G Y O U V E E E
E L T H I S S I T H E T S E B R A A N
W A I T F O R M E N D O M U O H T T U
A U G H T O T A R E N E G R I N T T B
R G H E W O T O O D U M B T O K N O W
I H R L D L Z Z U P S I H T E K I S C
F M I W O N D E R W O H J E N Z L E H
Z I P P I T Y D O O D A H Y W I L E O
O L L I N N A E N E R I T C O L U Y L
R G O T T O F I C R A Z Y F O R Y O U
E H T O N A T O O R R F I T A R D U T
```

Gearing Up • Page 54

```
I L B A C K S S T O O B G N I K I H
K A E O O U A E B I N O S E D T O L
B N E T V E I H T H I K N G O C O C
O T P M E P D C I N B A C K P A C K
O E I B E N K T G F O O R B A N L I
S R F I R S T A I D K I T I E T A P
T N N E T I C M K S C A B N M E N P
S R A L U C O N I B C C O O L E R I
B O C K P O C K R A W L O D A N L C
O S L E E P I N G B A G T B O O H K
```

Puzzle Answers

Sunny Seashore • Page 55

What a Zoo! • Page 57

South American Exhibit

Australian Exhibit

African Exhibit

Sail Away • Page 56

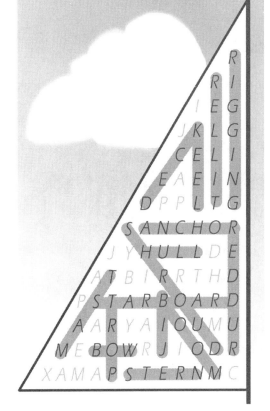

Famous Places • Pages 58–59

6 Florida
14 Hawaii
2 New York
3 Tennessee
15 Virginia
1 Arizona
5 California
10 New Mexico
7 Washington, DC
9 New York
12 N. Carolina
8 Missouri
13 Illinois
4 S. Dakota
11 Nevada

The EVERYTHING KIDS' Word Search Puzzle and Activity Book

Lots of Luggage • Page 60

KNOCK KNOCK
WHO'S THERE?
ALPACA
ALPACA WHO?

DRAOBYA
LUGGAGE
ALPWACA
VTNHET T
IUTFHRE
RPUGLNK
RNIKAYC
ALYLOUT
FPPAOCT
LEVART K

NOITANITSEDD
SECURITY
TERMINAL
ITCERUTRAPED
SEAT YROW

ALPACA THE TRUNK,
YOU PACK-A THE SUITCASE!

Tall Tale • Page 64

Why do giraffes
have long necks?

SO THEY
CAN'T SMELL
THEIR
STINKY FEET!

Pets at the Vet • Pages 62–63

ODSF
HOTOIT
CPHINC
LOACYCAS
IERNSHCR
TEEKARAP
ELSOSRTL
ZWAIAFYE
AHKFIRNT
SNEAKESE

HALMST
IZMI SSIMYDO
TOOGSA PZAKEEI
SPICDE ODRGROD
SHEWAAG ARSIERP
CRABBIT

PARAKSEETST
ITARANTULAI
THIANAKTHTS
ABBITKASPID
HARDSETPART
ISFDRAZILEL

CANARLYFICH
ABECDIEHKII
FICHNBFE
HKIIGRJ
HAMSTER
RLMQOGP

Farm Fun • Page 65

COW, SHEEP, PIG, BAT, HORSE,
DUCK, MICE, CHICK, GOOSE, GOAT

Puzzle Answers

Ocean Alive • Page 66

CRAB, WHALE, TURTLE, SEAL,
SHRIMP, SHARK, EEL, CLAM,
SEAHORSE, LOBSTER,
JELLYFISH, OCTOPUS

```
B A R C O E L T R U T
H S E A H O R S E W C
A E T N O C T O P U S
L I S S C E O M M P H
L A B E I M L N I W A
H E O A A N I A R B R
J E L L Y F I S H A K
S I C C A L L Y S W P
```

Man's Best Friend • Pages 68–69

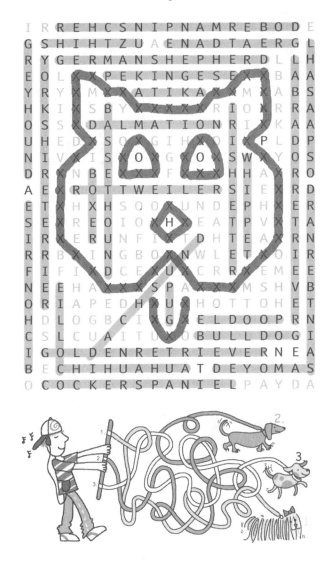

```
I R R E H C S N I P N A M R E B O D E
G S H I H T Z U A E N A D T A E R G L
R Y G E R M A N S H E P H E R D L L H
E O L X P E K I N G E S E X X B A A A
Y R Y X X A T I K A X X M X X R R A A
H K I S B Y X X X R I O X R R S A
O S S X D A L M A T I O N R I X P L D P
U H E D X S O X G I H X O I X P L D P
N I V X I S X O O X S W X Y O
D R X N B E X X F X X H H A X R O
A E X R O T T W E I L E R S I E X R D
E T X H X H S O O X U N D E P H X E
S E X R E O I O X H E A T P V X T A
I R X E R U N F I X T D H T E A X R N
R R B X I N G B O X N W L E T X O I R
F I F I X D C E X U X C R R X E M E E
N E E H A X X X S P A X X X M S H V B
O R I A P E D H X U X H O T T O H E T
H D L O G B C I G X E L D O O P R N
C S L C U A I T U X O B U L L D O G I
I G O L D E N R E T R I E V E R N E A
B E C H I H U A H U A T D E Y O M A S
O C O C K E R S P A N I E L P A Y D A
```

Holed Up • Page 67

```
    W O O D C H
  I Q U H I T W A
Q W S I S Q U I R S
E W O O D C H U C K N T
L F L M U N H K A U N A U C
I B A T M S I T U B U K R O
D E D O O P M A E K O T O
Y C Y R U R M T F A S Q L
B A B R S Q U I R R E L E A
G U U L E U N O O C C A R G
S G S N A K E G I C E A
  T B E R H E M O O S
  N I T B O T W O
    U L D B E N
```

Cold Creatures • Page 70

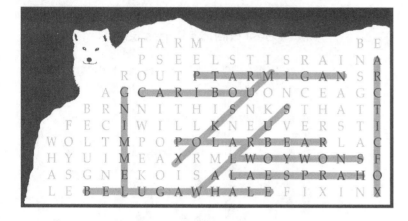

Desert Dwellers • Page 71

```
D M H O R A B O N D
E R A C H L A L A X
S O T G K I N G S R
E W T L E Y D E D E
R T E O S S G O P H
```

Animals in Danger • Page 72

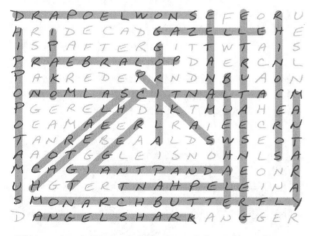

The extra letters spell: "Four decades after it was declared endangered, the American bald eagle is no longer in danger!"

Cool Car Collection • Pages 74–75

MACARONI	X L A N I D 🚗 A 🚗 B C D 🚗
SCARF	A B C D A E F G T H I J K
CARNIVORE	B L 🚗 E B M A 🚗 O N I M N
POSTCARD	C O P O C Q R S O T U V W
CARROT	D X Y F L Z A B N C D E 🚗
	F I F G D G H I J K L M V
CARTOON	G N S H E O 🚗 N I V O R E
SCARLET	🚗 P Q 🚗 F R S T U V W X Y
DISCARD	H Z A I D B S 🚗 E C R O W
CARDINAL	I J K L M N O P Q R S T U
SCARECROW	P O S T 🚗 D C D 🚗 R O T V
CARVE	E F 🚗 J G G H I J K L M W
CARTWHEEL	N O L K H P Q S S T U V X
	🚗 P E T I W 🚗 T W H E E L
CARPET	X Y T L J K L M N O P Q Y
CAROL	Z A B M 🚗 N O P Q S 🚗 F Z

Puzzle Answers

Check It Out • Page 76

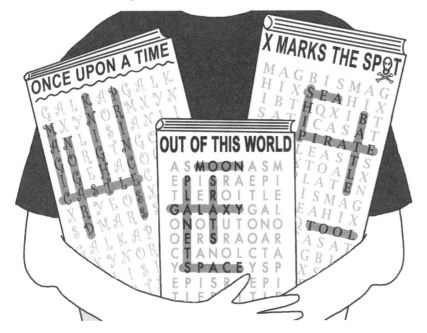

Origami Animals • Page 77

Delicious Desserts • Page 78

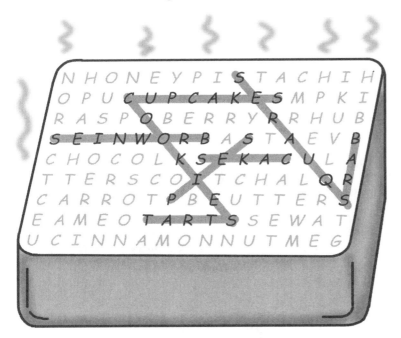

Aspiring Artist • Page 79

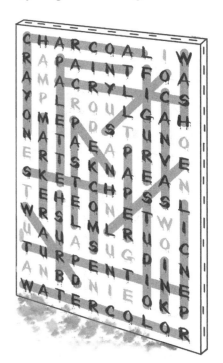

The EVERYTHING KIDS' Word Search Puzzle and Activity Book

Zap! Pow! • Page 80

```
N I W T O I M E A R G O T O
F A N T A S T I C F O U R N
M L I O C S H B W O N D A R
E N T A U F A M E T M N E
D I J S P P L T E N O O S T
O F A T H E A X A W R P F N
P S T A A R S M R Y I O O A
Y R U F I M T E V D O R R L
I E R T N A D N E C A O M N
T G T O B N O R N W A B E E
L N L I O T M T N I B O R E
L E E W L A U F L A S H S R
U V S L N U A N D R I C H G
C A P T A I N A M E R I C A
```

Stitching Time • Page 82

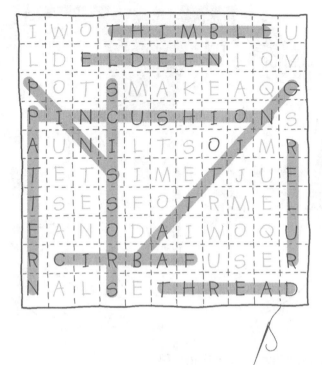

```
I W O T H I M B L E U
L D E L D E E N L O V
P O T S M A K E A Q G
P I N C U S H I O N S
A U N I L T S O I M R
T E T S I M E T J U E
T S E S F O T R M E L
E A N O D A I W O Q U
R C I R B A F U S E R
N A L S E T H R E A D
```

Darling Dolls • Page 81

```
C R Y E O B U N C
H D A I S Y H I A
E I P T R O B I N
R K E N N U R O D
R O N O N A T K Y
Y O N N T S H L I
C R Y S T A L S T
O B U N Y O S O M
C A N D H E D Y I
```

In the Orchestra • Page 83

```
T H E E T I G H T E
E E T R U M P E T N T T
W E I L B V G E O R V E R E
R T M U A R N E C L O P N A I I
R E P D E L O B O E U M N I E B A I
L S A L E C G Y A T T E B K R A I D N A
N P N A M N E E R S I U A O N A I N N M G P
A I A V I O L I N S R L S N R L H A O U P L
S O C R I D H L Y S O I F R E N C H H O R N E
B L U C E O E P O A N O I G H T O S N B A D L X M O
U M T O D L A O B I N N P C Y M B A L S A S I P N T
I N L R A G L S A E X T U B E T I O L N S R L R
A O U N D Y C E                    N Y O N E A S U
I M T E X P                          R I D H B E
A N D P                              R E D J
```

Puzzle Answers

Saving Stamps • Page 84

Having a Ball • Pages 86–87

GOLF BALL

TENNIS BALL

BASKETBALL

Take Me Out to the Ballgame • Page 88

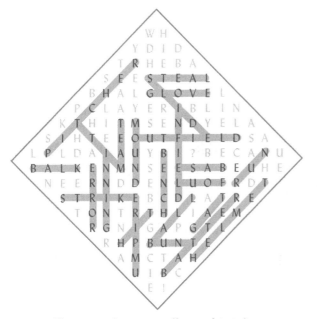

The extra letters spell out this joke:
Why did the baseball player blink his eyelashes
all day? Because he needed batting practice!

The EVERYTHING KIDS' Word Search Puzzle and Activity Book

Hit the Slopes • Page 89

Scramble • Page 91

KIRN = RINK
LOGA = GOAL
OCLKC = CLOCK
SOTH = SHOT
TAKES = SKATE
CIE = ICE
TICKS = STICK
DROBA = BOARD
CHEBN = BENCH
KUPC = PUCK
ULOF = FOUL

Swim Meet • Page 90

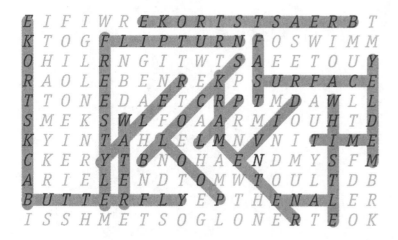

Spelling Ball • Page 92

Here are some of the words you can find in the "Spelling Ball":

ALIVE	OVER	SILVER
EVIL	PALE	SLIVER
LAP	PALER	TOIL
LEAP	PERT	TON
LION	PET	VELVET
LIVE	REAL	VETO
LIVER	REAP	VISION
NOISE	REAPER	VOTE
NOT	RELIVE	VOTER
NOTE	REVOTE	PAL(S)
OIL	SEAL	SLAP

The ten-letter bonus word is TELEVISION.

Puzzle Answers

Secret Soccer • Page 92

Fully Equipped • Pages 94–95

ARCHERY
BASEBALL
BASKETBALL
FOOTBALL
KAYAKING
LACROSSE
SKATEBOARDING
ICE SKATING
BIKING
SOCCER
TENNIS
WEIGHTLIFTING

Floor Exercise • Page 93

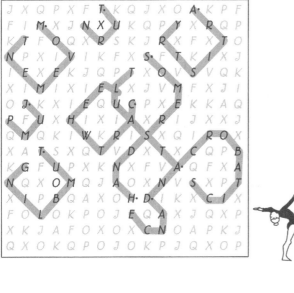

Extreme Sports • Page 96

Beautiful Ballerina • Page 98

Funny Fairy • Page 99

Puzzle Answers

Knight Night • Pages 100–101

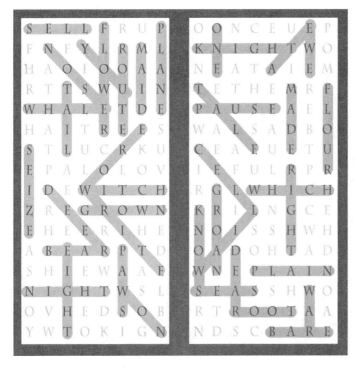

Presto Chango • Page 102

WAND   SCARF
BUNNY   CARDS
FLOWER
STAR
HAT
ROPE

Unusual Unicorn • Page 103

Special clothes that identifies a team = U N I F O R M
All of outer space and everything in it = U N I V E R S E
All the people in your city or town = C O M M U N I T Y
Imaginary animal with one horn = U N I C O R N
Gathering of old classmates = R E U N I O N
Long shirt that hangs to the knees = T U N I C
One-wheeled bike = U N I C Y C L E
Common summer plant with trumpet-shaped
   flowers = P E T U N I A
To join together = U N I T E
Only one of its kind = U N I Q U E

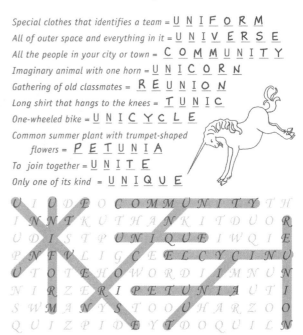

Pirate Booty • Page 104

1. SILVER
2. PEARLS
3. GOLD
4. SAPPHIRES
5. EMERALDS
6. DIAMONDS
7. RUBIES

Marvelous Mermaids • Page 105

Mermaids are __LOVELY__ fish-women that live __UNDERWATER__ in the __OCEAN__. They have a __TAIL__ instead of legs, and can __SWIM__ really fast. __LEGEND__ says that mermaids can __ENCHANT__ sailors when they __SING__.

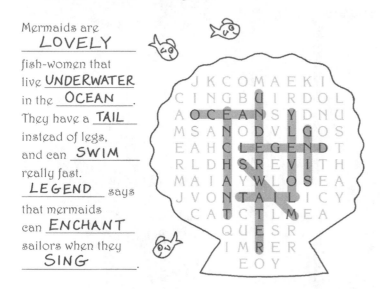

```
J K C O M A E K I
C I N G B U I R D O L
A O C E A N S Y D N U
M S A N O D V L G O S
E A H C L E G E N D T
R L D H S R E V I T H
M A I A Y W L O S E A
J V O N T A I L I C Y
C A T C T L M E A
Q U E S R
I M R E R
E O Y
```

Ask an Alien • Page 106

The words you are looking for:
LEADER, PLANETS, SPACESHIP, STARS, TECHNOLOGY, UNIVERSE, LIGHTS

The letters UFO appear in the puzzle grid ten times.

Greetings, Earthling!

WOW!

```
            T I S T
     W H A U F O H A T U
     S P A C E S H I P W F E
     I R L D L I G U H T I O N T
     E U S A K T E C H N O L O G Y Y
     I F S N I T U F O A I B I R D A
     P O L E A L N E N U I V T S S   P U E
  U N I D E N T K F I E D F L Y E N S O B F E C T
  O M A N I T I S S V E G R O V E R Y H A O R T T O
  R U F O I T E O W I T H A U T A U S I N G A N Y
  O U S S R O F S A O U R T F T S T L E A D E R O
    O U S U T C O R F M E S O U T W H X E R
    O I M I S S O R O S I U F O E I O
      H O N O I O E O H O S
```

Puzzle Answers

Custom Castles • Page 107

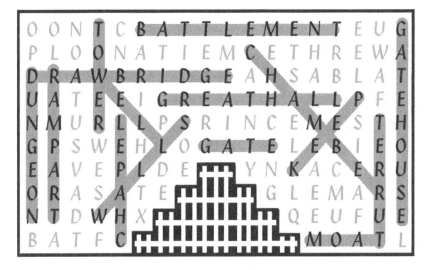

Dragon Breath • Page 108

Look Again! • Page 109

1. Perfect Pets

2. Driveway Fun

3. You're It!

4. Savings Sum

5. Gearing Up

6. Farm Fun

*crease folds
with thumbnail*

7. Origami Animals

8. Floor Exercise

9. Dragon Breath

Part 2

States Smarts

INTRODUCTION

The United States is a remarkable country, and we as Americans are lucky to live here. Have you ever wondered what this country is like? Maybe you know a bit about where you live, your hometown, maybe your home state, but there are fifty states in the United States. How much do you know about them?

Were you aware that the state of Alaska would fill up one-fifth of the total area of the rest of the United States all by itself? Were you aware that Hawaii has a state fish? Or that Massachusetts has a lake within its borders that has the longest name of any body of water in the whole United States? It's true!

If you're curious about your country and would like to learn more about what it is like, "from sea to shining sea," then this section is intended for you. If you want to know what there is to see and do if you visit other states in the Union, if you're curious about each state's history, if you'd like to know what kinds of things are made and sold in these states, if you'd like to know wacky and little-known facts about each state, then this is the book you've been looking for!

Beginning with New England in Chapter 10 and ending with the Pacific Northwest in Chapter 19, this book sweeps across the nation we call home, telling us a bit about where we live, what we do for fun, and what our future looks like. Mixed in are tidbits such as Fast Facts, Words to Know, and Try This, all intended to keep you focused on the fun side of learning about America.

May God bless her!

The states that make up the region we know as New England include some of the oldest states in the union. For example, Massachusetts was founded as a colony nearly 400 years ago. The American Revolution started in New England, as did the American anti-slavery movement nearly a century later.

New England has supplied our country with a number of its leaders—revolutionary leaders like Samuel Adams and his cousin John Adams and John's remarkable wife, Abigail, for example. John Adams later became our second president. His son, John Quincy Adams, was also president. In the 1960s, Massachusetts senator and war hero John Fitzgerald Kennedy became the thirty-fifth president.

New England is famous for its seasons, especially for autumn, when the leaves in its huge forests turn different colors. People from all over the world come to New England in the fall to witness the changing of the leaves. A delicious effect of the seasonal changes in New England's forests is the maple syrup industry!

MASSACHUSETTS: The Bay State
Geography and Industry

Massachusetts is both one of the smallest states and one of the most thickly populated states. Most of the people who live in Massachusetts live in the eastern part of the state, near the coast. The western part of the state has more mountains, with fewer cities, smaller towns, and a lot fewer people living there.

Because of its long and varied history, Massachusetts has a lot of places listed on the National Register of Historic Places, including three national historical parks: Lowell, Boston, and Minute Man.

Massachusetts is also home to many ponds and small lakes, such as the famous Walden Pond and Lake Chargogg.

Massachusetts has a lot of islands off of its coast, including such large ones as Nantucket and Martha's Vineyard. Rivers such

ALL ABOUT
Massachusetts

CAPITAL: Boston

LARGEST CITY: Boston

POPULATION: 6,349,097 (2000 Census)

STATE BIRD: Chickadee

STATE TREE: American Elm

STATE FLOWER: Mayflower

STATE MOTTO: *"Ense Petit Placidam Sub Libertate Quietem* (By the Sword We Seek Peace, but Peace Only under Liberty)"

STATEHOOD: February 6, 1788

POSTAL ABBREVIATION: MA

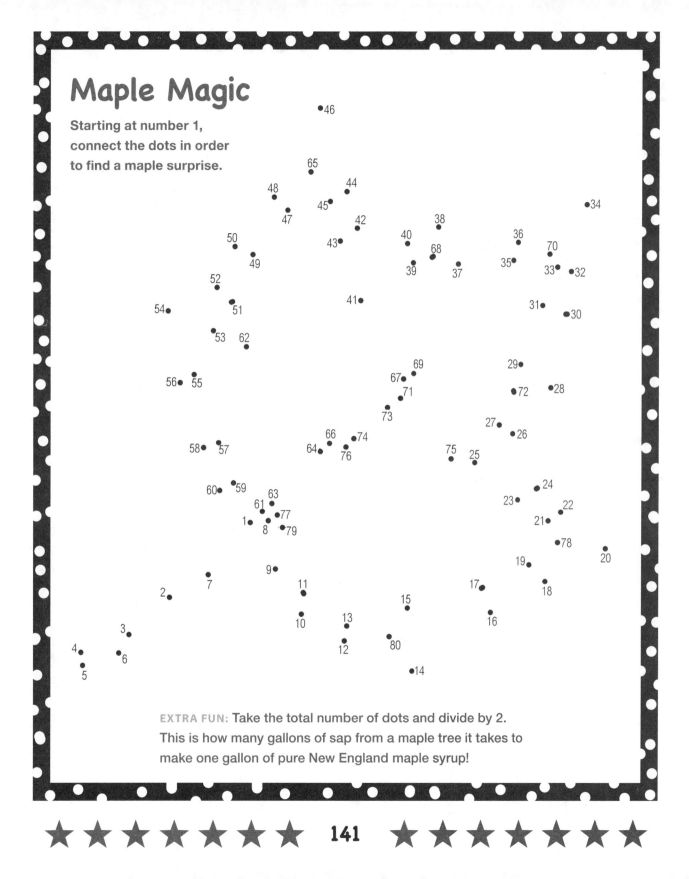

Maple Magic

Starting at number 1,
connect the dots in order
to find a maple surprise.

EXTRA FUN: Take the total number of dots and divide by 2.
This is how many gallons of sap from a maple tree it takes to
make one gallon of pure New England maple syrup!

WORDS TO KNOW

Lake Chargoggmaunchaugag-oggchaubungungamaugg

This is the longest name of any body of water in the United States. It is a Native American name that means "You fish on your side and I'll fish on my side, and nobody fishes in the middle," and was probably named in honor of an agreement between two tribes on how best to peacefully share access to it.

as the Merrimack are short and speedy, and helped provide the waterpower that the early textile mills of the 1800s needed in order to run faster than any had before. These textile mills were part of the Industrial Revolution in America.

Massachusetts' economy relies heavily on industry. In other words, a lot of the people who live in Massachusetts make things for a living. Electronic items like computer parts, electrical wires and cords, plus tools, a lot of plastics, and many other manufactured things are all made in Massachusetts. Massachusetts has so much manufacturing within its borders partly because when industries began to manufacture goods in the modern way, Massachusetts was one of the first places where companies set up modern plants with assembly lines.

History

The Commonwealth of Massachusetts is one of the original thirteen states, and the second oldest of the English colonies (after Virginia). Its capital city of Boston was founded in 1630 by Puritans seeking religious freedom.

The Puritans were a group of people who came from England to America because of their religious differences with England's official church, the Anglican Church. Originally, this group of people hoped to "purify" the Anglican Church of some of its religious practices that they didn't like. This is how they got the nickname "Puritans." Today the spiritual descendants of the Puritans are members of the Episcopalian Church of America.

Massachusetts has a rich history, and has many interesting things to see if you go visit, such as the battlefields of Lexington and Concord, where the American Revolution started. Also, the U.S. Navy's oldest active commissioned warship, a sailing vessel called the USS Constitution, is permanently docked in Boston Harbor. She is over two hundred years old!

RHODE ISLAND: The Ocean State

Geography and Industry

With a total area of 1,214 square miles, Rhode Island is the smallest of the fifty states. Also, after New Jersey, it is the most densely populated state, in spite of the fact that much of the western part of the state is heavily forested. Rhode Island is made up mostly of the land surrounding the large waterway known as Narragansett Bay (and the islands in it).

There is a lot to see and do in Rhode Island. The seaside community of Newport is world-famous for its history of yachting, and there are some amazing homes to visit there, including the ones built by the wealthy Vanderbilt family. In fact, with its miles and miles of coastline, Rhode Island has more oceanfront than some states twice its size!

Like Massachusetts to the north, Rhode Island's economy relies heavily on manufacturing. Industries represented within the state include textiles, jewelry making, electrical wire and cable manufacturing, and some agriculture. Fishing was once the most important industry in the state, but it no longer is, because it is not as profitable as it once was. Narragansett Bay is still home to a plentiful amount of shellfish.

Even though commercial fishing isn't as important as it once was, shipping is still a major industry in Rhode Island. After all, Narragansett Bay is a fine natural harbor.

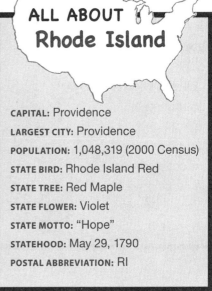

ALL ABOUT
Rhode Island

CAPITAL: Providence
LARGEST CITY: Providence
POPULATION: 1,048,319 (2000 Census)
STATE BIRD: Rhode Island Red
STATE TREE: Red Maple
STATE FLOWER: Violet
STATE MOTTO: "Hope"
STATEHOOD: May 29, 1790
POSTAL ABBREVIATION: RI

History

Rhode Island was first settled in 1636 by followers of a Puritan leader named Roger Williams. Williams had been banished from nearby Massachusetts because he preached that people ought to tolerate each other's religious differences. Later Anne Hutchinson likewise angered leaders of the Plymouth colony and was also banished. She also moved to Rhode Island in search of religious freedom and founded the present site of Portsmouth. As a result, Rhode Island is seen by many as the cradle of America's tradition of religious freedom.

WORDS TO KNOW

Textiles

Textile refers to both a number of types of finished cloth and also the fibers or yarns from which they are made. Items like cotton shirts, tablecloths, and carpets are referred to as textiles.

ALL ABOUT Connecticut

CAPITAL: Hartford

LARGEST CITY: Bridgeport

POPULATION: 3,405,565 (2000 Census)

STATE BIRD: American Robin

STATE TREE: White Oak

STATE FLOWER: Mountain Laurel

STATE MOTTO: *"Qui Transtulit Sustinet* (He Who Transplanted Sustains)"

STATEHOOD: January 9, 1788

POSTAL ABBREVIATION: CT

At the start of the Revolutionary War, Rhode Islanders were the first colonists to reject their allegiance to Britain and were also the first colonists to take action against the British by attacking British vessels. Although no large battles were fought in Rhode Island, regiments from the state participated in every major campaign in the war.

After the American Revolution, the shipping industry declined in Rhode Island. But Samuel Slater soon founded the first successful U.S. textile mill on the banks of the Blackstone River in what is today Pawtucket, Rhode Island. The abundance of waterpower at the site led to the rapid development of manufacturing, which is considered to be the start of the Industrial Revolution in the United States.

CONNECTICUT: The Constitution State

Geography and Industry

The Connecticut River (for which the state is named) runs through the middle of this state, cutting it in two. The Connecticut River Valley separates Connecticut's Eastern Highland from its Western Highland.

Connecticut was one of the original thirteen colonies that formed the early United States. Initially settled by Dutch traders beginning in the mid-1630s, then by Pilgrims from Plymouth Colony, and eventually by Puritans from Massachusetts Bay, Connecticut incorporated as an English royal colony by writing up the Fundamental Orders (the colony's main set of governing laws) in 1639. These laws were eventually replaced by a formal, written constitution in 1662.

Like its neighbors Massachusetts and Rhode Island, Connecticut is an important manufacturing center. Sewing machines, textiles, firearms, and heavy machinery, including engine parts, are all made in Connecticut. (Guns have been made continuously in Connecticut since the American Revolution!) Although farming is no longer a major industry in Connecticut, apples, dairy products, eggs, tobacco, and mushrooms are all still grown there and shipped around the country.

History

Two of early America's most savage Indian wars took place in Connecticut. First came the Pequot War, named for the largest and most powerful tribe of Native Americans in the area. It broke out in 1637 between the Pequot tribe and the Connecticut and Massachusetts Bay colonies (along with some Native Americans who fought with the colonists). The war ended with the virtual extinction of the Pequots.

The second of Connecticut's bloody Indian wars was King Philip's War, which began in 1674 in Connecticut and quickly spread throughout the New England colonies. Fought between the formerly friendly Wampanoag tribe and the English settlers, it also ended badly for the Native Americans. Thousands of them died or lost their homes.

NEW HAMPSHIRE: The Granite State

Geography

New Hampshire is bordered to the north by the Canadian province of Quebec. Maine borders New Hampshire to the east, Massachusetts to the south, and Vermont to the west. The Connecticut River forms the border between New Hampshire and Vermont.

New Hampshire is very mountainous and is home to the tallest mountain east of the Rocky Mountains: Mount Washington, which is 6,288 feet above sea level. Some of the best skiing in the eastern United States can be found in New Hampshire!

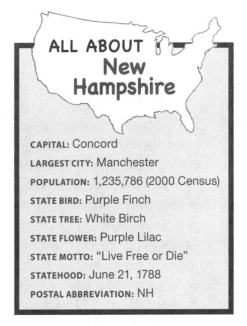

ALL ABOUT New Hampshire

CAPITAL: Concord
LARGEST CITY: Manchester
POPULATION: 1,235,786 (2000 Census)
STATE BIRD: Purple Finch
STATE TREE: White Birch
STATE FLOWER: Purple Lilac
STATE MOTTO: "Live Free or Die"
STATEHOOD: June 21, 1788
POSTAL ABBREVIATION: NH

History

The last of the original thirteen colonies to be established (in 1741, when it broke away from Massachusetts Bay), New Hampshire was the first of the future United States to declare its independence from Great Britain. Famous for its state motto ("Live

Free or Die") and for the White Mountains that run through it, New Hampshire is a state that prides itself on being very different even from its neighbors in New England.

One of the most important things to happen in New Hampshire after the American Revolution was the negotiation and signing of the Treaty of Portsmouth in 1905. Negotiated by President Theodore Roosevelt, the Treaty of Portsmouth ended the Russo-Japanese War (a war between Russia and Japan). This treaty not only ensured Japan's new status as a world power, but also showed that the United States was a powerful country that would use its own emerging world power status to help keep the peace from continent to continent.

Economy

New Hampshire began using the water in its rivers to power textile mills during the 1800s, as part of the beginning of the Industrial Revolution. These days, although much of the manufacturing in the state has shifted to high-technology supplies, there are still many manufacturers of leather goods, particularly of shoes and boots.

In recent years, tourism has become one of the most important industries in New Hampshire. During the winter months, people come from all over the country to ski in New Hampshire's rugged mountains. During the summers, the state's lakes, such as the huge Winnipeesaukee, are home to summer boaters. Fishing is no longer as important as it once was in the state, but still plays a role in the state's economy.

Two other industries that were once of major importance in New Hampshire are the lumber industry and the granite quarrying industry. The lumber harvested in New Hampshire is used in making paper. Lumber is about the only harvesting going on in New Hampshire. The mountains and the thin, flinty soil make it tough to grow food there. As for the granite quarrying industry, there is not as much demand for granite as a building material as there used to be. Steel makes up the foundations of most buildings nowadays.

Fun Facts

THE OLD MAN OF THE MOUNTAIN

The Old Man of the Mountain was a New Hampshire rock formation that looked very much like the profile of an old man. New Hampshire residents came to identify with this rock outcropping, and adopted it as their state symbol in 1945. The rocks that formed the natural sculpture had weathered over the years, though, and the entire structure collapsed in 2003.

Yee Ha!

They were hand crafted in Concord, NH, but were famous for carrying mail and passengers throughout the western United States! Can you help this Concord Coach deliver the mail from START to END of the route?

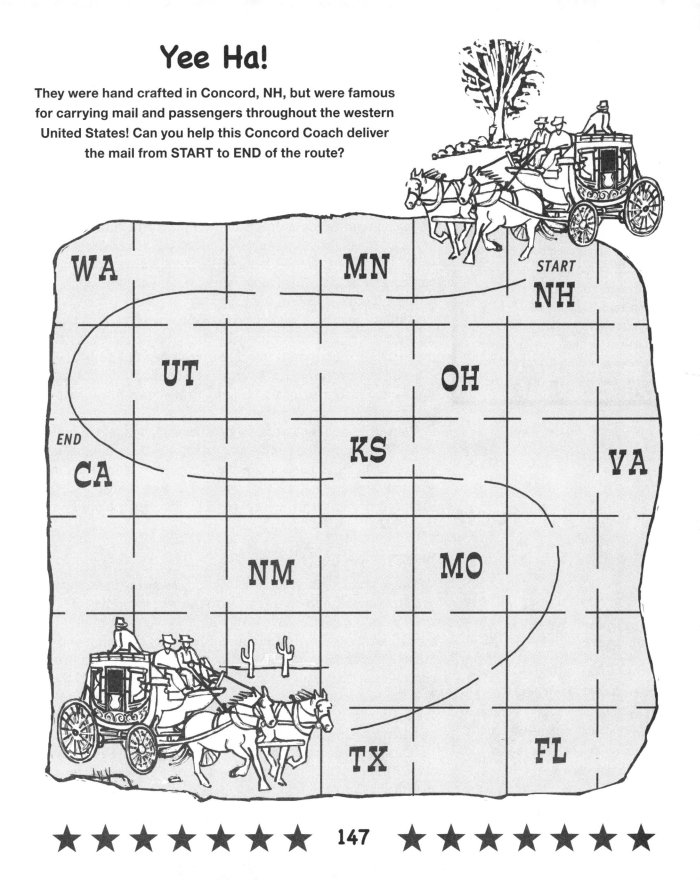

WA

MN

START
NH

UT

OH

END
CA

KS

VA

NM

MO

TX

FL

ALL ABOUT Vermont

CAPITAL: Montpelier

LARGEST CITY: Burlington

POPULATION: 608,827 (2000 Census)

STATE BIRD: Hermit Thrush

STATE TREE: Sugar Maple

STATE FLOWER: Red Clover

STATE MOTTO: "Freedom and Unity"

STATEHOOD: March 4, 1791

POSTAL ABBREVIATION: VT

Fun Facts

VERMONT GRANITE

Vermont's granite and marble quarries produce some of the most distinctive building stone in the world. Vermont marble in particular is thought to rival Italian marble in its beauty.

VERMONT: The Green Mountain State

Geography and Industry

Bordered on two sides by large bodies of fresh water, Vermont shares its western border with New York (where Lake Champlain forms part of the boundary), and its eastern border with New Hampshire (where the Connecticut River marks the entire boundary line). The Canadian province of Quebec is north of Vermont, and Massachusetts lies to the south. Vermont is a very mountainous state. Vermont's Green Mountains are some of the most rugged country in the eastern United States.

Unlike the other New England states, Vermont has a strong agricultural base. This is especially true when it comes to dairy products. Vermont's milk and cheese are world famous—as is Vermont ice cream! (Ben & Jerry's is a Vermont company.) Apples and maple syrup are also important agricultural products that come from Vermont.

Vermont has a reputation for producing high-quality marble. While New Hampshire marble was valuable in building early skyscrapers and millionaires' mansions, Vermont marble comes in so many varieties that it is highly prized as a finishing product (as in marble tile for bathrooms) and as a medium for sculpture.

History

Vermont's contribution to the Patriot cause during the American Revolution can be traced back to the very beginning of the war for independence. On May 10, 1775, Vermont militiamen (the famous Green Mountain Boys) under the command of Ethan Allen and Benedict Arnold seized Fort Ticonderoga (which controlled access to all of Lake Champlain) in the name of the new Continental Congress. They did so without firing a shot, taking the British garrison there completely by surprise during an early morning raid.

During the decades leading up to the American Revolution, three different English colonies (New York, New Hampshire, and

Massachusetts Bay) claimed the area now known as the state of Vermont as part of their own territories. As a result of their inability to settle their differences over Vermont, these three colonies blocked Vermont's attempts to join the United States as a new state during the late 1770s.

In response to this dilemma, Vermont declared itself an independent state. The state's government coined its own money, appointed ambassadors, set up a postal system, and did all the everyday functions of an independent government until finally allowed to join the Union as the first state that had not previously been an English colony (and the fourteenth state overall).

MAINE: The Pine Tree State

Geography and Industry

Maine's soil is rocky, and not very good for raising crops. The state originally had large forests filled with huge pine trees, but heavy logging has cleared much of the land. There is still plenty of wilderness to be explored in Maine, though, especially in the northern parts of the state. People come from all over the world to camp and hike in Maine's forests of white pine, and to boat and fish not only in its 5,500 lakes and streams but also on its irregular, rock-strewn, 3,500 miles of coastline.

Maine's economy relies heavily on timber sales, but not in the same way that it did when tall Maine trees were cut down to make ships' masts. Nowadays, Maine's trees are used mostly as pulp to make paper.

At one time, fishing was Maine's largest and richest industry. But the fishing industry has suffered recently, because the supply of fish is getting smaller. Many environmentalists think this is a result of what is called over-fishing. Over-fishing is what happens when fishermen don't leave enough of a type of fish for that species of fish to produce enough new fish to replace those that were caught that year. One exception to the over-fishing problem is the famous Maine lobster which is sold worldwide.

ALL ABOUT **Maine**

CAPITAL: Augusta
LARGEST CITY: Portland
POPULATION: 1,274,923 (2000 Census)
STATE BIRD: Chickadee
STATE TREE: Eastern White Pine
STATE FLOWER: White Pine Cone and Tassel
STATE MOTTO: "*Dirigo* (I Direct)"
STATEHOOD: March 15, 1820
POSTAL ABBREVIATION: ME

Fun Facts

MAINE'S TIMBER INDUSTRY

Timber has always been a major export for Maine. During the Age of Sail (when people traveled mostly by sailing ships), Maine's tall white pine trees were used to make ships' masts, which hold up the sails. In fact, the very first sawmill in the United States was built in Maine, on the Piscataqua River in 1623.

History

Up until 1820, Maine was a part of Massachusetts. In that year Maine entered the Union as a free state (meaning that slavery was illegal in the state), as part of a deal made in Congress between representatives of southern and northern states, called the Missouri Compromise. The Missouri Compromise was an agreement that allowed Missouri to enter the Union as a slave state). Since Maine would enter the Union at the same time, it would help keep the number of slave and free states in the Union equal. During the 1830s, Maine was the site of a border dispute between the United States and Canada. This conflict, called the Aroostook War, resulted in no deaths, and only a few bruises among the men who "fought" it. The long-term result of this so-called war was the Webster-Ashburton Treaty of 1842, which settled the boundary line between the United States and Canada not only in Maine, but along most of the rest of the border as well, making it the longest undefended international border in world history.

★ CHAPTER 11 ★
THE MID-ATLANTIC STATES

Fun Facts

NIAGARA FALLS

The falls of the Niagara River are a world-famous attraction that draws millions of people to see them every year. Every hour 5,000,000,000 gallons of water flow over the edge of the Niagara Falls.

WORDS TO KNOW

Floodplain

A floodplain is a flat piece of land next to a river, stream, or ocean that experiences occasional flooding.

The states in the Mid-Atlantic region run from New York in the north along the Atlantic shore of the east coast, to the Potomac River in the south. All five of the states in this region were among the original thirteen colonies that fought for independence from Great Britain and later ratified the U.S. Constitution.

The Mid-Atlantic States were also the birthplace of the westward settlement movement and the Transportation Revolution (1816–1850). These two sweeping events led to the beginnings of the railway, steel, coal, oil, and canal-building industries. As a result, some of the largest and most heavily populated cities in the United States are in the Mid-Atlantic States. Cities such as New York City, Philadelphia, Buffalo, Pittsburgh, and Baltimore all boomed in part because of their location during the Transportation Revolution.

NEW YORK: The Empire State

Geography and Industry

In the southeast, New York's Long Island is surrounded by three bodies of water: Long Island Sound, the Atlantic Ocean, and New York Harbor. Along its southern border, New York is bordered by New Jersey and Pennsylvania.

New York has a little bit of every terrain, except for desert, within its borders. In the southeast, there is the broad floodplain of the Atlantic. Running north from there is the Great Appalachian Valley, which includes the Hudson River and Lake Champlain. The Hudson cuts through the Allegheny Plateau, which rises into the Catskill Mountains.

The northern part of the state is mountainous, with the Adirondack chain running through it. Western New York is very hilly, with a number of lakes, including the Finger Lakes and Lake Oneida.

History

Before European settlement, New York was the home of many different tribes of Native Americans. The most powerful tribes were the Iroquois confederacy in western New York.

The Iroquois were not one tribe—they were actually five tribes! They called themselves the *Ho-de-no-sau-nee*, which means "People of the Longhouse." In the minds of the Iroquois, they all lived together, much the same way that a family will live in different parts of a house today. The Seneca lived furthest west, and were called the Keepers of the Western Door. The Mohawks lived furthest east, and were called the Keepers of the Eastern Door. The tribes in the middle were the Cayuga, Oneida, and Onondaga. Many of the descendants of the Iroquois still live in western New York as well as in southern Canada today.

The French and Dutch were the first Europeans to visit New York. They have left their words as place names all over the state—for example, bodies of water like Lake Champlain (pronounced "sham-PLAIN") and the Schuylkill River (pronounced "SKOOL-kil").

The Dutch (people from the Netherlands) founded the first permanent settlement in what is now New York when they bought an island at the mouth of the Hudson River in 1626. They paid local Native Americans with trade goods (blankets and colored beads) that would cost us about $25.00 in today's money for what is now Manhattan Island! Imagine buying the area where New York City now stands, and having money left over from your allowance. You'd be the next Donald Trump!

The Dutch called this colony New Netherlands, and called the city they built on Manhattan Island New Amsterdam. The English later fought a war with the Dutch and took New Netherlands away from them. They changed the name of the colony (and its largest city) to New York.

After America became a nation, New York City quickly became more and more important. It was even the national capital city for a brief time! Did you know that when New York became a state, the northern parts of Manhattan Island still had farms on them? It's true! But by the late nineteeth century, with the growth of manufacturing in New York City, the farms were long gone.

One of the major reasons for New York's emergence as the foremost city of the new nation was its harbor, lauded by

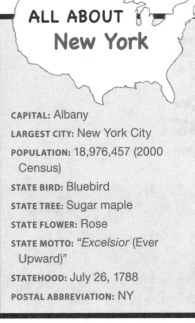

ALL ABOUT New York

CAPITAL: Albany

LARGEST CITY: New York City

POPULATION: 18,976,457 (2000 Census)

STATE BIRD: Bluebird

STATE TREE: Sugar maple

STATE FLOWER: Rose

STATE MOTTO: *"Excelsior* (Ever Upward)"

STATEHOOD: July 26, 1788

POSTAL ABBREVIATION: NY

The Iroquois Language

Did you know that the Iroquois language has no sounds that are made with your lips pressed together? It's true! Their names for themselves, as well as the rest of their language, do not include sounds like "m," "b," or "p." That is why they have names like Ho-de-no-sau-nee, and Hiawatha, and Thayendaneegeeah. Try saying these names without touching your lips together. Can you do it?

many as the finest natural harbor in the western hemisphere. This meant a boom in the trade that passed through New York City on its way between the American West and places overseas such as Europe and Asia. On top of the city's harbor, there also was the fact that New York state had built the famous Erie Canal, which made it very easy to get trade goods back and forth across the state between the harbor cities of New York, which was on the Atlantic coast, and Buffalo, which serves as an important port city at the eastern end of the Great Lakes.

PENNSYLVANIA: The Keystone State

Geography and Industry

The Appalachian Mountains pass right through the heart of Pennsylvania. With the Delaware River Valley helping form the eastern part of the state, Pennsylvania has everything from rugged mountains to smooth river bottoms.

But Pennsylvania isn't just a land of mountains and plains. It is also a land of large rivers. Along with the large and powerful Delaware (and the Susquehanna, which flows through the state and down into the Chesapeake Bay), Pennsylvania also has the mighty Ohio River, which begins in the western part of the state. In fact, the Ohio begins right in the middle of what is now the city of Pittsburgh! The city was originally the site of a fort built where the Monongahela and Allegheny rivers merge to form the Ohio River. This is where Pittsburgh's once famous Three Rivers football stadium got its name!

History

There were many powerful tribes of Native Americans living in what is now Pennsylvania before European settlement. These included the Delaware, the Suquehannock, and the Shawnee.

Many people don't know that there were more Europeans exploring and colonizing the New World than just the French,

English, and Spanish. In Pennsylvania and neighboring New Jersey, two other countries struggled to control new colonies: the Swedish and the Dutch!

The Swedes were forced out by the Dutch, who were then forced out by the English. The Duke of York (the brother of the English king) gave Pennsylvania to an English Quaker named William Penn. Why did he just give all this land away? It's because he owed Penn money! So he gave away a colony that English soldiers had taken away from the Dutch a few years before. Penn asked for the land as payment of the debt, because he wanted to start a colony there for other Quakers.

Pennsylvania was very important during the American Revolution. Everyone knows that the Declaration of Independence was signed on July 4, 1776. But do you know *where* it was signed? The Declaration of Independence was signed at Independence Hall in Philadelphia, Pennsylvania, and that place is now a national historical landmark. American and British forces fought a number of battles in Pennsylvania during the Revolution, at places including Brandywine and Germantown. Congress was forced to flee Philadelphia when the British army invaded Pennsylvania and captured the city. In order to keep an eye on the British, General Washington's Continental Army spent a terrible winter not far away, at Valley Forge.

Since the American Revolution, Pennsylvania has been an integral part of the Industrial Revolution. After all, the state is the site of the first oil well in the United States. It also has some of the largest coal deposits in the world. When the Industrial Revolution began, Pennsylvania was an ideal place for steel mills to spring up because the state had plenty of coal to power the mills. Men like Andrew Carnegie made millions from building up the steel industry, mostly in Pennsylvania!

You might know Andrew Carnegie's name because when he died he left most of his money to a fund that set up free public libraries all over the country. Many cities and towns that couldn't have afforded a library otherwise had one as a result of his generosity. Is there a Carnegie Library where you live?

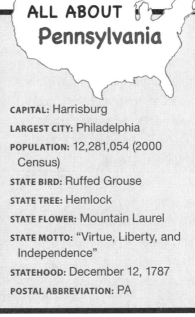

ALL ABOUT Pennsylvania

CAPITAL: Harrisburg

LARGEST CITY: Philadelphia

POPULATION: 12,281,054 (2000 Census)

STATE BIRD: Ruffed Grouse

STATE TREE: Hemlock

STATE FLOWER: Mountain Laurel

STATE MOTTO: "Virtue, Liberty, and Independence"

STATEHOOD: December 12, 1787

POSTAL ABBREVIATION: PA

Fun Facts

PHILADELPHIA, OUR CAPITAL!

Did you know that Philadelphia was the first capital of the United States? It's true! For a number of years both during and after the American Revolution, Philadelphia was our national capital. The capital moved to New York during President Washington's administration.

WORDS TO KNOW

Quaker

Quakers are a religious group that believes that everything in life was meant to be simple and straight-forward. They call themselves the Society of Friends, and got the nickname "Quakers" because during some early sermons preached among some of their members, the people shook violently while "possessed by the Holy Spirit"!

ALL ABOUT New Jersey

CAPITAL: Trenton
LARGEST CITY: Newark
POPULATION: 8,414,350 (2000 Census)
STATE BIRD: Eastern Goldfinch
STATE TREE: Red Oak
STATE FLOWER: Purple Violet
STATE MOTTO: "Liberty and Prosperity"
STATEHOOD: December 18, 1787
POSTAL ABBREVIATION: NJ

NEW JERSEY: The Garden State

Geography and Industry

New Jersey shares its northern border with New York. Aside from that, all of its other borders are formed by water: the Delaware River to the west, the Atlantic Ocean to the east, and Delaware Bay to the south. Northern New Jersey is very hilly, and southern New Jersey is very flat. The big rivers running through New Jersey are the Passaic and the Raritan.

New Jersey is one of the smallest of the United States (only Rhode Island, Massachusetts, Connecticut, and Delaware are smaller), but it is also one of the most populous. This means that New Jersey has a lot of people living in its borders. New Jersey ranks in the top ten of all the states in population numbers. That is a lot of people living in a very narrow space! New Jersey is a very crowded state in part because it is right between the huge eastern cities of Philadelphia and New York City. In fact, the metropolitan areas of both of these cities have expanded into New Jersey over the last few decades. As a result of this, many of the residents of New Jersey commute to jobs in other states!

History

Remember how eastern Pennsylvania was originally settled by the Swedes (people from Sweden)? Well, the same thing happened in New Jersey, which is just on the other side of the Delaware River from Pennsylvania. And just like in Pennsylvania, the Swedes were forced out by the Dutch, who after a few years lost a war with the English, who then claimed New Jersey and Pennsylvania for themselves. The Dutch left their mark in this area through the names of villages such as Hoboken (which is a large city today).

Two of the most important battles of the American Revolution were fought in New Jersey. Have you learned in school about General Washington's famous crossing of the Delaware? Maybe you've seen the famous painting, which shows him and his soldiers crossing the river in big boats. If you have, did you wonder where he was going when he and his army crossed the river?

Well, the answer is that he was going to New Jersey! Washington's army crossed the Delaware the night before Christmas, and attacked Hessian soldiers the next morning in their camp at Trenton. He and his troops took the Hessians completely by surprise, killed many soldiers, and captured many others. A few days later, Washington struck again, this time at Princeton, New Jersey (now home of the famous university that bears its name), and again won an overwhelming victory! These two battles were very important because up to that point, General Washington had not won many battles against either the British or the Hessians, and his winning at Trenton and Princeton gave the patriots everywhere hope that they would win independence from England.

New Jerseyite of Note

One of the ways in which New Jersey has had a major impact on the world since the end of the American Revolution was by helping launch the motion picture industry. Did you know that before there was a Hollywood, there was a Menlo Park? Menlo Park, New Jersey, that is. It's true, the first American movies were filmed in New Jersey!

And guess who filmed many of those movies? Thomas Edison. Have you heard of him? Yes, he invented the light bulb (well, he actually improved the design of another scientist, allowing a light bulb to burn for longer than a few minutes before it burned out), but he did much more, and he did it all in his laboratory in Menlo Park, New Jersey. In fact, one of his many nicknames was "the wizard of Menlo Park."

Aside from improving the light bulb, Edison also invented the phonograph (an old-fashioned record player). Ask your parents or grandparents what a

ALL ABOUT Maryland

CAPITAL: Annapolis

LARGEST CITY: Baltimore

POPULATION: 5,296,468 (2000 Census)

STATE BIRD: Baltimore Oriole

STATE TREE: White Oak

STATE FLOWER: Black-Eyed Susan

STATE MOTTO: *"Fatti Maschii, Parole Femine* (Manly Deeds, Womanly Words)"

STATEHOOD: April 28, 1788

POSTAL ABBREVIATION: MD

Maryland Seafood

Have you ever had a crab cake? The next time you go to the grocery store with your parents, find the crab cakes and see if you can find on their packaging where they were made. If they came from Maryland they're probably the best you'll ever eat!

phonograph is. They might even have one they can show to you. Phonograph records work a lot differently than CDs and MP3s work today! Other inventions that Edison improved include the typewriter, which did some of the things that computers do today (again, ask your parents or grandparents) and the motion picture camera. Some of the oldest home movies ever taken were shot in the 1890s in New Jersey, in and around Edison's laboratory in Menlo Park. In fact, Edison even started the first movie studio. When movies began to be shown around the country a few years later, many people called them "Edison shows."

MARYLAND: The Old Line State

Geography

Maryland is cut in two, right down the middle, by a huge body of water called the Chesapeake Bay. The part of the state that is separated from the rest of it by the big bay is called the Eastern Shore. The state shares its eastern border with Delaware and the Atlantic Ocean. To the north lies Pennsylvania, to the south is Virginia, and to the west is West Virginia. Between Maryland and Virginia is the District of Columbia, where the U.S. capital of Washington, D.C. is located. The state has many different types of landscapes. In the east and the southeast it is very flat, with lots of good farming land. The Piedmont (a chain of mountains) runs through the western part of the state, making it far more rugged than the eastern and the central parts.

History

Maryland was originally a colony run by Lord Baltimore, an English lord who named the colony for his wife and the largest city in it for his family. Lord Baltimore wanted a place that would welcome Catholics. At the time, Catholics were not treated very well back home in England. Although people of many faiths eventually settled in Maryland, it shared Rhode Island's beginning as a safe haven where people could worship as they chose.

Did you know that Maryland almost joined the Confederate States of America? It's true! Maryland was a southern state, where tobacco and cotton were grown and where slavery was legal. Many Marylanders thought that their place was fighting with their neighbors to the south against the northern states. In fact, many Marylanders fought on the southern side during the Civil War, even though their state never actually officially left the union!

One of these men who believed in the southern cause was a famous actor named John Wilkes Booth, who later shocked the country and the world by shooting and killing our sixteenth president, Abraham Lincoln. Booth often referred to the south as his home, and to slavery as a God-given right. No wonder he hated President Lincoln!

ALL ABOUT Delaware

CAPITAL: Dover

LARGEST CITY: Wilmington

POPULATION: 783,600 (2000 Census)

STATE BIRD: Blue Hen Chicken

STATE TREE: American Holly

STATE FLOWER: Peach Blossom

STATE MOTTO: "Liberty and Independence"

STATEHOOD: December 7, 1787

DELAWARE: The Diamond State

Geography and Industry

Delaware occupies the northern and eastern portion of what many Marylanders call the Eastern Shore, and what still others call the Delmarva peninsula (short for Delaware-Maryland-Virginia). It is one of the smallest peninsulas of the United States.

Have you ever heard of the DuPont Corporation? It's a company that makes lots of things, especially all kinds of plastic, plastic tools, and paint. The DuPont Corporation is a big business with its headquarters in Delaware, where a man named Pierre DuPont started it. His great-grandson, Pierre "Pete" DuPont IV, eventually became a congressman from Delaware, as well as a governor of the state.

History

Before European settlement, most of what is now Delaware was occupied by members of the Delaware tribe of Native Americans. In 1610 an English explorer named one of Delaware's capes "La Warre," in honor of Virginia Colony's governor, Baron de La Warr. This is where the name "Delaware" comes from.

As you learned in reading about New Jersey and Pennsylvania, the first Europeans to settle in the Delaware River Valley

Fun Facts

THE FIRST STATE!

Did you know that Delaware was the first of the original thirteen colonies (later the first thirteen states) that won their independence from England to ratify the U.S. Constitution? It's true! The people of Delaware are to this day very proud to call theirs the "first state," because of this!

State to State

**Choose the state names that
complete the silly riddles.**

HINT: **The pictures are a clue.**

New York   Utah

Maryland   Idaho

New Jersey   Delaware

Pennsylvania

What did

_____?

She wore her

_____!

What did

_____?

She hoed her

_____!

were the Swedes and the Dutch. In fact, Peter Minuit, who had once been the governor of New Netherlands (modern New York), was hired by Sweden to establish a colony in the New World. He established Fort Christina (named for Sweden's queen) on the present site of the city of Wilmington, Delaware, in 1631.

This brought the Swedish traders who came to settle around the colony into conflict with the Dutch, who had already claimed the entire Delaware Valley as their own. They fought a war with the Swedes that ended in 1654. The Swedes lost. Ten years later, the Dutch lost all of their possessions in North America to the English. England's king gave all of these lands, which included all of what is now Delaware, to the Duke of York.

For most of the rest of the colonial era, Delaware was a semi-independent part of the Pennsylvania colony. A few years later, Delaware became an English crown colony.

During the American Revolution, Delaware contributed many brave soldiers to the Continental Army. They became known as the Blue Hen's Chickens, because they fought with the ferocity of gamecocks.

WORDS TO KNOW

Gamecock

A gamecock is a rooster (male) chicken, usually bred to be an aggressive fighter. Before such things were outlawed, gamecocks were used in rooster fights (called cock fights), which people would bet money on.

CHAPTER 12

THE UPPER SOUTH

ave you ever had Kentucky Fried Chicken? Well, can you guess where it originally came from? The Upper South is where much of what is called "southern cooking" comes from. Recipes for meals like mac 'n' cheese, chicken and dumplings, and fried chicken were created in this region.

Some of the states in the Upper South have been called the Border States, because they run along the Mason-Dixon Line, which runs along Pennsylvania's border with Maryland, then along the Ohio River, all the way to the Mississippi. This line was originally established to end an argument over state boundaries between Maryland and Pennsylvania. But it is also well known for dividing the free states from the slave states until the Civil War.

All of these Border States participated in the Civil War, and almost all of them had their citizens fighting on both sides in that terrible struggle. The main reasons the Civil War was fought between the North and the South were questions like whether individual states had the right to make laws that were not allowed by the national government, and whether the practice of slavery ought to be protected (as many Southerners thought) or whether it ought to be abolished (as many Northerners thought).

VIRGINIA: The Old Dominion State

Geography and Industry

Virginia is a very large state now, but in the past it was even larger. Virginia once claimed all of the land that now makes up two different states, West Virginia and Kentucky, in addition to its present territory! In 1792, Congress created the state of Kentucky in the west, and in 1863, northwestern Virginia seceded from the rest of the state to form West Virginia.

Eastern Virginia is made up of the southern tip of the Delmarva Peninsula (named for the three states that share it: Delaware, Maryland, and Virginia) and a few islands in between the Atlantic Ocean and the Chesapeake Bay. This region is also called the Eastern Shore.

ALL ABOUT Virginia

CAPITAL: Richmond

LARGEST CITY: Virginia Beach

POPULATION: 7,078,515 (2000 Census)

STATE BIRD: Cardinal

STATE TREE: Dogwood

STATE FLOWER: Dogwood

STATE MOTTO: "*Sic Semper Tyrannis* (Thus Always to Tyrants)"

STATEHOOD: June 25, 1788

POSTAL ABBREVIATION: VA

The central part of Virginia includes two types of country. The tidewater section, which is right on the shore of Chesapeake Bay, is flat, humid, and very swampy in many places. Four big rivers run through the tidewater section: the James (where Jamestown is), the York, the Rappahannock, and the Potomac.

The other type of country in the central part of Virginia is called the Piedmont. The Piedmont is hillier than the flat tidewater section, and has a lot of fertile soil. Everything from wheat to gourds like squash and pumpkins to tobacco is grown in the Piedmont. Cattle are also raised there. The Piedmont rises higher and higher as it goes west, until it becomes the mountains of the Blue Ridge. The western part of Virginia is very rugged.

History

Many Native American tribes lived in Virginia before Europeans visited the region. The Powhatan confederacy was the largest group of native tribes in the area when English settlers landed at what is now Jamestown in 1607. They took their name from their leader, Powhatan. You have heard of Pocahontas, haven't you? Well, Pocahontas was Chief Powhatan's daughter.

When English ships first landed in Virginia in 1607, most of the men who came as part of the expedition were interested in one thing: gold! They had heard that in the New World, gold and silver were just lying around on the ground, waiting to be picked up.

At first, the members of the tiny new colony were only interested in finding the kind of treasure the Spanish had found in Mexico and Peru. They were so busy looking for it that they didn't bother to farm, trade for food, or raise livestock. As a result, they nearly starved to death.

But later generations learned a lesson from what the original settlers called the "starving time." They came to realize that in Virginia, it was easier to grow tobacco than to find gold. They could also grow wheat that would sell for good prices. By the time the American Revolution started, Virginia was a very prosperous colony.

TRY THIS!

Can you tell the difference between a pumpkin and a squash?

The plants themselves, not their fruit! Both plants are members of the gourd family. The next time you go to pick out a pumpkin for Halloween, ask the farmer if you can see his pumpkin patch. What types of plants are pumpkin plants? Are they bushes or vines? And what about squash? If you can't go to the country to try this, you can always look on the Internet.

WORDS TO KNOW

Powhatan

The powerful chief of the Powhatan confederacy of Native American tribes, this man was also the father of the famous Pocahontas. Actually, "Powhatan" was a title, like "king." Powhatan's real name was Wahunsonacock.

Virginia

When the English first landed in Virginia, they named their new colony in honor of their ruler, Queen Elizabeth I. People called Elizabeth I the Virgin Queen, which is how the settlers came up with the name Virginia.

Important Virginians

Four of the first five presidents of the United States were Virginians! These great men were George Washington, Thomas Jefferson, James Madison, and James Monroe. All of these future presidents contributed to the American cause of getting independence from the British during the Revolution. Washington was commander-in-chief of the Continental Army. He is largely credited with keeping his army going during the early years of the Revolution, when they were losing battle after battle.

Jefferson served in the Continental Congress, and wrote most of the Declaration of Independence. Jefferson was also America's first secretary of state (an official who takes care of this country's relationships with other countries), and also served as vice president before he became president in 1801.

Madison also served in the Congress, and was largely responsible for the U.S. Constitution (the system of government we still have in this country today). Madison is the man who came up with the idea of making the president, the Congress, and the Supreme Court equal branches of government, in order to make sure that one person didn't have too much power and become a tyrant.

Monroe served as an officer under Washington's command in the Continental Army, and later as a diplomat in Europe, negotiating treaties and trade agreements with other countries for the new American government.

Virginia and the Civil War

Virginia's location played a big part in the state's being the site of many of the major battles of the American Civil War. This was partly because Virginia was the northernmost state to secede from the Union and join the Confederacy, and partly because it was across the Potomac River from the Union capital of Washington, D.C. Also, after Virginia seceded, the Confederate capital moved to its largest city, Richmond. This placed the capital cities of both sides in the war within 100 miles of each other.

Many men from Virginia served on both sides during the Civil War. One of them was General Robert E. Lee, who resigned from the Union Army and went on to command the Confederate Army. Before he resigned his commission, he turned down President Lincoln's offer of command of the Union Army. When asked why he did not take the president's offer, Lee said, "I cannot go against my country." By that he meant Virginia.

WEST VIRGINIA: The Mountain State
Geography and Industry

West Virginia is one of the most heavily forested and most rugged of all the states east of the Mississippi River. Almost all of West Virginia is located on the Allegheny Plateau, which is a high stretch of land with a pretty flat top (as opposed to mountain ranges, which do not have flat tops). Fast-flowing rivers like the Big Sandy, the Kanawha, and the Monongahela cut through parts of West Virginia. The northern part is not on the plateau at all. It is part of the Ohio River Valley (the Ohio River runs along West Virginia's northwestern border).

Because of its high elevation, West Virginia gets a lot of snow every winter, and that in turn draws crowds of skiers every year. Also because of its high elevation, most of West Virginia is still undeveloped wilderness. It is a popular vacation spot for people who like to hike, boat, fish, and hunt. The state has a lot of state parks, and large national forests such as the George Washington National Forest and the Monongahela National Forest.

History

Before European settlement of the area, most of West Virginia was too rugged for the Native Americans to be interested in living there. After all, why would people live in a place where they couldn't grow any food or find many animals to hunt? However, the Shawnee, Miami, and several other tribes were able to settle in a few of the less rugged parts of West Virginia, mostly in the northern part of the state, in the Ohio River Valley.

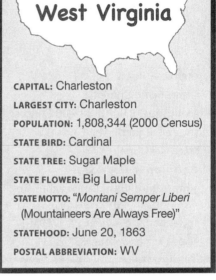

ALL ABOUT West Virginia

CAPITAL: Charleston
LARGEST CITY: Charleston
POPULATION: 1,808,344 (2000 Census)
STATE BIRD: Cardinal
STATE TREE: Sugar Maple
STATE FLOWER: Big Laurel
STATE MOTTO: "*Montani Semper Liberi* (Mountaineers Are Always Free)"
STATEHOOD: June 20, 1863
POSTAL ABBREVIATION: WV

WORDS TO KNOW

Secede

When the voting citizens of one part of a country or a state or a county decide that they no longer want to be part of that country or state or county, they are saying that they wish to "secede" from it, or leave it. The southern states during the Civil War tried to secede from the United States and form a separate government.

ALL ABOUT North Carolina

CAPITAL: Raleigh

LARGEST CITY: Charlotte

POPULATION: 8,049,313 (2000 Census)

STATE BIRD: Cardinal

STATE TREE: Pine

STATE FLOWER: Dogwood

STATE MOTTO: *"Esse Quam Videri* (To Be Rather Than to Seem)"

STATEHOOD: November 21, 1789

POSTAL ABBREVIATION: NC

Up until 1862, West Virginia was a part of the state of Virginia. Because of the mountains, tobacco and cotton would not grow in this part of the state. Because they didn't have the large plantations that their neighbors in the rest of Virginia had, slavery was not at all widespread in what later became West Virginia.

So when the rest of Virginia voted to secede from the Union, the counties that made up West Virginia voted to break away from Virginia! The people of West Virginia had the help of the Union Army, which protected them because they wanted to stay in the Union. Congress passed a law allowing West Virginia to enter the Union on June 20, 1863.

NORTH CAROLINA: The Tarheel State

Geography and Industry

From long, thin barrier islands in the east to the tallest mountains east of the Mississippi River to the west, North Carolina is home to a wide range of climates and terrains. Because of such barrier islands as Ocracoke and such famous capes as Cape Fear, Cape Lookout, and Cape Hatteras, North Carolina has a lot of large bays called "sounds." The most important of these are Pamlico and Albemarle Sounds, and they attract boaters, water-skiers, and fishing enthusiasts the year round. If you plan to visit North Carolina's shores, try to see places such as the Cape Hatteras National Seashore, and the Wright Brothers National Memorial at Kitty Hawk.

West of the barrier islands and the sounds lies the tidewater area. It is flat, humid, and riddled with swamps. Several large rivers run through it, including the Tar, Neuse, Cape Fear, and Roanoke rivers.

Farther west of the tidewater area is the Piedmont: rolling hills that are excellent farmland. The Piedmont rises at first gradually, then more steeply into the Blue Ridge Mountains, which are as rugged as any mountains east of the Rockies! The scenery is so breathtaking, and the climate is so mild, that western North Carolina is visited by campers and hikers year-round. North Carolina has four large national forests as well The Great Smoky Mountains

National Park, and the Appalachian Trail passes through western North Carolina, so there are plenty of places to camp, fish, or hike.

Like its neighbor Virginia, North Carolina produces a lot of tobacco, a cash crop with a long history in the state. In fact, North Carolina is the leading producer of tobacco in the world. Since smoking cigarettes in this country has declined over the past few years, farmers in North Carolina have begun to grow other crops in greater numbers. Sweet potatoes, peanuts, corn, and soybeans have been grown in North Carolina for a long time, and now they are beginning to replace tobacco in fields throughout the state.

History

Before European exploration and settlement, the largest tribes in what is now North Carolina were the Tuscarora in the central part of the state and the Cherokee in the mountain valleys of the western part of the state. The Tuscarora eventually went to war with the English colonists. The result was a disaster. After the Tuscaroras lost their fight with the colonists of North Carolina, they were forced to move all the way to western New York, where their cousins the Iroquois welcomed them as the sixth nation in their confederacy.

The Cherokees handled the advancing frontier very differently. They adopted European clothes, language, and many other customs, including their farming practices. (The Cherokees will be discussed in more detail in Chapter 4.)

You know from reading about Virginia earlier in this chapter that Jamestown was the first English settlement in North America. But, it wasn't the *first* English settlement in the New World. It was just the first permanent one! The first English colony in what is now the United States was not at Plymouth or Jamestown. It was Roanoke Colony, in what is now North Carolina.

Because it was so far away from England, Roanoke was difficult to establish, and it was hard to keep the colony supplied with food and even fresh water. This was a big problem. An expedition intended to resupply Roanoke found the colony deserted and its occupants gone without a trace and with no sign of a struggle! It seemed like the colonists had just disappeared. Carved into the

Fun Facts

THE WRIGHT BROTHERS

Kitty Hawk is the site of the first airplane flight in 1903. Two Ohio bicycle shop owners named Orville and Wilbur Wright used the strong winds of Kitty Hawk to help them get their first airplane off the ground. Today you can see the Wright Brothers' airplane at the Smithsonian Institution.

post of one of the colony's houses was a single word: CROATOAN, (which is a slight misspelling of the name of a local Indian tribe, the Croatan). Whether this was a clue about what happened to the colonists of Roanoke, no one knows for certain.

It was another sixty years before settlers from the Virginia colony moved south and began to successfully establish homes in what was then called the Carolinas (after the Latin name of the English king Charles I). The Carolina colonies were officially separated into North and South Carolina in 1712, the same year that the Tuscarora War broke out.

In 1861 North Carolina joined eleven other southern slave states (states where slavery was legal at the time) in seceding from the Union and establishing the Confederate States of America. Aside from having most of its ports captured by the blockading Union Navy, North Carolina saw little fighting during the civil war that followed secession.

In late April of 1865, the last Confederate army still in the field surrendered to Union forces in North Carolina. This occurred more than two weeks after General Robert E. Lee's main army surrendered at Appomattox in Virginia.

KENTUCKY: The Bluegrass State

Geography

If you're going to be in central and western Kentucky, don't miss the horse farms in the bluegrass region around Lexington, or the track where many of those horses race in the world-famous Kentucky Derby at Churchill Downs. Out west of the bluegrass is a region named after a kind of mint that grows there called the Pennyroyal. One sight to see in the Pennyroyal is Mammoth Cave. Mammoth Cave goes on for miles, and parts of it are open to the public.

History

Before European exploration and settlement, Kentucky was a no man's land for Native Americans. The land was fertile, and full

ALL ABOUT Kentucky

CAPITAL: Frankfort

LARGEST CITY: Louisville

POPULATION: 4,041,769 (2000 Census)

STATE BIRD: Cardinal

STATE TREE: Kentucky Coffee Tree

STATE FLOWER: Goldenrod

STATE MOTTO: "United We Stand, Divided We Fall"

STATEHOOD: June 1, 1792

POSTAL ABBREVIATION: KY

One to Grow On

Two sisters from Louisville, Kentucky wrote a simple song in 1893.
Every single person you know can sing this song and knows all the words!
What is it? To find out, fill in all the boxes with a dot in the center.

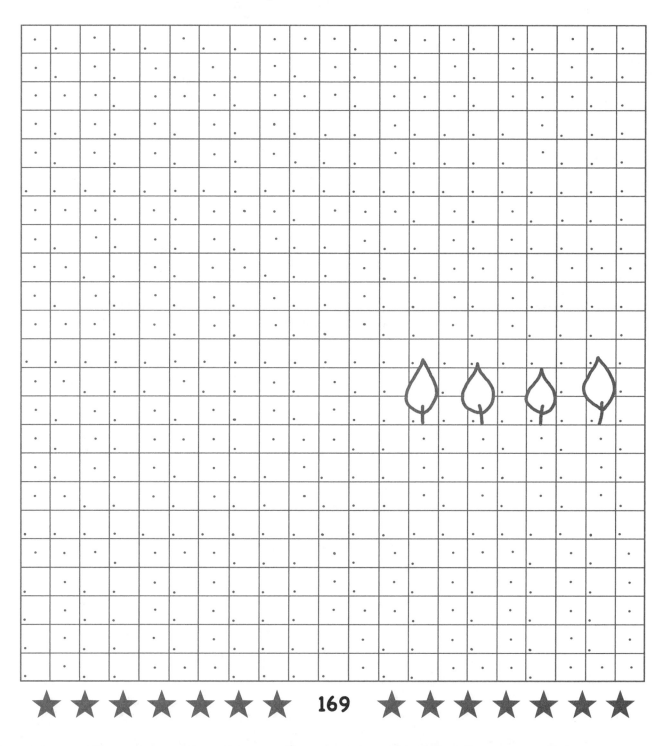

WORDS TO KNOW

Bluegrass

Bluegrass is the common name for the lawn and pasture grass in the eastern United States from Tennesse northward. Bluegrass has also come to mean the region of the United States around the Kentucky area that is known for its excellent soil, horse farms, and rolling hills of bluegrass.

of game animals. It was a great place to find food. This led to several large tribes such as the Shawnee, the Ottawa, the Delaware (who had been pushed out of the eastern colonies), the Cherokee, and the Tensa (Tennessee) fighting over these large hunting grounds. Because none of them could defeat all of their enemies, these tribes lived around Kentucky (but not in it), and ventured into it to hunt and fish, and to fight each other!

Kentucky was originally claimed by the French though they did not settle there or even enter the area. While the Native Americans ventured into Kentucky to fight each other, the French avoided the area, and instead traded furs just outside of the Kentucky border with the tribes.

After the English won Kentucky in a war with the French, their colonies on the Atlantic coast began sending settlers through the Cumberland Gap into Kentucky. The famous frontiersman Daniel Boone visited Kentucky for the first time in 1767. He founded one of the first permanent settlements in the area at Boonesboro in 1774. This wave of settlement led to savage fighting with Indian tribes living around Kentucky, especially the Shawnee.

Sitting between the Deep South and the lower states of the North, Kentucky was truly what historians call a border state. Kentucky's climate was not like that of states such as Alabama and Mississippi. In those states it was hot enough that plantation farming made money for farmers. Kentucky was too cold to grow much cotton or tobacco. Since it wasn't a good place for these crops, there wasn't as much need for slaves to work the fields in Kentucky.

But Kentucky was settled mostly by people from southern states such as Virginia (including Abraham Lincoln's grandfather, who sold his farm in Virginia to reside in Kentucky!), and in many ways was a truly southern state. So when the Civil War came, families and friendships in that state were torn apart.

Kentucky never seceded from the Union, although many Kentuckians fought on both sides of the war. The sons of a U.S. senator from Kentucky split down the middle: one fought for the North, and one fought for the South. In Kentucky the Civil War literally was a case of "brother against brother"!

A Famous Kentucky Taste

In 1930, Harland Sanders owned a gas station in Corbin, Tennessess and decided to start selling chicken cooked with his personal recipe of herbs and spices right at the station. His food quickly became popular, and the governor made him an honorary "Kentucky Colonel" six years later in! In 1952 the Colonel began opening chain restaurants. Kentucky Fried Chicken is still headquartered in Louisville, Kentucky.

TENNESSEE: The Volunteer State

Geography and Industry

Eastern Tennessee is very rugged, with a lot of forests and many narrow river valleys. Central Tennessee is like central Kentucky to the north: it is open country that has lots of bluegrass in it. Western Tennessee is some of the richest farmland in the United States. Much of the cotton grown in the United States comes from the fields of western Tennessee.

The Tennessee River flows through the central part of the state, then down into Alabama, and back north into western Tennessee, up through Kentucky, and on into the Ohio River. The Tennessee River is one of the largest and most important rivers in the south.

There is so much to see and do in Tennessee. With the Mississippi River next door, and the Tennessee River itself winding through the state, boating, water-skiing, and fishing are all very popular, to say nothing of bass fishing, which many Tennesseans take very seriously. And since Tennessee has more than twenty state parks, as well as parts of the Cherokee National Forest, the Great Smoky Mountains National Park, and the Cumberland Gap National Historical Park within its borders, there are plenty of places in Tennessee to camp and hike as well.

Tennessee has many historic places worth visiting. These include President Andrew Jackson's plantation, The Hermitage. Shiloh National Military Park marks the site of the Civil War battle of Shiloh in the west, and the Chickamauga and Chattanooga National Military Park does the same for the Chattanooga battlefield in the southeastern part of the state.

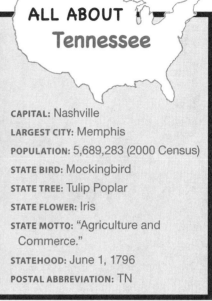

ALL ABOUT Tennessee

CAPITAL: Nashville
LARGEST CITY: Memphis
POPULATION: 5,689,283 (2000 Census)
STATE BIRD: Mockingbird
STATE TREE: Tulip Poplar
STATE FLOWER: Iris
STATE MOTTO: "Agriculture and Commerce."
STATEHOOD: June 1, 1796
POSTAL ABBREVIATION: TN

Fun Facts

THE "STATE" OF FRANKLIN

East Tennesseans formed a state government in 1784 because they felt abandoned by North Carolina. The state "existed" for four years but it was never recognized by the U.S. government.

TRY THIS!

Graceland

Have you ever heard your parents talking about the famous singer Elvis? Elvis's home is now a museum in Tennessee that's called Graceland. Make up a game with your friends about who can name the most Elvis songs. Or ask your parents to help you dig up some of their Elvis records and see if you can count how many times Elvis mentions Graceland in the lyrics.

Also, Tennessee is the home of Nashville, which is the country music capital of the world. If blues is more your thing, then Memphis, in the western part of Tennessee, might be a better place for you to visit, because Memphis is a hotbed of blues music!

History

Before the first Europeans visited Tennessee during the 1540s, tribes of Native American peoples like the Shawnee, Cherokee, and Chickasaw lived in the area. Hundreds of years earlier, the region was dominated by the Mound Builder culture. These people constructed various styles and sizes of mounds for burial, ceremonial, and residential purposes. The mounds can be found all over Tennessee.

During the American Revolution, Tennessee was part of North Carolina (just like Kentucky to the north was a county in Virginia). East Tennessee was already settled by a number of Carolinians, including a heroic Revolutionary War leader named John Sevier.

Tennessee nearly split up during the Civil War. Eastern Tennessee was mountainous and not a good place to grow plantation crops such as tobacco and cotton. Like the people in the mountains of West Virginia, the people who lived in eastern Tennessee's Great Smoky Mountains supported the Union during the war, and did not want to secede. The rest of Tennessee was plantation country, and supported slavery. Most of the people living there (aside from the slaves themselves, obviously!) wanted to secede.

It turned out to be a costly choice. Aside from Virginia, no state saw more fighting during the Civil War than Tennessee. Union troops in the western part of the state invaded the south by fighting their way along the main rivers in the state. Rivers were surrounded by valleys that made it easy for armies to move together.

Because of its position as a place from which to launch not one but two invasions of the south, getting and keeping control of Tennessee was very important to the Union during the Civil War. In fact, it was so important that in 1864, when President Lincoln was running for re-election, he took as his running mate a senator from Tennessee who had refused to give up his seat in Congress when his home state seceded.

CHAPTER 13

THE DEEP SOUTH

S wamps. Mint juleps. Moss-covered plantation houses. These are the images that come to mind when people think of the Deep South. And yet there is so much more to the Deep South than that! Florida has long beaches, a colorful Caribbean subculture, and Disney World in Orlando. South Carolina has gorgeous beaches as well, with Myrtle Beach being one of its most famous.

And the food! If you like it deep-fried, you'll like the Deep South! They even deep-fry vegetables in the Deep South (like fried okra). And then there's the barbecue, and the cornbread!

The Deep South is a place of many contrasts. It has mountains and lowlands, swamps and prairies, forests and bayous. It is also a land of large, powerful rivers such as the Mississippi, Alabama, Tennessee, and Tombigbee.

SOUTH CAROLINA: The Palmetto State

Geography and Industry

South Carolina is one of the most stereotypically "southern" of southern states. In the Palmetto State, "barbecue" is a noun as well as a verb, the weather is hot, cotton is grown all over, and plantations still dot the landscape.

The southern part of the state is covered in cypress swamps, and the northeastern part of the state has wonderful white-sand beaches, which are a year-round tourist attraction. Places such as Myrtle Beach, the Sea Islands, and the Grand Strand draw people from all over the world. So does the beautiful city of Charleston in the south, with its historic old homes, and the Fort Sumter National Monument marking where the Civil War began.

The Blue Ridge Mountains run through the northwestern part of the state, making it more rugged than the other two sections, which are coastal areas. Lots of vegetables (especially many kinds of squash) are grown in the northwestern hills of the state.

ALL ABOUT South Carolina

CAPITAL: Columbia

LARGEST CITY: Columbia

POPULATION: 4,012,012 (2000 Census)

STATE BIRD: Carolina Wren

STATE TREE: Palmetto

STATE FLOWER: Carolina Jessamine

STATE MOTTO: "*Dum Spiro Spero* (While I Breathe, I Hope)"

STATEHOOD: May 23, 1788

POSTAL ABBREVIATION: SC

Indigo (a plant that produces the blue dye of the same name) and rice have been cash crops in the Palmetto State for centuries. South Carolina is also a leader in the textile industry. This is because so much cotton is grown in the state, and because there are fast-flowing rivers such as the Edisto, Pee Dee, Santee, and Savannah that are great sources of power for cotton mills. If you're wearing a cotton shirt with a label that says Made in the U.S.A., it's pretty likely that it was made in South Carolina.

WORDS TO KNOW

Cash Crop

A cash crop is a crop that is grown strictly for the purpose of obtaining money as opposed to a crop meant to feed the farmer's family or livestock.

History

Before the coming of the Europeans, South Carolina was home to such powerful Native American tribes as the Catawba in the north, the Yamasee along the coast in the south, and the Cherokee in the mountainous northwest.

The first Europeans in what is now South Carolina were the members of a Spanish exploring expedition led by Lucas Vásquez de Ayllón. They occupied a site somewhere on the South Carolina coast during the year 1526. But they soon abandoned it.

By 1562, the Spanish mission system had worked its way up from Florida, and had gotten as far as what is now Charleston. The Spanish abandoned their missions in the Charleston area when the English began to colonize what they first called the Carolinas in the 1660s. This colony eventually split into two separate colonies: North and South Carolina.

The people who colonized South Carolina came from other parts of Europe besides England. There were Scots and Irish settlers, and French settlers as well. These French settlers were religious refugees called Huguenots (pronounced "HYOO-guh-nots"). While most of the people of France were Catholics, the Huguenots were Protestants, and were treated unfairly because of it. This was why many of them chose to come to the New World, where they could worship in their own way, without being bullied.

Fun Facts

A NEW WAY TO FIGHT

During the first years of the revolution, South Carolina did not see much action aside from hit-and-run raids by rebel units on British forces. The leaders of these rebel units became famous for their ingenuity and daring. Men such as Francis Marion (so crafty that he was nicknamed the Swamp Fox) and Thomas Sumter with their cunning, Indian-style tactics, helped change the way wars were fought.

Slavery and Secession in South Carolina

In the years between the Revolution and the Civil War, slavery became even more important in South Carolina than it had been before the United States won its independence. This was due partly because of Eli Whitney's invention of the cotton gin. Cotton became very important to South Carolina, and its textile industry boomed. That meant more cotton had to be grown. The fastest way to do that was to get more slaves, and put them to work planting and picking cotton, which led to acquiring more slaves and planting more land with cotton, and so on.

This made South Carolina politicians and property owners resist other peoples' attempts to free the slaves and to get rid of plantation life completely. In the minds of these South Carolinians, slavery stopped being a "necessary evil," and became a positive force for southern society.

South Carolina politicians wanted to see the South's way of life protected, and for them, that meant no limits on slavery in America. During a speech he gave in June of 1858, Abraham Lincoln declared, "[a] house divided against itself cannot stand. I do not believe this government can endure permanently half-slave and half-free." In 1860, Lincoln was elected president and South Carolina's leaders were so worried that he would abolish slavery throughout the country that they voted to leave the Union. They ordered the state's militia to seize federal forts and armories within South Carolina's borders.

One such federal fort was Fort Sumter, which protected the Charleston harbor. When rebel gunners fired their cannons at the fort in an effort to get its commander to surrender, the Civil War began. The date was April 12, 1861.

As it turned out, there was very little fighting in South Carolina during the four-year struggle that followed. Aside from the Union navy occupying the Sea Islands as part of a blockade of all southern ports, South Carolina saw no major military activity within its borders until the very end of the war.

GEORGIA: The Peach State

Geography and Industry

The southern tip of the Blue Ridge Mountains rises in Georgia's northwestern sector, and forms one of the state's three geographic regions. These mountains are part of the Appalachian chain, and run all the way north into West Virginia!

Georgia's two other regions are the hilly Piedmont, which slopes down from the Blue Ridge across the central part of the state, and the southeastern coastal plain, which includes the large Okefenokee Swamp. Georgia also shares the Sea Islands with South Carolina, its neighbor to the north.

Georgia's rivers help form most of its borders with the states that surround it. The Savannah River runs along Georgia's border with South Carolina. The Chattahoochie in the west forms part of Georgia's boundary with Alabama, and the St. Mary's in the south is the marker for part of the Georgia-Florida border.

Georgia has the southern end of the Appalachian Trail in its northwestern section, and as a result, has many places within its borders to hike and camp. Many Georgians also love to hunt and fish. Along Georgia's coastline, surf fishing is incredibly popular. Places such as Warm Springs, the Sea Islands, and the Civil War battlefield national monuments at Chickamauga and Kennesaw Mountain draw millions of tourists every year.

Cotton used to be the "king" crop in Georgia, but that hasn't been true for decades. These days, the top products are peanuts, lumber, tobacco, and corn. The state is covered in pine forests, and because of its warm climate and long growing season, these trees can be grown quickly and harvested more often than in other timber-producing states.

History

Did you know that Georgia began as a prison? It's true! When Georgia was founded as a British royal colony in 1733, it was

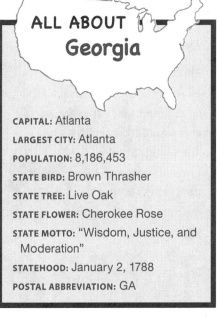

ALL ABOUT Georgia

CAPITAL: Atlanta

LARGEST CITY: Atlanta

POPULATION: 8,186,453

STATE BIRD: Brown Thrasher

STATE TREE: Live Oak

STATE FLOWER: Cherokee Rose

STATE MOTTO: "Wisdom, Justice, and Moderation"

STATEHOOD: January 2, 1788

POSTAL ABBREVIATION: GA

Fun Facts

PEANUTS

Do you like peanuts? If you do, odds are that the ones you've eaten came from Georgia. Georgia is the country's largest producer of peanuts. Former president (and Georgia resident) Jimmy Carter started out as a peanut farmer.

WORDS TO KNOW

The Trail of Tears

The trail of tears was a 116-day journey of several thousand Cherokees from their homes in Georgia to a reservation in Oklahoma. The Georgia state government forced the Cherokees to make this trip. The journey was so poorly planned and badly managed that nearly 4,000 Cherokees died on the trip.

illegal to owe money that you couldn't pay. People often went to jail until they could pay their debts. Georgia's founder James Oglethorpe thought that one way to help people in this position was to offer to send them to a colony in America, rather than send them to a jail in England, where they couldn't pay off their debt because they weren't free to work. And so Georgia (named for George II, the English king at the time) was born.

Before European settlement, Native American tribes such as the Cherokee (who lived in the Blue Ridge mountains of the northwest) and the Muskogean-speaking Creek (who lived in the river valleys of the west) lived in Georgia. Other, smaller Muskogean-speaking tribes lived along Georgia's swampy southeastern coast.

As the Georgia frontier advanced inland, it ran into the lands of the Cherokees beginning shortly before the American Revolution. At first the Cherokee fought the settlers moving into their land. Then they had a brilliant idea.

The Cherokee began to adopt the ways of the European settlers. They dressed like their white neighbors, settled down to raise cotton and tobacco, even owned black slaves and used them for labor on Cherokee plantations!

This accommodation of American settlers did not help the Cherokee in the long run, though. By the early 1830s, gold had been discovered on Cherokee land, and most of them were forced to give up their homes in Georgia and move west to a reservation set aside for them in distant Oklahoma.

Whereas Georgia escaped the American Revolution without having a major battle fought within its borders, the Civil War that came ninety years later utterly destroyed most of the property in the state. Union general William Tecumseh Sherman led a large army southeast from Tennessee and through the heart of Georgia, all the way to the sea. Sherman's troops seized all farm supplies (including grain) and most of the farm animals of the people who lived in their path.

What they didn't take, Sherman's army burned. This included the large and prosperous city of Atlanta. Sherman became so hated in Georgia that for generations after the war, if you toasted General Sherman anywhere in Georgia, you were literally asking for a fight!

Pickles?

Of all the states, Georgia is the biggest producer of the "three Ps." Follow the directions below to cross items out of the grid. When you are done, you will know what the three Ps are!

POMEGRANATES	PEAS	PAPAYAS
PARSNIPS	PEANUTS	PEARS
PECANS	PENCILS	PEPPERS
PALMETTOS	PIMENTOS	PUMPKINS
PASTA	PUZZLES	PRETZELS
POPCORN	PORK	PINEAPPLES
PAPRIKA	PENNIES	PLOWS
PATIOS	POTATOES	PEACHES
PICKLES	PUDDING	PASTRIES
PLUMS	PETUNIAS	PANCAKES

Cross out all items that...

...are not edible

...have double letters

...start with PA

...have the letter K

...are less than 6 letters

...are more than 7 letters

...have the letter O

Fun Facts

ST. AUGUSTINE

You know about Jamestown in Virginia, and about Plymouth in Massachusetts, but do you know about St. Augustine in Florida? It is the oldest city in North America. Spanish settlers established it in 1565, almost fifty years before Jamestown!

FLORIDA: The Sunshine State

Geography and Industry

Florida is mostly a giant peninsula surrounded on three sides by salt water, and is possibly the flattest state in the Union. It's true! Florida is even flatter than such plains states as Kansas and Nebraska. It's also a huge state, one of the largest in the country.

Have you ever visited a wetland? Well, Florida is home to the Everglades, which is a unique type of country: it is part swamp and part cypress forest, and all wetland. In fact, it's one of the largest wetlands in the world. Like many other things in Florida, the Everglades country is huge. It covers a lot of the southern tip of the state, and much of it lies within the Everglades National Park.

In the north, Florida is covered by a combination of pine and palmetto forests. There are many swamps in the northwestern part of the state as well, in addition to such large rivers as the Perdido River and the St. Mary's River. On Florida's east coast there are a lot of barrier islands: long, thin islands that protect the coastline from the tides, and naturally prevent erosion.

Speaking of islands, don't forget the Florida Keys. They are a chain of islands that extend southwestward from the southern tip of Florida for hundreds of miles out into the Gulf of Mexico. And they even have a highway that runs between them!

History

Native Americans have been active in Florida for at least the past 10,000 years. When Juan Ponce de Leon explored Florida for Spain in 1519, there were thousands and thousands of Native Americans (mostly members of a language group called the Apalachee) living there. We know very little about these people, because so many died after the explorers came into their land. The Spaniards who followed Ponce de Leon to Florida in the decades afterward brought European diseases like smallpox, influenza, and whooping cough that made the Indians sick enough to die. On top of that, the Spanish explorers who came to Florida, looking for the same gold and silver they had found in South America and Mexico, tried to enslave the native population, killing many of them outright in the struggle. It was a horrible time to be a Native American in Florida!

In 1819, Spain sold Florida to the United States for $5,000,000. Why? First, the Spanish military had been weakened by recent wars in Europe. The Spanish government was afraid that the United States would simply move in and take Florida from Spain without Spain receiving anything in return. Second, at about this time, an American army under the command of General Andrew Jackson chased Seminole Indians from southern Georgia into Florida. The Spanish were not able to stop Jackson and his militia. This incident convinced the Spanish that if they didn't sell Florida to the United States, they would soon lose it anyway.

By 1845 Florida had enough American citizens living in its borders to become a state. Just sixteen years later, Florida sided with the other southern states, and helped found the Confederacy.

Florida saw almost no fighting during the Civil War. The Union Navy did seize a few strategic coastal towns, though. After the Civil War, Florida experienced a huge real estate boom. People made millions buying and selling Florida property.

Real estate is still an important and money-making industry in Florida even today. But can you guess what Florida's most important industry is today? Here's a hint: "I'm going to Disney World!" That's right, tourism is the answer. Every year, millions of people from all over the world visit Florida on vacation, and not just to see Disney World. They also visit Miami's restaurants and shops, take boat cruises that begin in Jacksonville, and enjoy the miles and miles of beaches all along Florida's coastline.

WORDS TO KNOW

Seminole

Seminoles are members of the Creek Nation of Indians. Their name means "separators," because they left the Creek homeland in Alabama and moved south, into Florida, during the eighteenth century. From Florida, the Seminoles encouraged runaway slaves and members of other tribes to join them and intermarry with them.

ALABAMA: The Yellowhammer State
Geography and Industry

Alabama has a few mountains in the northeast (it's part of the Cumberland Plateau). Aside from them, the state is very flat. The Piedmont section in the middle part of the state rolls down to the coastal plain, which lies around the huge harbor of Mobile Bay. The Tennessee River winds through Alabama's northern section, then back into Tennessee. And the Alabama and Tombigbee rivers flow through the central section and drain into the Gulf of Mexico in

ALL ABOUT
Alabama

CAPITAL: Montgomery

LARGEST CITY: Birmingham

POPULATION: 4,447,100 (2000 Census)

STATE BIRD: Yellowhammer

STATE TREE: Southern (Longleaf) Pine

STATE FLOWER: Camellia

STATE MOTTO: *"Audemus Jura Nostra Defendere* (We Dare to Defend Our Rights)"

STATEHOOD: December 14, 1819

POSTAL ABBREVIATION: AL

Fun Facts

HOME OF THE CONFEDERATE CAPITAL

Did you know that Richmond, Virginia, was not the original capital of the Confederate States of America? Because Virginia did not secede from the Union until many months after the states of the Deep South did, the capital was originally located in Montgomery, Alabama.

the south. These large, navigable river systems are popular year-round with boaters and fishermen.

Alabama is the site of some of the largest caves in the United States as well. One particular set, which was lived in continually by Native Americans for thousands of years, can be found at Russell Cave National Monument. Another popular Alabama tourist attraction is Mound State Monument, where early Native American burial mounds have been preserved.

As with its neighbors Georgia and Mississippi, cotton used to be the only real product of Alabama. These days manufacturing is very important in this state, where power is cheap and plentiful because of the hydroelectric dams on the Tennessee River. Roaster chickens are also raised in Alabama (as they are in Mississippi).

History

Before European settlement, Alabama was home to many large Native American tribes. The Cherokee lived in the northeast, the Creek in the southeast, the Choctaw in the southwest, and the Chickasaw in the northwest. All of the tribes except for the Cherokee spoke dialects of the Muskogean language, and because of Alabama's fertile black soil and year-round warm weather, they were all farmers.

The Spanish explored Alabama first. Cabeza de Vaca visited the region in 1528, and Hernando de Soto in 1540. De Soto's men were terribly destructive. They fought many of the local tribes and burned many native towns.

The French were the first Europeans to permanently settle in the region. They established a fur-trading post in Mobile Bay in 1702. For the next century, the fur trade was the major reason for European settlement in the region.

By the early 1800s, American settlers from Tennessee and Georgia had begun to plant cotton in Alabama, and the numbers of the Americans in the region boomed. Crowded westward by American settlement, the Creek nation went to war to protect their lands. American militia troops under the command of Tennessee general Andrew Jackson defeated the Creek confederacy at the battle of Horseshoe Bend in 1814. As a result, the Creeks gave up their lands, and agreed to be moved to what is now Oklahoma. The Choctaw and Chickasaw soon followed them there.

When the Civil War broke out in 1861, few southern states were as ready for a fight as Alabama. It was among the first states to follow South Carolina's example and secede from the Union. Although (like South Carolina) Alabama provided many soldiers for the southern cause during the war, it saw very little fighting (also like South Carolina). The exception to this was the huge naval battle at Mobile Bay in 1864. The Union won it, and continued to blockade the South's trade with Europe.

MISSISSIPPI: The Magnolia State

Geography and Industry

Mississippi has many different types of land within its borders. In the northern part of the state there are hills and river valleys cut by small, fast-flowing rivers. The southern part is taken up mostly by the broad floodplain of the Mississippi River. This plain is called the Mississippi Delta, and runs between the mouth of the Mississippi River in the west and that of the Yazoo River in the east.

After Eli Whitney invented the cotton gin and made cotton such an important crop, places like Mississippi became very important centers of the growth of cotton. Although not as important as it once was, cotton is still grown all over Mississippi's delta region today. With cotton not being grown so much anymore, a lot of Mississippi's rich farmland is currently devoted to cattle-ranching and chicken-raising. If you've ever had roaster chicken, it probably came from Mississippi.

History

Before European exploration and settlement, Mississippi was home to large tribes of Native Americans such as the Choctaw, Chickasaw, and Natchez. The Spaniards visited the region first, and Hernando de Soto's men discovered the Mississippi River in 1541.

The French, in 1699, established a trading post on the coast, near Biloxi. Over the next century, the area changed hands between the

ALL ABOUT Mississippi

CAPITAL: Jackson

LARGEST CITY: Jackson

POPULATION: 2,844,658

STATE BIRD: Mockingbird

STATE TREE: Magnolia

STATE FLOWER: Magnolia

STATE MOTTO: *"Virtute et Armis* ("By Valor and Arms")"

STATEHOOD: December 10, 1817

POSTAL ABBREVIATION: MS

WORDS TO KNOW

Delta

A delta takes its name from the Greek letter *delta*, which is triangular in shape. Greek visitors to the Nile River noticed that the river dumped a lot of the soil it carried from upstream at its mouth, that this soil was excellent for farming, and that the shape of the river's floodplain was roughly triangular in shape. This is why the Greeks called the area the delta.

French, Spanish, and English numerous times. In the treaty that ended the American Revolution, the English ceded most of what is now Mississippi to the United States. The southern part came to the United States as part of the Louisiana Purchase in 1803.

Just as they did in Alabama, by the 1820s, cotton-growing American settlers displaced the Native American population, and began to take the rich farmland in the delta. By the time the Civil War began in 1861, Mississippi was a cotton empire. Its plantation owners made millions from the British demand for the crop, and slavery flourished.

As a result, the state joined the other states of the Deep South in seceding from the Union. In fact, Mississippi also supplied the Confederacy with its first and only president: former Mississippi senator and U.S. Secretary of War, Jefferson Davis.

Like Virginia and Georgia in the east, Mississippi was a battleground state during the Civil War. The important battles of Shiloh, Jackson, and Vicksburg were all fought in Mississippi. The loss of Vicksburg to the Union forces is considered by many historians to be the turning point in the American Civil War.

Where are my glasses?

Start in one of the corners and read the letters in order around the grid and into the middle. You must find which corner to start, and in which direction to read! When you are finished, you will have the silly answer to this riddle: Why is Mississippi such an unusual state?

S	F	O	U	R	E	Y	E	S
A	A	N	'	T	S	E	E	!	A
H	C	L	L	I	T	S	D	N
T	I	E	S	U	A	C	E	B

CHAPTER 14

THE MIDWEST

The Midwestern states might also be called the Great Lakes states, because each of them (even the mostly land-locked Indiana) at least partially borders the Great Lakes. Such large continental rivers as the Ohio and the Mississippi are also important in tying the states of this region together.

Most of the states of the Midwest are part of what is now known as the Rust Belt, as well. This is a part of the country that built up huge manufacturing plants because of its closeness to coal and oil deposits, its central location, and its good transportation routes to other parts of the country (first by riverboat, then by railroad) and to the world.

Several of the cities in this section of the country have been very important to the development of American industry, including Detroit, Cleveland, Milwaukee, and especially Chicago. The Midwest region of the country ties the other sections together.

OHIO: The Buckeye State

Geography

Ohio is bordered to the south by the river for which it is named. To the north lies Lake Erie. Ohio is mostly flat, with some rolling hills in the southeastern part of the state. Before European settlement, Ohio was a big, unbroken hardwood forest. Most of that huge forest is gone now, replaced by some of the richest farmland in the country. Wheat is grown in Ohio, nearly as much as is grown in the plains states!

In the Ohio River Valley, you can find a number of large earthen mounds. These were left by a group of Native Americans that archaeologists call the Hopewell civilization. Other people refer to these people as the Mound Builders. This civilization, which disappeared hundreds of years before European exploration of the region, built mounds that measure as high as sixty-five feet off the ground, and in some places they cover

ALL ABOUT Ohio

CAPITAL: Columbus
LARGEST CITY: Columbus
POPULATION: 11,353,140 (2000 Census)
STATE BIRD: Cardinal
STATE TREE: Buckeye
STATE FLOWER: Scarlet Carnation
STATE MOTTO: "With God, All Things Are Possible"
STATEHOOD: March 1, 1803
POSTAL ABBREVIATION: OH

acres of ground! Some of these mounds are circular; others are in the shape of animals such as snakes. You can find many of these interesting mounds in the Hopewell Culture National Historical Park.

History

After the end of the Hopewell civilization, other tribes entered the Ohio country and prospered there. Tribes such as the Miami, the Shawnee, and the Erie settled in the region. During the seventeenth century, the Erie fought a long war with the Seneca, a member tribe of the Iroquois confederacy, which lived in western New York. The two tribes fought over control of the fur trade in the Ohio region. The Erie lost, and were absorbed by the Seneca, who took over the Erie hunting grounds as their own.

During the eighteenth century, most of the tribes in the Ohio country sided with the French in a series of wars with the English. Because the French had claimed all of the lands drained by the waters that flowed out of the mouth of the Mississippi and into the Gulf of Mexico, they had a claim to the Ohio country as well, because the Ohio River flows into the Mississippi.

When the French lost their lands in North America as part of the treaty that ended the Seven Years' War (1756–1763), many of the Native Americans in the Ohio Valley joined in what later became known as Pontiac's Rebellion. This wave of violence led to the eventual removal of all Native American tribes to west of the Mississippi River.

After the American Revolution, the British ceded Ohio to the United States as part of the Old Northwest Territory. Ohio became its own territory in 1799, and a state in 1803.

Shortly after Ohio became a state, it became a battleground of the War of 1812, which the young United States fought with Great Britain. One of the most important battles of this war was an American naval victory over the British on Lake Erie, within sight of the Ohio shore.

WORDS TO KNOW

Drain

When geographers use this term they are usually using it as a verb, to explain which rivers and streams "drain" a region. In other words, saying that a river "drains" a region means that the water that flows out of the area goes by way of this river (and its tributary streams) to the ocean.

Fun Facts

OHIO: THE MOTHER OF PRESIDENTS!

Ohio has supplied more presidents to our country than any other state, eight presidents in all! Aside from William Henry Harrison (who was born in Virginia, and moved to Ohio when it was still a territory), all of these presidents were born and raised in Ohio: Ulysses S. Grant, Rutherford B. Hayes, James A. Garfield, Benjamin Harrison, William McKinley, William Howard Taft, and Warren G. Harding.

Industry in Ohio

Ohio has changed a lot in the 200 years since it became a state. Because it had a lot of natural resources like oil, coal, and natural gas, Ohio was a natural choice for people who were looking for places to build factories to produce goods like cloth. Later, as the Industrial Revolution helped make it easier to produce high-grade steel products, Ohio's coal deposits were one reason that the state became a center of steel production in the United States.

The other reason Ohio became so important in industry was its water access to other markets. In the southern part of the state, the mighty Ohio River fed into the Mississippi, and out of the Gulf of Mexico and to foreign markets. In the north there was Lake Erie, which fed eventually into the St. Lawrence River, and again, out to sea, and to foreign markets in places such as England, which was a large market for American steel during the nineteenth century.

As a result of this, Ohio became a very important state in the Union, before, during, and after the Civil War. Many of America's military and political leaders came from Ohio during this century, including Union generals Ulysses S. Grant and William Tecumseh Sherman, and a number of U.S. presidents.

Important Ohioans

There are many great explorers among those Ohioans who have gone on to national and international fame. These include John Wesley Powell, who explored the Grand Canyon in the late nineteenth century, and Annie Oakley, the great American sharpshooter.

Then, of course, there are the Wright Brothers, who invented the airplane in 1903. They owned a bicycle shop in Dayton, Ohio, even though they are remembered for their flights at Kitty Hawk in North Carolina. Because of the contributions of the Wright Brothers, we have the later accomplishments of John Glenn, one of America's first astronauts (and later a U.S.

senator from Ohio), and Neil Armstrong, another American astronaut and the first man to walk on the moon (in 1969). Other great Ohioans include Daniel C. Beard, who founded the Boy Scouts of America, and A.B. Graham, who founded the 4-H club movement.

Get in Shape

Ohio's flag is unique among the 50 states. Why?

Connect the dots, and break the "Vowel Switch" Code to find out!

1.
•6

•2

Tha stuta flug if Ihei es treungolur, weth twi pientad tuels.

3.

•4

5•

ALL ABOUT Indiana

CAPITAL: Indianapolis

LARGEST CITY: Indianapolis

POPULATION: 6,080,485 (2000 Census)

STATE BIRD: Cardinal

STATE TREE: Tulip Poplar

STATE FLOWER: Peony

STATE MOTTO: "The Crossroads of America"

STATEHOOD: December 11, 1816

POSTAL ABBREVIATION: IN

Fun Facts

INDIANA LIMESTONE

The majority of the limestone used in buildings in this country comes from southern Indiana.

INDIANA: The Hoosier State

Geography and Industry

Indiana is right in the middle of both the Midwest and the United States itself. In fact, north Indiana is one of the most frequently crossed parts of the country because of its closeness to the transportation hub in the city of Chicago in the neighboring state of Illinois. More planes, trains, trucks, and cars cross northern Indiana than most other parts of the United States combined.

Northern and central Indiana are pretty flat, and ideal farmland. In fact, even though manufacturing is Indiana's biggest type of industry, 75 percent of the state is still farmland. Most of the available land is used to grow wheat, corn, soybeans, and hay. Another important Indiana crop is popcorn! Nearly half of the popcorn eaten in America is grown and packaged in Indiana. After all, Orville Redenbacher was an Indiana native.

Northwestern Indiana has a lot of heavy industry (mostly things like steel production), again because it is so close to Chicago. Southern Indiana is made up mostly of rolling limestone hills, in which groundwater has bored out immense underground caves. The major rivers in Indiana include the Ohio (which marks Indiana's southern border), the Wabash, and the Indiana.

History

The Mound Builders discussed in the section on Ohio also lived and built monuments in Indiana. After the decline of their civilization, Native American tribes such as the Shawnee, Miami, Wyandot, and Delaware (who had been pushed west first from Pennsylvania, then from Ohio by European settlement) lived in what is now Indiana.

These tribes all sided with the British during the American Revolution, and continued to fight against the United States even afterward, because they were trying to keep American settlers off of their land. One of their leaders was a Shawnee Chief named Tecumseh. He was respected on both sides of the conflict for his bravery and his honesty. Tecumseh tried to unite the tribes of the Ohio Valley with other tribes west of the Appalachian Mountains, such as the Creeks and Cherokees in the south. He wanted to get these tribes to band together to keep the whites out of the lands west of the mountains.

While Tecumseh was away in the south trying to persuade the Creeks to join his confederacy, his followers fought a battle with American soldiers under the command of General (and future president) William Henry Harrison. This battle took place on November 7, 1811, on the banks of Tippecanoe Creek.

Although it was pretty much a draw, this battle made a name for Harrison, who made a political career of the event. He ran for the presidency nearly thirty years later with the campaign slogan "Tippecanoe and Tyler Too!" (John Tyler of Virginia was his running mate.)

Tecumseh sided with the British during the War of 1812. He was later killed in what is now Ontario, Canada, at the Battle of the Thames. When he died, Native American resistance to white settlement in Indiana collapsed, and most of the remaining Native American tribes in the area were relocated by the U.S. government to lands west of the Mississippi River.

TRY THIS!

Ancient Native American Food: Popcorn

Did you know that Native Americans had popcorn as part of their daily diet nearly 80,000 years ago? It's true! In fact, there was a bag of popcorn brought to the first Thanksgiving. This led to the first American cold cereal: popcorn with milk poured over it, served at breakfast. If you'd like to try an early American favorite pour some milk over your plain popcorn. It may not be sweet like today's cereals but you'll be able to taste how cereal began!

Crossing Indiana

Indiana has more interstate highways per square mile than any other state. Maybe that's why its state motto is "The crossroads of America"!

See if you can find the one route that ENTERs and LEAVEs Indiana. You can travel over and under on the roads, but must stop at road blocks or dead ends!

ENTER

LEAVE

ILLINOIS: The Prairie State

Geography and Industry

Illinois gets its name from the large rolling prairies that cover the state. As with most of the Midwest, there are no mountains to speak of in Illinois. The state is both bordered and affected by a number of large rivers: the Mississippi in the west, the Ohio and Wabash in the southeast, and the Illinois River, the largest river in the state, which runs across Illinois to drain into the Mississippi itself.

Although noted for its large prairies, the state has a number of hardwood forests in various portions of it, including the vast tracts to be found in the Shawnee National Forest. Places like the Cahokia Mounds have remnants of large burial mounds left behind by the ancient Mississippian civilization, too.

Illinois is located close to the geographic center of the country, and as a result, its largest city, Chicago, is the central transportation hub in the United States. Transcontinental flights routinely stop over in Chicago's O'Hare Airport, one of the world's largest. Also, the city has been the eastern endpoint of a number of national railroads for over a century. Freight that gets shipped through Chicago frequently gets shifted from the railroad to a container ship, which in turn can take it out of the Great Lakes, through the St. Lawrence Seaway to parts of the East Coast or overseas markets.

History

Well before the arrival of European explorers in the region, a mound-building Native American civilization known today as the Mississippian culture had a huge presence in what is now Illinois. The ruins of this culture can still be viewed at places such as Cahokia, in the southern part of the state. At one point Cahokia was home to nearly 40,000 people and the site of a large earthen mound that stood 100 feet high and nearly 1,000 feet long. The Mississippian culture declined because of

ALL ABOUT Illinois

CAPITAL: Springfield

LARGEST CITY: Chicago

POPULATION: 12,419,293 (2000 Census)

STATE BIRD: Cardinal

STATE TREE: White Oak

STATE FLOWER: Native Violet

STATE MOTTO: "State Sovereignty, National Union"

STATEHOOD: December 3, 1818

POSTAL ABBREVIATION: IL

WORDS TO KNOW

Prairie

The word prairie comes from the French word for "meadow" and refers to a type of landscape that contains mostly grasses and herbs and a few trees. Prairies tend to have a moderate or temperate climate.

food shortages and warfare sometime between 1250 and 1400 A.D.

After the Mississippian culture fell apart, Algonquian-speaking tribes such as the Winnebago, the Illini, and the Sauk and Fox moved in to the area, living and farming in the state's large river valleys. When the Europeans came, they were initially French and mostly fur traders. In time, they lost the land to the English, who gave up the area to the United States as part of the treaty ending the American Revolution.

As a result of the Black Hawk War of 1832, the U.S. government "removed" the Native Americans living in this area to lands across the Mississippi River. The Illinois country began to rapidly fill up with people interested in farming the region's rich black soil. To this day, Illinois produces huge quantities of crops such as wheat, soybeans, corn, and sorghum, in addition to livestock such as cattle and hogs. Because of its location and the availability of railroads to bring cattle and hogs from rural Illinois and such plains states as Kansas and Nebraska, Chicago also quickly became the center of the meat-packing industry.

After the Civil War, manufacturing in Illinois boomed. Because ironmongers had figured out how to make high-grade steel in large quantities, Chicago quickly got something it hadn't had before: a view! Chicago was the site of a massive explosion of skyscraper building during the decades right before the turn of the nineteenth century.

Because of both its booming manufacturing base and its central location in the United States, Chicago also became the catalog sales capital of the world in the late nineteenth century. Sears, Roebuck & Company (among many other catalog sales businesses) started out as a catalog store based in Chicago. In other words, you could order goods from it to be delivered anywhere that had postal service, but you couldn't go to the store, because there was no store to go to, only a supply center in Chicago.

Fun Facts

BUY YOUR HOUSE FROM A CATALOG!

At one time, there didn't seem to be anything a person couldn't buy from a Sears catalog, including a house! Beginning in 1908, Sears offered to ship a customer a house ready to be assembled for anywhere from $100 to just over $600, depending on what kind of house the buyer wanted. Sears sold about 100,000 of these houses until it discontinued the program in 1940.

MICHIGAN: The Wolverine State

Geography and Industry

Michigan is one of the most oddly and interestingly shaped states in the union. It is really nothing more than two peninsulas that are surrounded by a lot of lake water and not physically connected to each other at all! These two peninsulas are called the Lower Peninsula and the Upper Peninsula, respectively.

The Lower Peninsula is roughly hand-shaped, and juts out into two of the Great Lakes (Michigan and Huron). The majority of Michigan's population lives in this peninsula. Michigan's largest city, Detroit, is near the "thumb" of the hand-shaped peninsula. The Lower Peninsula is mostly lowland forest and rolling hills.

Michigan's Upper Peninsula is northwest of the Lower Peninsula and across Lake Michigan from it. It extends eastward from northeastern Wisconsin, with Lake Superior to the north and Lake Michigan to the south. Less than ten percent of Michigan's population lives here. It has lots of forest land, and the western portion is pretty rugged. These mountains have lots of copper and iron deposits. People come from all over the Northeast to ski in Michigan's western mountains, and to summer on its cool and temperate northern Lake Superior shore.

Most of Michigan's economy for the past century has been tied to Detroit's massive auto industry. As American car makers have lost their foremost position as makers of cars, the entire state has suffered. The last couple of decades in particular have been tough times in Detroit.

History

Michigan, before European exploration and settlement, was inhabited by Algonquin-speaking tribes of Native Americans such as the Chippewa, Ojibwa, Ottawa, Mingoes, and Potawatomi. French explorers and fur traders visited Michigan beginning in the seventeenth century. They founded trading posts at

ALL ABOUT Michigan

CAPITAL: Lansing

LARGEST CITY: Detroit

POPULATION: 9,938,444 (2000 Census)

STATE BIRD: Robin

STATE TREE: White Pine

STATE FLOWER: Apple Blossom

STATE MOTTO: "*Si Quaeris Peninsulam, Amoenam Circumspice* (If You Seek a Pleasant Peninsula, Look about You)"

STATEHOOD: January 26, 1837

POSTAL ABBREVIATION: MI

Michigan: The "Hand" State

Michigan's Lower Peninsula is shaped like a hand. You can locate places in the state by looking at your left hand with the palm down, the thumb extended out a bit, and the fingers extended outward. For example, Chicago, Illinois would be placed on the left part of your wrist and Detroit would be near your thumb. Give this a try and see what other sorts of "hand directions" you can come up with!

such spots as Detroit and Michilimackinac. Detroit in particular became an important French fort, because it commanded access to the upper Great Lakes, with its site on the strategic Detroit River.

When the French lost all of their holdings to the British in 1763, Michigan became a British possession for just over twenty years. In 1783, it changed hands again, going to the Americans in the Treaty of Paris, which ended the American Revolution. For a time Michigan was part of the Old Northwest Territory, then of the Ohio Territory, then of the Indiana Territory.

When Michigan was ready to become a state itself, it got into a border dispute with neighboring Ohio. This dispute was called the Toledo War, because the site of what is now Toledo, Ohio, at the southwestern end of Lake Erie, was smack in the middle of the disputed territory. Ohio eventually won the "war" (which had only one injury and no deaths), and claimed Toledo as its prize. As compensation for losing the Toledo corridor, the federal government gave the entire Upper Peninsula over to Michigan when it became a state, in early 1837.

WISCONSIN: The Badger State

Geography and Industry

While its neighbor Minnesota is often called the Land of 10,000 Lakes, Wisconsin could easily be called the State Next Door, Which Has 8,500 Lakes. Much of northern Wisconsin is taken up by the same sorts of moraine lakes that dot neighboring Minnesota. These lakes range from huge (Lake Winnebago) to some that are small enough to be nothing more than ponds. And yet there are thousands of them!

These lakes aren't the only examples of glacial sculpting of Wisconsin's countryside. The Wisconsin Dells are another example. This rock formation is a deep canyon, about five miles in length, along the Wisconsin River. The Dells were dug out of very old sandstone by an advancing glacier during the last ice age.

Water is an important factor in Wisconsin life. Not only does it fill Wisconsin's many lakes, it also forms most of Wisconsin's borders: to the east, there's Lake Michigan, and to the north there's Lake Superior. The Mississippi River runs along Wisconsin's western edge, forming a natural border between Wisconsin and its neighbors Minnesota and Iowa. The Wisconsin River runs south through much of the state, then turns west just north of the state's capital city of Madison and runs into the Mississippi.

Wisconsin is still mostly farmland. It is a dairy state. Its farms produce large amounts of milk, cheese, and cream for coffee, tea, and (of course) ice cream! The state is also an important producer of potatoes, hay, alfalfa, apples, and the largest producer of cranberries in the United States.

Timber products have always been an important export of Wisconsin's forests, especially in northern Wisconsin. Also in the north, the Gogebic Range of mountains is a source of copper and iron. Lead is widely mined in southern Wisconsin, and has been for centuries.

History

Some of the earliest inhabitants of what is now Wisconsin were the mound builders of what we now call the Mississippian culture. They built and farmed in the region for around 1,000 years, disappearing around 1500. The Native American tribes who lived in Wisconsin when the first European explorers arrived included the Menominee, the Sauk and Fox, the Winnebago, the Kickapoo, and the Sioux. Just about the time the first explorers and fur traders arrived in the area, these tribes were already being pushed out of Wisconsin by eastern tribes such as the Huron, the Ottawa, and Ojibwa, who had in their turn been pushed westward by European settlement farther east.

The French originally claimed Wisconsin as part of their North American possessions. They established their first trading posts in the area of Green Bay during the 1660s. For the next century the French conducted a thriving fur trade with most of

ALL ABOUT Wisconsin

CAPITAL: Madison

LARGEST CITY: Milwaukee

POPULATION: 5,363,675 (2000 Census)

STATE BIRD: Robin

STATE TREE: Sugar Maple

STATE FLOWER: Wood Violet

STATE MOTTO: "Forward"

STATEHOOD: May 29, 1848

POSTAL ABBREVIATION: WI

WORDS TO KNOW

Moraine Lake

"Moraine" is a term that can mean anything left behind by a retreating glacier: boulders, trees, mounds of soil—and, yes, lakes. Moraine lakes are usually deep holes dug by an advancing glacier and then filled by the melt water left behind when it retreats.

Fun Facts

GET YOUR MOTOR RUNNING

Perhaps Wisconsin's most famous industrial product is the Harley-Davidson motorcycle. The Harley-Davidson company was founded in Racine, Wisconsin, in 1903. That year it produced three motorcycles. Since then, it has produced hundreds of thousands of motorcycles!

the local tribes. The one exception to this was the Fox tribe, who fought a fifty-year-long war with the French.

The French lost Wisconsin along with the rest of their North American possessions to the British in 1763. Twenty years later, the British gave up Wisconsin as part of the settlement of the American Revolution. Wisconsin was originally part of the Old Northwest Territory (which included all of what is now Ohio, Indiana, Illinois, Michigan, and Wisconsin, and part of Minnesota). Later, it became part of first the Illinois, then the Michigan Territory in 1818.

By the 1820s Wisconsin's lead mines had been opened up and were producing, and timber was being sold from land cleared for farming. By 1832, the remaining Native American tribes (mostly the Sauk and Fox) had had enough. They rebelled, were ruthlessly defeated in the short Black Hawk War, and removed to land west of the Mississippi River.

Wisconsin became a territory in 1836, and a state in 1848. Shortly before it became a state, Wisconsin lost claims to land surrounding Chicago, in northern Illinois, and also to what became Michigan's Upper Peninsula.

During the 1850s Wisconsin political leaders helped found the Republican Party, because Wisconsin was a firm anti-slavery state and the Republican Party was intended to be an abolitionist political party first and foremost. During the Civil War, many Wisconsinites served in the Union Army.

Wisconsin's radical streak stayed alive during the post–Civil War industrial boom. Politicians in Wisconsin founded the Progressive Party, and although the Party was eventually swallowed up by the Republican and Democratic parties, for a while the Progressives did elect some prominent leaders.

MINNESOTA: Land of 10,000 Lakes

Geography and Industry

Obviously, Minnesota, like its neighbor Wisconsin, has a lot of lakes. Most of these lakes were formed by a retreating ice sheet during the last ice age. Minnesota is also the state where the Mississippi River, the largest and most important river in America, gets its start. From its source at Lake Itasca in Minnesota, the mighty Mississippi runs over 2,300 miles to its mouth on the Gulf of Mexico, in Louisiana!

Rivers are as large a part of Minnesota's geography as are the state's many lakes. There are three major river systems in Minnesota. There is the Mississippi, which flows south; there is the Red River system, which flows north into Canada; and the eastern part of the state is drained by streams that flow eastward into Lake Superior.

Geographically speaking, Minnesota is a very diverse state. It has huge forests in the northern part of the state, several iron-rich mountain ranges in the eastern part of the state (the Mesabi, Cuyuna, and Vermillion ranges), and prairies in the central and southern parts of the state that make for very rich farmland.

Places like Voyageurs National Park and the Grand Portage and Pipestone National Monuments draw thousands of visitors per year. Minnesota is also a fishing paradise, with all of its lakes and streams and its access to Lake Superior.

History

Minnesota was dominated by the Ojibwa in the east and the Sioux on the western prairies when the French arrived to trade for furs in the mid-seventeenth century. The northeastern part of the state was ceded first to the British and then to the United States in the 1760s and the 1780s, respectively. The majority of the state was acquired by the United States in the Louisiana Purchase of 1803. The northern part came to the United States

ALL ABOUT
Minnesota

CAPITAL: St. Paul

LARGEST CITY: Minneapolis

POPULATION: 4,919,479 (2000 Census)

STATE BIRD: Common Loon

STATE TREE: Red Pine

STATE FLOWER: Showy Lady's Slipper or Pink and White Lady's Slipper

STATE MOTTO: "L'Etoile du Nord (The Star of the North)"

STATEHOOD: May 11, 1858

POSTAL ABBREVIATION: MN

Fun Facts

MINNESOTA: NOT THE LAND OF 10,000 LAKES!

It's true! Minnesota's nickname is a mis-name. There are actually more than 10,000 lakes in Minnesota. In fact, there are over 12,000 in the state. This means that whoever came up with Minnesota's nickname got it wrong by over 2,000 lakes!

TRY THIS!

Visit the Spam Museum!

Did you know that there is a museum devoted to the canned meat known as Spam? It's true! It's in Minnesota (home of Hormel, the company that makes Spam), and it's called The Spam Museum. It's located at 1937 SPAM Boulevard, in Austin, Minnesota (1937 is the year that Hormel introduced Spam to the public).

in an 1818 treaty establishing part of the border between the United States and Canada.

Minnesota became a territory in 1849. The Panic (economic depression) of 1857 hit the territory very hard, because so many people had invested in various land schemes that wound up losing them money. Statehood came in 1858, and the Civil War in 1861.

While most of the army was away fighting in the southern states, the Minnesota Sioux went to war in 1862 against the U.S. government. It was a bloody uprising. Nearly 300 people on both sides were killed before the Sioux were suppressed.

Another momentous event that occurred in 1862 had a large impact on Minnesota. That year, Congress passed the Homestead Act, which gave "160 acres and a mule" to every settler who could stake out and farm a given tract of land for five years. Settlers flocked to Minnesota as a result.

During the post–Civil War period, large iron deposits were found in Minnesota's eastern mountains. For decades afterward, miners worked these deposits, until they were all but depleted. To this day, the largest open pit iron mine in the world is in Minnesota.

Several of America's most established food brands began in Minnesota. These include Pillsbury and Hormel.

CHAPTER 15

THE NORTHERN PLAINS

Stretching unbroken from the Canadian border in the north down to the Oklahoma country in the south, the Great Plains both divide and bind together the North American continent. This part of the country is now known as America's Breadbasket because it grows enough grain collectively to feed the people of the world several times over. Wheat, oats, barley, and corn are grown all over the Great Plains.

And yet most people once called this region the Great American Desert! Before the steel plow was invented, there wasn't any blade strong enough to cut through the prairie sod of the plains, and so Americans viewed the Great Plains as an obstacle to be crossed on their way to places on the West Coast, like California.

The plains states are places of wide skies and broad horizons, of sudden tornadoes and baking hot, cloudless days. They are bordered by huge mountains in the west, and the broad Mississippi in the east. And they are crossed from northwest to southeast by a number of vast river systems of their own.

ALL ABOUT North Dakota

CAPITAL: Bismarck

LARGEST CITY: Fargo

POPULATION: 642,200 (2000 Census)

STATE BIRD: Western Meadowlark

STATE TREE: American Elm

STATE FLOWER: Wild Prairie Rose

STATE MOTTO: "Liberty and Union, Now and Forever, One and Inseparable"

STATEHOOD: November 2, 1889

POSTAL ABBREVIATION: ND

NORTH DAKOTA: The Peace Garden State
Geography and Industry

North Dakota is equal parts desolate (the western part of the state) and fertile (the eastern part of the state). The Missouri and Red rivers both flow through the state, and farming (wheat, flax, and corn) is good along their valleys. But the western part of the state is high desert, where very little grows. This region was so hard to travel through that early explorers nicknamed it the "badlands." The name stuck.

Nowadays people don't try to avoid the badlands. They go out of their way to see these rugged rock formations. Tourism has become an important industry in North Dakota.

North Dakota is almost entirely an agricultural state, and it is one of the most rural states left in the nation. There is little industry to speak of besides mining, farming, and ranching in North Dakota. Oil was discovered in the 1950s, and is North Dakota's leading mineral export. Not long after, natural gas fields were uncovered as well. There are also salt, sand, gravel, and lime mining operations in the state.

Weather-wise, North Dakota is a tough place to live. The climate is harsh: hot, humid summers, sometimes plagued by tornadoes or drought, and frigid winters, consistently among the coldest in the continental United States. Because of its location in the far northern part of the country, directly south of Canada's great plains, there is nothing to keep polar weather from sweeping down along the Canadian Shield and directly into North Dakota.

History

Before European fur traders visited the region, semi-nomadic tribes such as the Arikara (Ree), Hidatsa (Gros Ventres), and Mandan farmed North Dakota's fertile river valleys for part of the year, then hunted buffalo during the other part. When the horse was introduced to the northern plains starting in the sixteenth and seventeenth centuries, tribes such as the Sioux, Cheyenne, Ojibwa, Cree, and Assiniboin abandoned farming, and moved out on the plains to follow the great buffalo herds year-round.

The Lewis and Clark Expedition spent the winter of 1804–05 with the Mandan tribe before making their way to the Pacific coast. Within twenty years, the Mandans had been literally wiped out by European diseases such as smallpox, cholera, whooping cough, mumps, and measles.

We know these diseases as childhood diseases, and today, hardly anyone dies from them. But the Native Americans did not have any immunity to these diseases, and so died by the thousands from them. This had happened to other tribes

Fun Facts

WHO ARE THE DAKOTAS NAMED AFTER?

North and South Dakota take their names from a band of the Sioux called the Dakota. There are other bands, with names like Lakota, etc., but the two states are named after the ones whose name starts with the "D"!

WORDS TO KNOW

Rural

A rural area is the opposite of an urban area, which means that a rural area is a relatively unpopulated place—still wild, with no cities and few roads or houses. Cultivated farmland is also considered a rural area, since it guarantees that there is no room for a city.

Fun Facts

ROOSEVELT THE COWBOY

In the 1880s future U.S. President Theodore Roosevelt established a working cattle ranch in the badlands of western North Dakota. Roosevelt spent three years working as a cowboy on his own ranch. He identified himself as a cowboy at heart for the rest of his life!

farther east as Europeans explored and settled North America, but out on the plains it seemed to happen even faster.

In 1818 the United States acquired part of the Red River Valley from British Canada, in exchange for some land drained by the Missouri River farther north. This land became part of the Dakota Territory when it was organized in 1851. The territory included land that eventually became the states of North and South Dakota, Wyoming, and Montana. Also in 1851, the first permanent American settlement was established in North Dakota, at a place called Pembina.

During the next few decades, the Native Americans living on the plains fought a series of wars with the U.S. Army, trying to stop the tide of white settlement. The Sioux and the Cheyenne fought especially hard. North Dakota was finally being settled because the new transcontinental railroad made travel and shipping of goods through and across the area much easier.

Things got really bad in the 1870s, with Sioux and Cheyenne warriors raiding all across the northern plains. By 1877, Native American resistance had ended.

The very next year, the first cattle ranch was established in North Dakota. Among those easterners who eventually came west to try their luck raising cattle was a young New Yorker named Theodore Roosevelt.

North Dakota became a state in late 1889, just minutes ahead of South Dakota, its neighbor to (not surprisingly) the south. Both states list the same day (November 2, 1889) as the day they became states.

Rock 'n' Roll

Break the letter codes to get the silly riddle and its silly answer!

HINT: You will need to write the alphabet on a piece of paper, and write the numbers from 1 to 26 underneath. A=1, B=2, C=3, etc.!

23rd	F+2	1st	R+2	♭	19th	before P	21st	S+1	J-2
A+3	E-4	L-1	after N	V-2	Z-25	14th			
18th	M+2	3rd	J+1		F+1	S-1	Q-2	T+1	16th
8th	1st	19th		D+2	M+2	21st	P+2		
L+1	5th	14th		Z-3	8th	Q-2			
4th	M+2	P-2	'	20th		19th	G+2	14th	I-2	?
after L	Q-2	V-1	M+1	20th					
Q+1	21st	before T	8th	before N	N+1	after Q	5th		!

SOUTH DAKOTA: The Mount Rushmore State

Geography and Industry

South Dakota has three separate geographic regions within its borders: the prairies in the east, the Great Plains in the middle, and the Black Hills in the west. The Black Hills are a small range of mountains that rise up to a height of 7,000 feet at their highest point, right in the middle of the plains. They have been sacred to the surrounding tribes of Native Americans for centuries. Because the Black Hills are covered with forests, an early explorer described them as "an island of trees in a sea of grass."

★ ★ ★ ★ ★ ★ ★ **205** ★ ★ ★ ★ ★ ★ ★

ALL ABOUT South Dakota

CAPITAL: Pierre

LARGEST CITY: Sioux City

POPULATION: 754,844 (2000 Census)

STATE BIRD: Ring-Necked Pheasant

STATE TREE: Black Hills Spruce

STATE FLOWER: Pasqueflower

STATE MOTTO: "Under God the People Rule"

STATEHOOD: November 2, 1889

POSTAL ABBREVIATION: SD

TRY THIS!

Hot Springs

Evans' Plunge, in Hot Springs, South Dakota, is fed by a natural hot spring. Hot springs are usually a result of volcanic activity in the region. Are there any hot springs near where you live? Go to your library or use the Internet to find out.

The Missouri River Valley is very wide where it runs south through the central part of South Dakota. Other important rivers in the state include the Cheyenne, the Big Sioux, the James, and the White. The climate in South Dakota is pretty much the same as that of North Dakota, with frigid winters and hot, humid summers.

Tourism is very important to South Dakota's economy, and the massive patriotic sculpture of Mount Rushmore is visited by millions of tourists every year, as are such attractions as Badlands National Park and Wind Cave National Park. There is also some hot spring activity in the region, and there are spas at places like the appropriately named Hot Springs.

Farming is also important, and South Dakota is a major producer of grains (wheat, barley, oats, etc.), corn, sunflowers, flax, sorghum, and soybeans. Where oil is North Dakota's major mineral product, gold is South Dakota's.

The Sioux and the Black Hills

When the first French fur traders visited the region during the eighteenth century, two large tribes of Native Americans lived in what is now South Dakota. The Sioux were horse-breeding, buffalo-hunting nomads, and the Arikara lived and farmed the wide river bottoms in the valleys of the Missouri and South Dakota's other large rivers. The Sioux considered the Black Hills sacred (their descendants still do), in much the same way that Jews, Christians, and Muslims today have considered the lands of Israel and Palestine sacred for centuries.

By the 1840s the Sioux were in sole possession of South Dakota, having chased the Arikara north into North Dakota and Canada. They did not enjoy sole ownership of the region for long. As happened in North Dakota, the transcontinental railroads began to open up South Dakota to settlement beginning in the 1850s.

The Homestead Act of 1862 made settlement of South Dakota even more appealing to thousands of farm families

looking for "free" land. The Sioux didn't like this, and went on the warpath several times during the 1860s. Finally, the Sioux and the U.S. government signed a treaty in 1868 giving the Sioux a reservation in their sacred Black Hills. It seemed as if there might be peace in South Dakota after years of tension between the Native Americans and white settlers.

These good feelings lasted less than six years. In 1874, gold was discovered in the Black Hills, and gold fever struck South Dakota. Try as it might, the U.S. Army could not keep gold-hungry prospectors out of the Sioux's reservation. War soon followed.

At first, the Sioux and their allies won some brilliant victories against the army. They defeated a cavalry detachment under General Nelson Miles at the Battle of the Rosebud, and lured Colonel George Armstrong Custer and his Seventh Cavalry to their doom at the Little Big Horn in 1876. Sioux leaders such as Sitting Bull and Crazy Horse rallied their warriors time and again to fight for their sacred Black Hills.

But eventually, as had happened so many times before, the whites had better weapons and more soldiers. By 1877, the last of the Sioux wars was over. The United States "bought" the Black Hills from the defeated Native Americans (no money was ever paid out). Just over a decade afterward, South Dakota became the fortieth state.

As late as 1980, the U.S. government offered the Sioux $100,000,000 as compensation for taking the Black Hills from them. The Sioux have refused all such offers. They say they want the Black Hills back.

IOWA: The Hawkeye State

Geography and Industry

The terrain of Iowa is a combination of rolling hills and broad prairies. The Mississippi River borders Iowa on the east, and

ALL ABOUT Iowa

CAPITAL: Des Moines

LARGEST CITY: Des Moines

POPULATION: 2,926,324 (2000 Census)

STATE BIRD: Eastern Goldfinch

STATE TREE: Oak

STATE FLOWER: Wild Rose

STATE MOTTO: "Our Liberties We Prize and Our Rights We Will Maintain"

STATEHOOD: December 28, 1846

POSTAL ABBREVIATION: IA

Fun Facts

THE WORLD'S SHORTEST AND STEEPEST RAILROAD

Did you know that there is a railroad that has a 60-degree grade (that is *steep*!) and is less than 300 feet long? It's true! The world's shortest railroad is in Dubuque, Iowa, and measures only 296 feet!

two-thirds of Iowa's rivers and streams flow eastward into the Mississippi. The Missouri River flows along Iowa's western border. Iowa was once covered by hardwood forests, but logging and clearing of the area for farming destroyed much of them. Farm fields also took their toll on Iowa's original prairies in much the same way.

Iowa has some of the richest farmland in the world. Almost three-quarters of the state's land is still farmland! In Iowa, farmland means a bit of hay, a bit of oats, and some soybeans, but most of all it means corn. And that corn in turn often goes to feed prize-winning Iowa hogs (which means that these hogs are "corn-fed," naturally!).

Aside from farming, Iowa also supports such farming-dependent industries as food processing (which makes sense, because so much food is produced in Iowa). Another important industry is the manufacture of farm machinery (which also makes sense!).

Outdoor recreation including hunting and fishing are pivotal to Iowa. Iowa is in the path of migratory birds like ducks and geese. These birds and the European pheasant, among others, are hunted in the autumn. With so many rivers running in and around Iowa, there is year-round fishing there as well.

History

Long before the coming of the Europeans to what is now Iowa, the Mississippian culture flourished here. These people were mound builders, like their neighbors throughout the Mississippi and Ohio River valleys. Their culture collapsed and they disappeared around 1500.

When the first French explorers visited the region, there were a number of Native American tribes living there. These included the Sauk and Fox, the Sioux, and the Iowa (a tribe from which the state gets its name).

After the United States acquired Iowa as part of the Louisiana Purchase in 1803, settlers began moving across the Mississippi River and cutting down Iowa's forest and plowing under its prairies, converting the state to agriculture. After the disastrous Black Hawk War (1832) the remaining Native Americans were removed across the Missouri River to Indian Territory (what is now Oklahoma). Within a decade Iowa had not just river access to eastern markets for its corn and other vegetables, but railroad access as well.

NEBRASKA: The Cornhusker State

Geography and Industry

The Missouri River forms part of Nebraska's northeastern border. The other major river system that passes through Nebraska is the Platte. The Platte is formed in western Nebraska where the North Platte and South Platte rivers meet. The Platte itself flows into the Missouri near Nebraska's largest city, Omaha. Eastern Nebraska is very fertile soil, and it's mostly farmland, especially along the river bottoms. The majority of Nebraska's population lives in eastern Nebraska. Eastern Nebraska's farmers grow mostly grains such as wheat and barley, or hay and alfalfa for feeding hogs and cattle and other animals.

Cities such as Lincoln and Omaha are the hubs of the insurance industry, which is centered in eastern Nebraska.

Western Nebraska is cattle country. Nebraska is currently the second leading cattle-producing state in the United States! Western Nebraska has lots of sand dunes and sandstone rock formations. These formations shelter small valleys of grass that are ideal ranges for cattle grazing.

One of these formations is Scott's Bluff, which is very close to Nebraska's western border with Wyoming. It's at the center of the Scott's Bluff National Monument, which is part of the Oregon

ALL ABOUT Nebraska

CAPITAL: Lincoln
LARGEST CITY: Omaha
POPULATION: 1,711,263
STATE BIRD: Western Meadowlark
STATE TREE: Cottonwood
STATE FLOWER: Goldenrod
STATE MOTTO: "Equality Before the Law"
STATEHOOD: March 1, 1867
POSTAL ABBREVIATION: NE

Trail, and is quite a tourist spot. Other places in Nebraska that are popular with tourists include the Fort Niobara Wildlife Refuge and Father Flanagan's Boys Town in Omaha.

History

Mound-building Native Americans who were members of the Mississippian culture lived in eastern Nebraska up until the culture disappeared, around 1500. The first Europeans visited the region not long afterward when Spanish conquistadors under the command of Francisco Vasquez de Coronado entered Nebraska, looking for gold. They didn't find anything but native villages and rolling prairie.

Such Native American tribes as the Pawnee, Ponca, Osage, and Oto lived in what is now Nebraska when the French arrived to trade for furs in the eighteenth century. The Ponca, Osage, and Oto farmed in the fertile eastern river valleys. The Pawnee were nomads who hunted buffalo out in western Nebraska.

The French claimed Nebraska for themselves, and in 1803 they sold it to the United States as part of the Louisiana Purchase. Explorers such as the Lewis and Clark Expedition (1804–06) and Zebulon Pike's expedition (1806) helped map out much of the area for the United States. It was just a few years later (1813) that the first permanent settlement in Nebraska was established: a trading post at Bellevue.

Beginning in 1819, steamboats ran up and down the Missouri River. Omaha quickly boomed into a bustling river port. When settlers began moving west, along what eventually became known as the Oregon Trail, on their way to settle the Pacific Coast, Nebraskans made a lot of profit by selling them supplies.

In 1854 Nebraska became a territory as a result of the complicated Kansas-Nebraska Act, which allowed people in U.S. territories to vote and decide for themselves whether or

WORDS TO KNOW

Nomad

Nomads are groups of people who don't live in any single position, place, or situation for very long. Most of the buffalo-hunting plains tribes of North America were nomadic.

Unicameral

Nebraska is the only state in the Union to have a state government that is unicameral. This means that rather than having two houses, such as a house of representatives and a senate, as our national government does (a bicameral legislature), the state legislature of Nebraska has only one house. There is no state senate in Nebraska.

not their territories (and eventually their states) would be slave states (states where slavery was legal) or free states (states where slavery was outlawed). During the Civil War that followed soon after, Nebraska was a free territory, and entered the Union shortly after the end of the war, in 1867.

KANSAS: The Sunflower State

Geography and Industry

Kansas is wheat country. It is an even tableland that rises gradually from the lowland prairies in the eastern part of Kansas to the much drier western plains that border the foothills of the Rocky Mountains, in neighboring Colorado. The major rivers that drain the state are the Arkansas and the Kansas rivers, both of which flow southeastward through Kansas on their way to the Mississippi (although the Kansas River flows into the Missouri River first).

The climate is good for wheat, but can be hard on humans. Hot and humid in the eastern part and hot and dry in the western part during the summer months (which are also tornado season), Kansas can be bitterly cold during the winter (which is the blizzard season).

As stated above, Kansas is a wheat state. In fact, many people would say that Kansas is *the* wheat state! Kansas is the number-one-producing wheat state in the country. For a very long time, farming was Kansas's leading industry. In addition to wheat, the state also produces plenty of sorghum and corn, and beef cattle.

But farming is no longer Kansas's leading industry. Nowadays Kansas is a leading maker of computer parts and transportation equipment such as airplanes. Lots of planes are now built in Wichita, which has become an aerospace town.

ALL ABOUT Kansas

CAPITAL: Topeka
LARGEST CITY: Wichita
POPULATION: 2,688,418 (2000 Census)
STATE BIRD: Western Meadowlark
STATE TREE: Cottonwood
STATE FLOWER: Native Sunflower
STATE MOTTO: *"Ad Astra per Aspera* (To the Stars Through Adversity)"
STATEHOOD: January 29, 1861
POSTAL ABBREVIATION: KS

WORDS TO KNOW

Tornado

A tornado is a weather phenomenon that causes air to spin in ever-tighter circles until it forms what is known as a funnel cloud. This spinning storm can be like a top, sliding all over a vast area and crushing everything in its path. Tornadoes are usually very destructive and often fatal, so be careful if you ever see one in person!

History

The first Europeans to visit Kansas were the members of the Spanish conquistador Coronado's expedition, which passed through in 1541. They were searching for gold. They found a mostly flat, rolling country cut by huge, fast-flowing rivers.

When the French arrived to claim the region as their own and make it part of the sprawling Louisiana country in the late seventeenth century, there were several large tribes of Native Americans living in what is now Kansas. These tribes included the Kansa (for whom the state is named), the Osage, the Wichita, and the Pawnee.

When horses were introduced into the region, many of the Native Americans quit farming in the eastern part of the state, and moved out onto the plains to become nomadic buffalo hunters. The Pawnee in particular became skilled trackers and hunters on horseback. Many of them later worked for the U.S. Army as scouts in the government's wars against other tribes.

Because much of Kansas was covered in prairie grass that was too thick to be plowed, it was seen as part of the Great American Desert. Is it any wonder that many of those Native Americans you've been reading about in the previous chapters wound up getting sent to the "desert" part of Kansas? Many others were removed even farther south into what was then called Indian Territory, and what we today call Oklahoma.

Because it was close to Missouri and other southern border states, Kansas got caught up in the struggle over slavery during the decade preceding the American Civil War (1861–65). There was a bitter struggle between people who had moved to Kansas from slave states, such as Missouri, and wanted Kansas as another slave state for the Union, and those people who had come to settle Kansas from the northern free states.

This was a mini civil war that preceded the larger one that occurred across the country just a couple of years afterward. This fight and the territory itself were referred to as Bleeding Kansas.

CHAPTER 16

THE SOUTHERN PLAINS

You Live Where?

Figure out the word equations and picture puzzles to learn some silly but real names for cities in the Southern Plains!

, TX

, TX

X + 🍐 + iment, AK

🦉-WL + 🔑-EY+AY , OK

10¢ 📦, TX

, OK

The Southern Plains stretch from Missouri into Colorado, from the Gulf of Mexico to the Guadalupe Mountains in the west. They are broad and flat in places, rolling and hilly in others, and they rise into interesting rock formations and tablelands called mesas in others.

The Southern Plains experience serious extremes of temperature over the course of the year: cold in the winter and blazing hot in the summer. They are subject to some of the worst hailstorms and tornadoes in recorded history. These states have amazing mineral wealth, including oil, natural gas, and coal. They have rich farmland, and a couple of them (Louisiana and Texas) have huge and interesting populations.

The Southern Plains are also a rich mix of different cultures. Originally settled in places by the French and Spanish (and the Mexicans), and occupied continuously in others by a variety of Native American cultures, these states are a fascinating mosaic of the diversity the United States is capable of, even while the skyline seems unrelentingly the same throughout the region.

MISSOURI: The Show Me State

Geography and Industry

The Missouri River splits the state into three parts. The northern part is flat prairie that is like the land in Iowa. Also like Iowa, this part of Missouri is very rich farmland. Farmers grow lots of corn there, and raise livestock such as cattle and hogs. The Missouri River valley is also largely farmland, although

★ ★ ★ ★ ★ ★ ★ ★

the state's large cities—Kansas City in the west and St. Louis in the east—have attracted much heavy industry.

St. Louis lies at the juncture of the Missouri and Mississippi rivers. This location has led to both remarkable growth and quite a lot of history for the city that has long been considered the gateway to the west. This is in no small part because St. Louis sits at a crossroads of various parts of the nation. It is right at the center where north meets south, and both meet west. This makes it a bit of a cultural melting pot.

Directly south of the Missouri River lie the Ozark highlands, which include both mountains and foothills. The eastern part is more rugged, with the western part more rolling hill country.

The southwestern part of the state is part of the Great Plains, and rolls westward into Oklahoma. The main crops grown on these plains are livestock fodder, such as hay and alfalfa. Since cattle, sheep, and hogs are raised in this region as well, farmers don't have to go far to find customers for their crops!

Around Cape Girardeau in the southeast is the "bootheel" part of the state. This part of the state was swampland when Missouri was originally settled. Around the time that the United States acquired the territory as part of the Louisiana Purchase in 1803, a drainage system was devised that allowed the swampland to be converted into cotton plantations.

Missouri is not just an agricultural state, though. In cities like St. Louis, the aerospace industry is well represented. Airplane parts are made throughout the state also. In Kansas City, cars, trucks, other types of transportation equipment (buses, tractors, etc.), and vending machines are built.

History

Before European exploration and settlement of the area, there were a number of Native American tribes who lived in

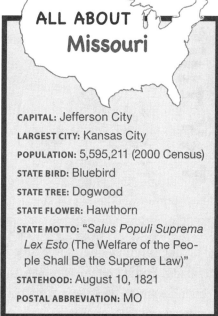

ALL ABOUT Missouri

CAPITAL: Jefferson City
LARGEST CITY: Kansas City
POPULATION: 5,595,211 (2000 Census)
STATE BIRD: Bluebird
STATE TREE: Dogwood
STATE FLOWER: Hawthorn
STATE MOTTO: "*Salus Populi Suprema Lex Esto* (The Welfare of the People Shall Be the Supreme Law)"
STATEHOOD: August 10, 1821
POSTAL ABBREVIATION: MO

Fun Facts

MISSOURI'S "BOOTHEEL"

When Missouri was ready to become a state, it turned out that it was a few thousand people short of the number required to become a state. So Congress shaved off what we now call the "bootheel" from the Arkansas Territory, and added it to Missouri in order to make its population high enough to qualify it for statehood!

TRY THIS!

Places to See

If you're in St. Louis, make sure you check out the Peace Arch. It's an amazing piece of architecture. Other places to see in Missouri include Kansas City's Nelson-Atkins Museum of Art, the Museum of the American Indian in St. Joseph, and the Harry S Truman Memorial Library in Independence.

the region, including the Osage, the Oto, and of course, the Missouri, for whom the state is named. The French were the first Europeans to settle in the region, establishing a lead mine at Sainte Genevieve in 1735. To this day, lead mining is an important part of Missouri's economy.

From 1735 until 1763, the French controlled Missouri. In 1763, they ceded Missouri along with the rest of their North American lands to the Spanish. Under Napoleon, the French got Missouri (and the rest of French Louisiana) back from the Spanish, but with the condition that they never turn it over to the United States. Napoleon promptly broke that agreement, and sold the entire area to the United States for about $3,000,000. What a bargain that turned out to be!

Missouri entered the Union as a result of the Missouri Compromise (see the Maine section of Chapter 1 for an explanation of the Missouri Compromise) in 1820. Because many of the people from the United States who moved in to help settle Missouri were originally from the South, and because Missouri had some land near Cape Girardeau that was under cotton cultivation, Missouri came into the Union as a slave state.

Surprisingly enough, when the Civil War finally came between the North and the South, Missouri stayed in the Union, although citizens of the state fought on both sides of the conflict, as was the case in other border states (see Chapter 3, Kentucky).

ARKANSAS: The Natural State

Geography and Industry

Like Missouri to the north, Arkansas is both on the western bank of the Mississippi River and bisected by a large river flowing eastward through the state into the Mississippi. Also like Missouri, the river running through Arkansas bears the same name as the state (the Arkansas River).

Other important rivers in Arkansas include the White, the Ouachita (pronounced WA-shee-taw), and the Red. The Red River marks part of Arkansas' western border with Texas.

Arkansas is a very hilly state. In the north lie the Ozark Mountains, and to the southwest are the Ouachita Mountains. The Ozarks are so rugged that the people who settled there became highly isolated and very independent.

The lowlands along the Mississippi and Arkansas River systems are rich farmland where cotton is still a major crop. Since the Civil War, though, Arkansas has grown many other crops. These other crops include two that are now much more important than cotton: rice and soybeans. Catfish are actually raised on Arkansas fish farms for sale to restaurants and grocery stores. Broiler chickens, turkeys, and dairy products also play a significant role in the state's economy.

Arkansas has many other products aside from agricultural products. These include things like natural gas, petroleum (oil), lumber, furniture, chemicals, aircraft parts, automobile parts, and other types of machinery.

Although hiking and camping are important recreational activities in Arkansas, they are not as popular as hunting and fishing are. This includes fishing for (you guessed it) catfish!

History

Before European exploration and settlement, Native Americans lived in Arkansas dating back to at least 500 A.D., when Native Americans called the Bluff Dwellers settled into caves along the Arkansas River. They were followed by Mound Builders of the Mississippian civilization, who built their trademark mounds in the major river valleys of the region. By the time of first contact with Europeans, such tribes as the Oto and the Osage were living in the region, splitting their time between farming and hunting/gathering.

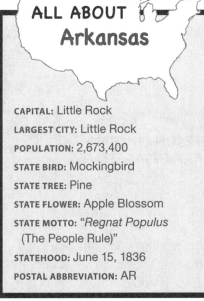

ALL ABOUT Arkansas

CAPITAL: Little Rock

LARGEST CITY: Little Rock

POPULATION: 2,673,400

STATE BIRD: Mockingbird

STATE TREE: Pine

STATE FLOWER: Apple Blossom

STATE MOTTO: "*Regnat Populus* (The People Rule)"

STATEHOOD: June 15, 1836

POSTAL ABBREVIATION: AR

WORDS TO KNOW

Bisect

The word *"bisect"* means to split or cut in two.

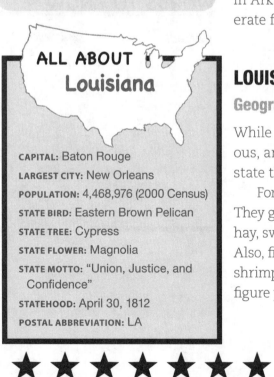

Fun Facts

TYSON CHICKEN: ARKANSAS TITAN!

Have you ever had Tyson chicken? Ask your parents if you don't know for sure. If you have, you likely had chicken from Arkansas, since almost all of the chicken sold by Tyson is raised in Arkansas. In fact, over *one billion* chickens are raised in Arkansas for sale for the dinner table each year alone!

ALL ABOUT Louisiana

CAPITAL: Baton Rouge

LARGEST CITY: New Orleans

POPULATION: 4,468,976 (2000 Census)

STATE BIRD: Eastern Brown Pelican

STATE TREE: Cypress

STATE FLOWER: Magnolia

STATE MOTTO: "Union, Justice, and Confidence"

STATEHOOD: April 30, 1812

POSTAL ABBREVIATION: LA

Spanish explorer Hernando de Soto and his expedition visited Arkansas in the early 1540s. De Soto and his men crossed and recrossed the state, headed first away from the Mississippi and into Oklahoma, then back to the Mississippi, all while looking for gold and silver.

The French eventually settled Arkansas during the seventeenth century, although during the French colonial period there were never as many people living in Arkansas as were living in New Orleans to the south, or around St. Louis to the north. Along with the rest of French Louisiana (the area of North America under French control west of the Mississippi River), Arkansas changed hands a number of times in the eighteenth century, before being sold to the United States as part of the Louisiana Purchase in 1803.

Having entered the Union in 1836 as a slave state, Arkansas seceded with ten other southern states in 1861. Battles such as Pea Ridge were fought in the northern part of the state, but the most important Civil War action that occurred in Arkansas was the naval battle between Union and Confederate forces for control of the Mississippi River.

LOUISIANA: The Pelican State

Geography and Industry

While it's true that there are swamps in Louisiana, and bayous, and cays, and crocodiles, there is a lot more to the Cajun state than hurricanes, hoodoos, and humidity.

For example, Louisiana is a leading agricultural producer. They grow an amazing amount of food: corn, pecans, soybeans, hay, sweet potatoes, sugarcane, rice, cotton, and strawberries. Also, fishing is a very important industry in Louisiana. Oysters, shrimp, and crayfish are all plentiful in Louisiana's waters, and figure prominently in local (Cajun) cuisine.

Like its neighbors Texas and Oklahoma, Louisiana has large deposits of crude oil (petroleum) and natural gas. Most of Louisiana's oil deposits are offshore, and the state has a thriving oil industry that includes large refineries that turn crude oil into motor oil and gas. These refineries and the rest of the oil industry employ large parts of Louisiana's population.

Timber (mostly pine forests) covers over half of the state. As a result, lumber and paper are also very important exports from Louisiana.

Louisiana has hundreds of small offshore islands, and the mighty Mississippi completes its 2,000-plus-mile journey across the continent and flows into the Gulf of Mexico in southern Louisiana. The coastal region is very rainy, fitting the stereotype of a swampy Louisiana made up of little other than marshes. There are large lagoons made up of standing fresh water. The largest of these is Lake Pontchartrain, which is the lake on the banks of which the city of New Orleans was built.

Speaking of New Orleans, it is one of the most colorful and distinctive cities in America. The birthplace of jazz and blues music, and home to Cajun cuisine, New Orleans is a very popular tourist attraction, especially during the early spring, which is Mardi Gras season. "Mardi Gras" is French for "Fat Tuesday," and it takes place in the famous French Quarter of the city. It is a tradition that has been ongoing in New Orleans since 1838!

Central, western, and northern Louisiana are a little like the French bayou country. Central Louisiana is full of pine forests and prairies, and northern Louisiana is very hilly. Baton Rouge, the state capital, is located in central Louisiana.

History

Louisiana was originally the home of such Native American tribes as the Choctaw, Natchez, and Caddo. The Spanish were the first Europeans to visit the region, but established

WORDS TO KNOW

Bayou

A bayou is a small slow-moving stream or creek usually found in low-lying areas.

Cajun

When France lost its Canadian colony of Acadia to the English, the English forced many of the Acadian settlers to leave. Thousands of these settlers moved to the other major French holding in North America: the Louisiana bayou country around New Orleans. Since they moved there nearly 300 years ago, the name "Acadian" has been corrupted to "Cajun."

Fun Facts

CRAYFISH

Crayfish are freshwater lobsters. They are smaller than their ocean-going cousins, and are highly prized by Cajun cooks. Nearly 100 percent of all crayfish caught and eaten in the United States are caught in Louisiana!

no lasting presence. In 1682 Robert de La Salle came south down the Mississippi to its mouth in what is now Louisiana, and claimed all of the lands drained by the river for France. The lands on the western side of the Mississippi were named Louisiana in honor of La Salle's king, Louis XIV of France.

New Orleans was founded in 1718. It quickly became the largest and most important city in French Louisiana. After the English took the French Canadian province of Acadia, thousands of French-speaking Acadians moved down the Mississippi and settled in French Louisiana. Today, there are as many as 500,000 of their descendants living in southern Mississippi, southern Louisiana, and eastern Texas.

After the United States acquired all of Louisiana in 1803, settlers poured into the area from the neighboring southern states and territories. The Louisiana territory entered the Union as the state of Louisiana in 1812, the same year that the United States fought its second war with England.

At the time that the Civil War broke out, there were more slaves than free people living in the state. Louisiana seceded in 1861. Because of its location next to the mouth of the Mississippi, Louisiana saw much fighting, especially along the Mississippi River. New Orleans was captured by Union forces in early 1862, and the entire river was under Union control by July 1863, when the last Confederate fortress on the river (Vicksburg) surrendered.

Life in LA

Louisiana has been the hangout for two different kinds of critters that both start with the letter P. One critter is historical, and the other is still there today! First, connect the dots. Then, break the "First to Last" and the "Vowel Switch" codes to learn about these Louisiana residents.

heT

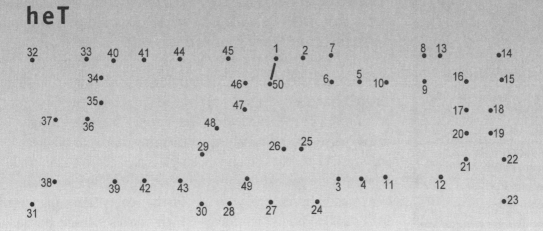

eanJ afitteL adh a ideawayh ni ouisianaL.

Tha briwn

es tha Lioeseunu stuta berd.

ALL ABOUT
Oklahoma

CAPITAL: Oklahoma City

LARGEST CITY: Oklahoma City

POPULATION: 3,450,654 (2000 Census)

STATE BIRD: Scissor-Tailed Flycatcher

STATE TREE: Redbud

STATE FLOWER: Mistletoe

STATE MOTTO: "*Labor Omnia Vincit* (Labor Conquers All Things)"

STATEHOOD: November 16, 1907

POSTAL ABBREVIATION: OK

WORDS TO KNOW

Sooner!

In 1890, the last great land rush of the nineteenth century took place in what is now western Oklahoma. Free land was available for the taking to anyone who could stake out a claim to it before anyone else did. This is where we get the word "sooner." The people who got their claims filed fastest were there sooner than anyone else!

OKLAHOMA: The Sooner State
Geography and Industry

Have you ever heard the song lyric from the musical Oklahoma that goes: "O-kla-HOMA where the wind goes whippin' down the plain"? (Ask your parents, or maybe your grandparents, about it.) Well, that lyric pretty much sums up Oklahoma's geography. Although it has some high mesas in the panhandle (western) part of the state, and the Ouachita Mountains in the southwest, the state is overwhelmingly open plains, with lots of wheat farming, and lots of grazing land for cattle and sheep. Large rivers cross Oklahoma from the northwest to the southeast, all headed for drainage in the Mississippi, which is farther east. These big rivers include the Red (which forms Oklahoma's southern border with neighboring Texas), the Canadian, and the Cimarron.

The weather on Oklahoma's plains can get pretty extreme. In the winter it gets very cold, because the wind whips from farther north, and there is nothing (hills, mountains, etc.) to stop it. In the summers the sun bakes the plains pretty thoroughly.

As mentioned above, wheat is an important crop in Oklahoma (it replaced cotton after the Civil War as Oklahoma's most important crop). And as with neighboring states like Louisiana and Texas, oil and natural gas are *very* important mineral exports of the Sooner State. The first oil well was drilled in 1888, and since then, countless billions of dollars have come to Oklahoma as a result of oil and natural gas sales!

History

Before European exploration and settlement, tribes like the Oto, the Osage, the Kansa, the Arapaho, and the Kiowa all lived in what is now Oklahoma. Interestingly enough, there was a time after the United States acquired Oklahoma when more Native Americans settled in eastern Oklahoma. This was because the United States designated parts of the Louisiana Purchase at various times as Indian territory.

TEXAS: The Lone Star State

Geography and Industry

Often when we think of Texas, we think of the desert and the plains. But Texas (like many other states) is surrounded by water. The Gulf of Mexico and the Rio Grande River border the Lone Star State on the southern side, the Sabine makes up a lot of its eastern border with Louisiana, and most of its northern border with Oklahoma is made up by the Red River.

Texas is huge! Not only is it the largest state in the continental United States (only Alaska is larger), it is the second-largest state population-wise (behind California).

In the east, Texas has hills covered in pine forests that spread between the Trinity River and the Sabine River where it borders Louisiana. These pine trees have led to the region developing quite a logging industry. There used to be huge cotton plantations here before the Civil War, but now rice is king. Most of the rice produced in Texas is produced in East Texas. There is also a lot of heavy industry in this region, with the cities of Port Arthur and Beaumont having much manufacturing within their city limits.

The north-central part of the state is prairie that has some of the richest soil in the country. And Dallas, which is in this region, has one of the fastest-growing industrial areas. Oil companies, agricultural conglomerates, and electronics and computer companies all have combined to help make Dallas an industrial force in the twenty-first century.

The high plains region in northern Texas has a lot of grazing land for cattle, even though it can get very cold there during the winters. (Texas is the number-one producer of beef in the

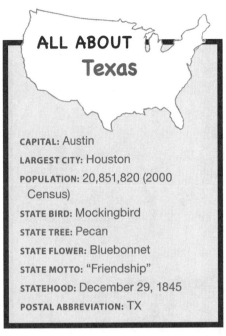

ALL ABOUT Texas

CAPITAL: Austin

LARGEST CITY: Houston

POPULATION: 20,851,820 (2000 Census)

STATE BIRD: Mockingbird

STATE TREE: Pecan

STATE FLOWER: Bluebonnet

STATE MOTTO: "Friendship"

STATEHOOD: December 29, 1845

POSTAL ABBREVIATION: TX

country.) West Texas is very arid and has a lot of rocky hills, rising as it does toward the neighboring Rocky Mountains. The Rio Grande border with Mexico is thousands of miles long.

Tourism is becoming a large industry in Texas. Padre Island National Seashore is a popular vacation spot, and the Johnson Space Center in Houston sees thousands of visitors annually. Outdoor recreation areas like Lake Meredith and Amistad National Recreation Areas and Guadalupe Mountains National Park offer breathtaking scenery for camping, fishing, hiking, and hunting.

History

Ancestors of the Caddo lived in Texas for thousands of years before the first Europeans visited. The Caddo lived mostly in the northwest, along the Red River, and were farmers who stayed put, rather than plains-dwellers. The Texas plains were home to tribes such as the Comanche, the Kiowa, and the Apache.

Spanish refugees from the Pueblo Revolt in New Mexico were the first Europeans to settle in Texas (see Chapter 9, New Mexico for more on the Pueblo Revolt). The French tried to settle along the Gulf Coast just three years later, moving westward from their base in Louisiana. This galvanized the Spanish settlers into strengthening their own claims to the region.

Around 1803, many Americans in the southern states were looking to Texas as prime cotton-growing country. Presidents such as James Monroe and John Quincy Adams tried to buy the region from Spain, but the Spanish were not interested.

After Mexico gained control of the land in the Mexican War of Independence, they did not want to part with Texas either, but they allowed Americans to emigrate there as settlers, as long as the Americans swore allegiance to the Mexican government. This rule worked only too well, because by 1830 there were three times as many American-born settlers in Texas as there were Mexicans. The Mexican government tried to crack down on the Americans in Texas and limit their trade with the

WORDS TO KNOW

Tejas!

Texas gets its name from the name of the first Spanish mission that was founded in the Lone Star State. The mission was established by Franciscan priests near the Neches River in 1690, and was called Mission San Francisco de los Tejas. "Tejas" meant "friends" and was referring to the local Native American population.

United States, but these attempts backfired, and pushed the Americans in Texas to think of independence from Mexico.

In late 1835 war broke out, and the Mexican dictator Antonio Lopez de Santa Anna invaded Texas at the head of a large Mexican army. He swore that he would crush the growing Texan rebellion. After wiping out the defenders of the Alamo and massacring several hundred Texan soldiers who had surrendered at Goliad, Santa Anna was caught completely by surprise by General Sam Houston's much smaller Texan army at the climactic battle of San Jacinto in 1836. Wounded and captured himself, Santa Anna granted Texas independence the next day, in exchange for his freedom. He later repudiated the treaty he signed, saying he did it because he was given no choice.

Texas Becomes a State

Texas was an independent republic for nearly a decade after it won independence from Mexico. Texans overwhelmingly wanted to be part of the United States, but there were obstacles to statehood. American politicians who feared worse relations with Mexico (which still claimed Texas) and wanted to halt the spread of American plantation slavery repeatedly blocked Congress's attempts to incorporate Texas.

By 1844 Texas's government was broke and in need of a bail-out. The English and French both offered to help, and that made the United States so nervous about having Texas in debt to European nations that President John Tyler was able to convince Congress to finally offer to annex Texas that year.

When the Civil War came, Texas seceded with the other states. Because of its vast open ranges and large supplies of cattle and grain, it was soon considered one of the "breadbaskets of the Confederacy." Once the Union Navy took control of the Mississippi River, though, Texas (along with Arkansas and Louisiana) was cut off completely from the rest of the South.

Totally Texas

Use the directions to figure out which words to cross out of the puzzle grid. When you are finished, read the remaining words from left to right and top to bottom. You will learn the silly answer to the math mystery!

Cross out...

...the three words of the Texas nickname.

...words that rhyme with DOOR.

...six-letter words that end in Y.

...numbers without the letter O.

"Talbott took twenty turtles to Texas to taste tacos."
How many letters T are in that?

twelve	there	lone
are	simply	four
more	thirteen	only
two	star	thirty
plenty	letters	ten
T	store	in
twenty	that	state

CHAPTER 17

THE INTERMOUNTAIN WEST

I magine a region with a skyline of jagged peaks that reach higher skyward than anywhere else in the continental United States. This is a place of broad plains and wide, rapid-running rivers, where everything is giant-sized. This is the Intermountain West, and the mountains are the Rockies.

Nothing is small in the Intermountain West. These mountains make mountains elsewhere in the country (like the eastern seaboard) seem more like hills. All of the large rivers that flow eastward across the Great Plains and into the Mississippi originate in the Intermountain West. Rivers such as the Missouri, the Arkansas, the Red, the Canadian, the Platte, and the Rio Grande all begin in the Rocky Mountains. So do the two great rivers of the west—the Colorado in the southwest and the Columbia (which rises in the Canadian Rockies) in the northwest.

MONTANA: The Treasure State

Geography

Montana takes its name from the Spanish word for "mountain country," but it is much more than a mountain state. Nearly two-thirds of Montana is on the western part of the Great Plains, and some parts of it are as flat as a table! These plains are one reason Montana is often called the Big Sky state, because on the Montana plains, the horizon is so low that most of what you see there is sky. Montana has mighty rivers running through it, such as the Missouri, the Milk, the Sun, and the Yellowstone (all of which actually drain into the Missouri).

However, Montana is "mountain country" for a reason. The Rocky Mountains run right through the western part of the state, and they include such famous ranges of mountains as the Cabinet Mountains and the rugged Bitterroot Range. The Continental Divide runs along the ridge of the Rockies, from northwestern Montana to the south central part of the state.

Montana is still mostly unpopulated. There are fewer than a million people in the state, which is not very many when you consider that Montana is the fourth largest state in America (only Alaska, Texas, and California are larger)! Montana's main industry these days is tourism, which has replaced mining and ranching.

There are so many places to see in Montana! There is Glacier-Waterton International Peace Park, Yellowstone National-al Park, and the Little Bighorn National Monument, which was the site of Custer's Last Stand. There are also plenty of places to hunt and fish, boat, hike, and camp, especially near Flathead Lake, a huge body of water just south of Glacier National Park.

Although not as essential as they once were, mining (especially gold, silver, zinc, platinum, and lead), cattle- and sheep-ranching, and agriculture are still very important to Montana's economy. Montana's farmers grow crops like wheat, barley, hay, and sugar beets.

History

Before Europeans first visited North America, Native Americans lived in Montana, on the edges of the plains, and would go onto the plains every once in a while to hunt buffalo. After Europeans brought the horse to America, many of these tribes moved out to live full-time on the plains as nomads, following the buffalo herds and hunting them year-round.

These nomadic peoples included the Cheyenne, the Gros Ventres (French for "Big Bellies"), the Arikara, the Crow, the Blackfoot, the Flatheads, and the Sioux (pronounced "soo"). Most of these tribes still live in Montana today. Their reservations dot the state, and Native American tribes are active participants in caring for the environment. These tribes all have their own governments, their own law codes, and their own police and fire departments!

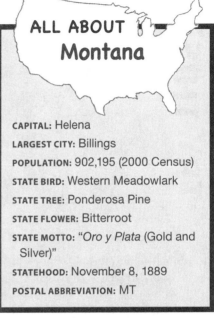

ALL ABOUT Montana

CAPITAL: Helena
LARGEST CITY: Billings
POPULATION: 902,195 (2000 Census)
STATE BIRD: Western Meadowlark
STATE TREE: Ponderosa Pine
STATE FLOWER: Bitterroot
STATE MOTTO: "*Oro y Plata* (Gold and Silver)"
STATEHOOD: November 8, 1889
POSTAL ABBREVIATION: MT

WORDS TO KNOW

Continental Divide

In the Rocky Mountains, which are the tallest point on our continent, the Continental Divide is the exact center point on the crest of the Rockies where water on one side of the mountains runs downhill and eventually enters the Atlantic Ocean and water on the other side of the mountains runs downhill and flows into the Pacific Ocean.

TRY THIS!

Make Your Own Continental Divide!

Make a mound of dirt in your backyard (get your parents' permission before you dig!). Try giving it a spine, like the top part of a tent. Now take your garden hose and pour a trickle of water along the spine, or crest, of your mountain range. What happens to the water? Does it run down one side, or the other, or both? If it runs down both, you're pouring the water right on top of the spine of your mountain range. So you've not only just made your own mountain range, you've just made your own continental divide!

Most of the state became the property of the United States after the Louisiana Purchase in 1803. That treaty gave the United States a claim to all of Montana up to the continental divide, but the western part of the state was still mostly unexplored at that time.

The Lewis and Clark expedition changed all that. They visited Montana both on the way to the Pacific coast and when returning to the east. They explored much of the state, and followed the Missouri to its source in the Rocky Mountains.

During the fifty years between Lewis and Clark visiting the region and the discovery of gold in Montana in the 1850s, there was a brisk fur trade going on. Companies such as the North West Fur Company and the American Fur Company established trading posts in the area, looking especially for beaver hides, which could be made into tall top hats.

Although Native Americans did most of the fur-trapping during this period, there were independent trappers from the east who competed with them. Many of these men lived among the local tribes and adopted their ways, including marrying and starting families with Native American women.

When gold was discovered in 1852, there was a mad rush into the region by people looking to get rich. These prospectors caused trouble with tribes like the Sioux and Cheyenne, who went to war several times to stop gold-seekers from invading their lands. During one of these wars, the Sioux lured soldiers under the command of Lt. Colonel George Armstrong Custer into an ambush in what is now eastern Montana, along the Little Bighorn River. Custer and all of his troopers (225 men) were killed within a thirty-minute period.

It was a huge victory for the Sioux and Cheyenne. However, within a year, the members of the tribes who had fought at Little Bighorn had almost all been captured and placed on a new reservation. By late 1877, even Sitting Bull, the Sioux chief and medicine man who had led the Sioux so skillfully, had fled north to Canada.

WYOMING: The Equality State

Geography and Industry

Wyoming is one of only two states in the Union that is a perfect rectangle. Can you guess the name of the other one? (It's Colorado, Wyoming's neighbor to the south.) Like Montana, Wyoming is part mountain state and part plains state. The Bighorn, Teton, and Wind River ranges of the Rocky Mountains all run through western Wyoming. So do the Laramie, Medicine Bow, and Absaroka ranges. Wyoming really is a mountain state!

The Powder River runs through the central part of the state, just east and south of where South Dakota's Black Hills run into Wyoming's northeastern corner. The mighty Snake River starts in Wyoming's western mountains and then runs into Idaho.

And there is the Yellowstone country. Lake Yellowstone is the largest lake in the state, and is the center of world-famous Yellowstone National Park, which is the world's first national park. Yellowstone National Park is home to a large herd of buffalo, lots of grizzly bears and wolves, and cougars and other predators that are endangered elsewhere. Also, Yellowstone is an area where there is a lot of volcanic activity, so there are many geysers and hot springs in the area.

Less than twenty miles south of Yellowstone National Park lies Grand Teton National Park, and it is gorgeous! Majestic peaks rise over the valley of the Snake River as the river makes its way into southern Idaho. The Continental Divide runs right through both of these amazing parks!

Wyoming's main economic venture is still cattle and sheep ranching. Just as the state has as many mountains and as much scenery as Montana and Colorado, it also has as much mineral wealth. Petroleum drilling is especially important.

ALL ABOUT Wyoming

CAPITAL: Cheyenne
LARGEST CITY: Cheyenne
POPULATION: 493,782 (2000 Census)
STATE BIRD: Meadowlark
STATE TREE: Cottonwood
STATE FLOWER: Indian Paintbrush
STATE MOTTO: "Equal Rights"
STATEHOOD: July 10, 1890
POSTAL ABBREVIATION: WY

Fun Facts

OLD FAITHFUL NOT SO FAITHFUL?

Do you know about Old Faithful, the world-famous Yellowstone geyser? It was named Old Faithful because it was thought to be so reliable. Well, it's not! Old Faithful erupts in a tall cascade of water *on average* every sixty-five minutes, but it doesn't erupt nearly that regularly. The time between its eruptions can run anywhere from thirty to ninety minutes.

History

When the first French fur traders visited Wyoming, such tribes as the Crow, Cheyenne, Shoshone, and Sioux lived there. The Sioux lived in and around the Black Hills, the Crow lived in the south central part of the state, and the Cheyenne lived in both the north central and eastern part of the state (which is why the state's capital city, located in that region, is named after them). When white settlement began to push the Sioux out of their hunting grounds in South Dakota and the Black Hills region, they in turn pushed the Crow westward into the mountains.

The first American to visit what later became Wyoming was a former member of the Lewis and Clark expedition, a man named John Colter. Colter visited the Yellowstone region, saw its wonders, and told people about them when he returned east of the Mississippi. They laughed at him and thought he was lying. People back then talked about what they came to call Colter's Hell the same way that people today talk about Atlantis and Shangri-la.

The Oregon Trail runs east to west across Wyoming. It was the main route that people used to cross the continent and go to either Oregon or California before the coming of the railroads. In fact, in many places in Wyoming, you can still see the 150-year-old ruts left in the trail by the wheels of the settlers' wagons!

Wyoming became a territory in 1868. In 1869 women in Wyoming were the first w men in the United States to get the right to vote. Wyoming became a state in 1890, and in 1924 continued to be out in front in the struggle for women's rights, when Nellie Tayloe Ross was elected the first woman governor by any state (she was elected to finish out her deceased husband's term). Later on the same day, another woman, Miriam Ferguson, continued the trend by being elected governor of Texas!

WORDS TO KNOW

Suffrage

Unlike the way it sounds, the word "suffrage" has nothing to do with suffering. It means the right to vote in government elections. Not until 1919, less than 100 years ago, did every state give women the right to vote!

IDAHO: The Gem State

Geography and Industry

Idaho is a state full of contrasts: heavily forested northern mountains, semi-arid southern flatlands, mountain lakes, and the broad Snake River cutting a canyon across its own floodplain.

Along the narrow Idaho panhandle (which is less than fifty miles wide) in the northernmost part of the state, there are medium-sized mountain ranges such as the Cabinet Mountains, and gorgeous lakes such as Lake Coeur d'Alene, Priest Lake, and Lake Pend Oreille.

In the north and central parts of the state, Idaho is covered by high, rugged mountains such as Mount Borah, which is close to 13,000 feet high! The Bitterroot Range lies in the north, and in central Idaho are the towering Sawtooth Mountains. Between the Sawtooths and the broad Snake River Valley to the south are the smaller Salmon River Mountains.

The Snake River flows across southern Idaho from its source in northwestern Wyoming, to form part of the state's western border with Oregon. It has been dammed in a number of places so that its water could be used to irrigate dry land that is fertile but lacking in rainfall. This lets southern Idaho produce lots of agricultural products, especially potatoes, beans, peas, sugar beets, hay, and wheat. Cattle ranching also continues to be a very important industry in Idaho.

But agriculture is no longer the major money maker it once was, and mining in the state is on the decline. However, high-tech industries have become important, especially telecommunications companies and computer software companies.

One of Idaho's newest and fastest-growing industries is tourism. The state is lovely, and has several different types of outdoor recreation areas, including the skiing available at places like Sun Valley, and boating in places like Hells Canyon National Recreational Area.

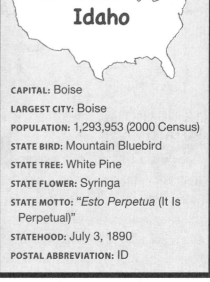

ALL ABOUT Idaho

CAPITAL: Boise
LARGEST CITY: Boise
POPULATION: 1,293,953 (2000 Census)
STATE BIRD: Mountain Bluebird
STATE TREE: White Pine
STATE FLOWER: Syringa
STATE MOTTO: *"Esto Perpetua* (It Is Perpetual)"
STATEHOOD: July 3, 1890
POSTAL ABBREVIATION: ID

Fun Facts

THE IDAHO POTATO

Do you like potatoes? Then more than likely you have eaten an Idaho potato, because Idaho leads the country in potato production. Many scientists think that potatoes do so well in southern Idaho because the climate is very similar to the climate in the Andes where potatoes evolved.

HELLS CANYON

Can you guess what the deepest canyon in North America is? It's not the Grand Canyon or Bryce Canyon—it's Hells Canyon in Idaho. At one point this canyon runs nearly 8,000 feet below the mountain peaks that surround it. You could stack five and half Empire State Buildings in a canyon that deep!

History

The first explorers of European descent to visit Idaho were the Lewis and Clark expedition, which followed the Snake River down to the Columbia and onward to the Pacific Ocean in 1805. At the time that Lewis and Clark entered Idaho, Native American tribes such as the Western Shoshone, Bannock, and Ute lived in the southern part of the state, the Nez Perce lived in western Idaho, and the Coeur d'Alene, Pend Oreille, and Kootenai lived in the north.

During the next forty years the only regular non–Native American visitors to Idaho were fur traders. They weren't the only whites to enter the region, though. The trading post at Fort Hall in southeastern Idaho was the point where the California Trail split off from the Oregon Trail and dipped south, headed toward northern California. None of the settlers who came west in those early years stayed in Idaho. They all pushed westward to either Oregon or California. That changed in the 1850s when gold was discovered in Idaho. Settlers poured into the region. Native Americans began to resist the settlement of their lands by whites seeking gold, government troops were called in, and the tribes were suppressed by the late 1850s.

The most famous Native American resistance to whites taking their land in Idaho occurred during 1876–77. The Nez Perce in western Idaho refused to move to a reservation, and fled their homes. They slipped into Montana, and almost made it into Canada, but were trapped and surrendered at Bear Paw Mountain, just a few miles south of the Canadian border. Chief Joseph and most of his people went to a reservation in eastern Washington. A few years later, many Nez Perce were able to return to their homes in Idaho.

Gold was discovered again in Idaho during the 1880s in Idaho's panhandle. The gold vein that miners found wasn't very big, but it led to the discovery of one of the largest veins of silver in the world. For the next 100 years, silver was mined out of several places in north Idaho. The mines ran dry in the early 1980s.

COLORADO: The Centennial State

Geography and Industry

Like Montana and Wyoming, Colorado has breathtaking scenery, and both high mountains and rolling plains. Eastern Colorado is part of the Great Plains, and is very hot and dry in the summer, then terribly cold during the winter. The other two geographic sections are the Rocky Mountains, which run from north to south through the central part of the state, and the Colorado Plateau, which is in the west.

Colorado's mountains are the tallest in the Rockies, and among the highest on the continent. In fact, Colorado has fifty-one of the eighty mountains in North America that are over 14,000 feet high!

The Rockies are made up of the Sangre de Cristos range, the Park Range, the Sawatch Mountains, the San Juan Mountains, and the Front Range. They are separated by wide basins called "parks." These include North Park, Estes Park, and South Park. Such mighty rivers as the Arkansas, the Red, the Colorado, both the North and the South Platte, and the Rio Grande all begin in Colorado's central mountain ranges. What's more, these mountains are covered with heavy forests of mostly conifers.

Western Colorado is a large plateau that is crossed by a number of canyons cut into the rock by fast-flowing rivers such as the Gunnison. Eastern Colorado is notable for its agriculture (cattle and sheep ranching especially), and the central region of the state is known for both high-tech (computer parts, software) and low-tech (metal production, electrical parts, etc.) industry. But the industry for which Colorado is world-famous is tourism.

Because it has so many outdoor recreational activities (hiking, biking, hunting, fishing, and skiing), Colorado has become a popular vacation spot. Resorts like Vail, Aspen, and Steamboat Springs attract people from all over the world.

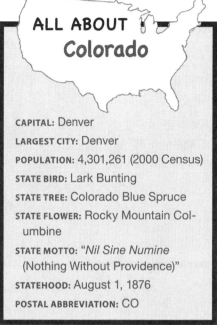

ALL ABOUT Colorado

CAPITAL: Denver
LARGEST CITY: Denver
POPULATION: 4,301,261 (2000 Census)
STATE BIRD: Lark Bunting
STATE TREE: Colorado Blue Spruce
STATE FLOWER: Rocky Mountain Columbine
STATE MOTTO: *"Nil Sine Numine* (Nothing Without Providence)"
STATEHOOD: August 1, 1876
POSTAL ABBREVIATION: CO

WORDS TO KNOW

Conifer

Conifers are trees that have needles instead of leaves, and drop cones instead of acorns when they're reproducing. Conifers are also evergreens, meaning that their needles stay on their limbs year-round.

WORDS TO KNOW

Centennial

The word centennial comes from a Latin phrase that means 100th anniversary.

History

Native Americans lived in the mesa country of southwestern Colorado for thousands of years before the coming of European explorers. First were the Basket Makers, who lived in the canyons of the mesa country. The Anasazi cliff-dwellers followed and built adobe houses along the walls of the same canyons that the Basket Makers had occupied before them.

At the time that American explorers such as Zebulon Pike (who discovered and named the famous Pike's Peak in 1806) visited Colorado, there were a number of different Native American tribes living on Colorado's plains. These tribes included the Arapaho, the Kiowa, the Southern Cheyenne, and the Ute.

During the 1840s, the plains tribes of Colorado went to war with white settlers to try to hold on to their lands. At the same time, the United States fought a war with Mexico. The Americans won both of these wars, and took much of northern Mexico, including what later became central and western Colorado, as part of the peace settlement of 1848.

As happened with many of the other Rocky Mountain states, Colorado experienced a huge explosion in population when gold was discovered near the present-day site of Denver in the early 1850s. The rush of gold prospectors and other settlers into the region pushed the local Native American tribes to war several times over the next twenty years.

White settlers in the region tried to organize a territory that they called Jefferson in 1859, but Congress refused to recognize them. So they acted illegally as a territorial government for nearly two years, until Congress finally passed a law that organized Colorado as a territory. Coloradans tried twice to become a state before Congress finally recognized the territory as one in 1876. Because this year was also the 100th anniversary of the signing of the Declaration of Independence, Colorado became known as the Centennial State.

UTAH: The Beehive State
Geography and Industry

Western Utah is a dry lake bed. Thousands of years ago, it was the bottom of the massive Lake Bonneville. The Great Salt Lake is all that is left of this ancient lake. Central Utah is a long, narrow, fertile valley. Most of Utah's cities lie in this corridor. Eastern Utah is very mountainous in the north, and has a network of deep, beautiful canyons. These include the world-famous Bryce Canyon and Zion Canyon. Many of these formations were created by the Colorado River, which flows northeast to southwest across the southeastern corner of the state.

There are many other natural wonders to see in Utah. They include Canyonlands and Arches (both national parks), and national monuments such as Golden Spike, Dinosaur, Grand Staircase-Escalantre, and Rainbow Bridge. There are ancient cliff dwellings in Capitol Reef National Park.

Mining is a very important part of Utah's economy. There is a lot of copper, gold, magnesium, and petroleum. Other metals, such as silver, lead, tin, and uranium, are mined there as well.

Because the terrain is so dry and rocky, the amount of land used for agriculture is very small. In the land that is usable as farmland, barley, corn, hay, and wheat are grown. Cattle, sheep, and poultry are also raised in large quantities.

Tourism is a growing industry in Utah. Not only do the canyons and rock formations of the east and the southern deserts draw many visitors every year, but so does the world-class skiing in places such as Park City, which is in the Wasatch Mountains in the northeastern part of the state.

History

Like neighboring states Colorado, New Mexico, and Arizona, Utah was occupied over a thousand years ago by cliff-dwellers who built in Utah's canyons using adobe. By the time the

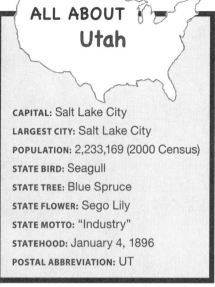

ALL ABOUT
Utah

CAPITAL: Salt Lake City
LARGEST CITY: Salt Lake City
POPULATION: 2,233,169 (2000 Census)
STATE BIRD: Seagull
STATE TREE: Blue Spruce
STATE FLOWER: Sego Lily
STATE MOTTO: "Industry"
STATEHOOD: January 4, 1896
POSTAL ABBREVIATION: UT

Spanish visited the region, the major Native American tribes living in Utah were the Western Shoshone, the Ute, and the Paiute.

Trappers like Jim Bridger worked throughout Utah, looking for beaver in the early 1800s. Bridger was the first white man to see the Great Salt Lake (in 1824). He was also the guide who led Brigham Young's first Mormon wagon trains to northern Utah.

Utah and the Mormons

The Mormons were established as a religious sect in the early 1800s by Joseph Smith, in upstate New York. As they gained in numbers, they moved several times, relocating to Ohio, then to Missouri, and after that to Illinois.

Later, Brigham Young was responsible for the Mormon migration to the far west. He hired Jim Bridger to lead the way. They arrived in the valley of the Great Salt Lake on July 24, 1847.

By 1850, all of Utah and part of what later became Nevada was designated by the U.S. government as the Utah Territory. However, it took nearly half a century and the threat of civil war before Utah became a state. This was mostly because the Mormons practiced polygamy, which means a man marrying more than one wife. Polygamy was illegal in the United States, but Mormons practiced it as part of their religion. In 1858 they had a series of skirmishes with U.S. troops sent to the territory to remove Brigham Young as governor. James Buchanan replaced Young as governor, but Young remained head of the Mormon Church.

A Transportation Revolution

On May 10, 1869, Leland Stanford, a California railroad owner, drove the ceremonial "golden" spike in the first transcontinental railroad tracks. The spike was driven in at Promontory Point in the northern part of Utah. With the opening of the railroad, travel between the west coast and the east coast went from taking months to taking days.

Fun Facts

THE GOLDEN SPIKE NOT SO GOLDEN?

The only problem is that the "golden" spike wasn't really golden! It's true! Pure gold is far too soft to be pounded into a wooden railroad tie with a hammer. So the builders used a spike that was made of an alloy of different metals, including gold, and covered in gold plating.

CHAPTER 18

THE SOUTHWEST

Sweeping from the borders of the southern plains all the way to the Pacific Ocean, the states of the Southwest are made up of vast deserts, high mountains, large rivers, and magnificent forests. This is the region that houses the mighty Grand Canyon and the ancient Sequoia trees of northern California, the wide Mojave Desert, and both the high Rocky Mountains and the rugged Sierra Nevada.

The Southwest has states with small populations, such as New Mexico, and the state with the largest population, California. It is both incredibly rural, with thousands of square miles where no human lives, and also incredibly urban. Orange County in California, for example, has more people living there than live on the entire continent of Australia!

There are rivers such as the Rio Grande, the Colorado, and the Sacramento running through the Southwest, and they drain millions of square miles of land into the Gulf of Mexico, the Gulf of California, and the Pacific Ocean. The Pacific Ocean runs along the western edge of the region, and on that coast there are fine natural harbors such as San Francisco Bay, Drake's Bay, and San Diego Harbor, to name just a few.

NEW MEXICO: Land of Enchantment
Geography and Industry

New Mexico straddles the Continental Divide in the western part of the state. Eastern New Mexico is covered by dry plains that get very little water. The Rio Grande River runs south from its source in Colorado through the state, and forms neighboring Texas's long border with Mexico. The mountain ranges that form spurs of the Rockies include the Sangre de Cristos, which rise to heights of nearly 14,000 feet in places.

ALL ABOUT New Mexico

CAPITAL: Santa Fe

LARGEST CITY: Albuquerque

POPULATION: 1,819,046 (2000 Census)

STATE BIRD: Roadrunner

STATE TREE: Pinon

STATE FLOWER: Yucca

STATE MOTTO: "*Crescit Eundo* (It Grows as It Goes)"

STATEHOOD: January 6, 1912

POSTAL ABBREVIATION: NM

Because water is so scarce in New Mexico, there is little fertile land. The land that is available is used mostly for grazing. Cattle and sheep raising are still major industries in New Mexico.

There are very few fruits and vegetables grown in New Mexico aside from hay, onions, potatoes, and grapes grown in the Rio Grande Valley. These grapes are used to make wine. In fact, New Mexico was the first place in the United States where vineyards were planted and grown, going back to 1610!

Parts of New Mexico are made up of limestone bluffs that are the remains of an ancient undersea reef. These bluffs have been eroded by wind and rain, and have been sculpted into gorgeous and strangely shaped mesas. Underground, the limestone in this region has been eroded by groundwater to form huge limestone caves, complete with stalactites and stalagmites!

Like other states with the Rocky Mountains running through them, New Mexico is rich in minerals. These include ore like copper, manganese, silver, tin, and uranium. Turquoise is found in the state in large quantities. There is a lot of natural gas in New Mexico, but not much petroleum or coal.

One out of every four people who hold a job in New Mexico works for the U.S. government. There are many military bases in the state, and some national observatories (places where scientists use telescopes to study the stars). Los Alamos, where the first atomic bombs were designed and built, is still a working government laboratory.

New Mexico gets millions of tourists every year. Aztec Ruins National Monument (which marks Pueblo ruins, not Aztec ones, despite the name!) and Carlsbad Caverns National Park are just a couple of the most popular places for tourists to go in the state. In the north, the very old city of Taos is the site of a number of art festivals that also draw lots of visitors every year.

WORDS TO KNOW

Stalactite/Stalagmite

What's the difference between stalactites and stalagmites, the rock deposits that look like icicles in underground caves? A stalactite hangs from the ceiling, and is formed by limestone deposits left behind by groundwater dripping from the ceiling toward the floor. Some of the limestone gets left behind on the floor where the water drips, and builds up into formations called stalagmites.

CARLSBAD CAVERNS

The Carlsbad Cavern system contains over eighty different caves, including Lechuguilla Cave, which is the deepest cave in the United States! It was discovered in 1986, and has been measured down to a depth of nearly 1,567 feet (That is deeper than a 110-story skyscraper!). It has not been completely explored yet, so it might be even deeper!

Spanish Explorers

As was the case with most of the states in the Southwest, the Spanish were the first Europeans to visit New Mexico. Before they came to New Mexico during the 1500s, the land was occupied by a flourishing Pueblo civilization that had been in place farming the river bottoms of the Rio Grande and other rivers such as the Pecos.

The first Spaniards to visit the region were the conquistadors who followed Captain General Francisco Vasquez de Coronado north from Mexico in 1540. Coronado was looking for the mythical Seven Cities of Cibola, which were supposedly so full of gold that the natives paved their streets with it. Although he rode all the way into what is now western Kansas, all Coronado found were Pueblo farmers and plains tribes.

He did, however, leave a lasting impression on the Native Americans of New Mexico. Coronado and his men were needlessly cruel to the tribes they encountered. As a result, over and over again during the following two centuries, the Pueblos and the Apaches (who lived in western New Mexico and what is now Arizona) fought very hard against the Spanish as they tried to establish a colony and a mission system.

History

In 1609 a colonial government was established at Taos, which is one of the oldest continuously inhabited European-built cities in North America. By 1680, the Spanish colonial government had again so angered the local Native Americans that the tribes once again went to war. This time, things were different; the Spanish lost, and they had to flee from New Mexico. The Pueblos and Apaches were able to keep the Spanish out of New Mexico for over twelve years!

Just over a century later, Mexico won its independence from Spain. That year New Mexico (which included what is now Arizona) became a Mexican province. The Mexicans were interested in trade with their neighbors to the north, and encouraged American traders to come to Mexico to do business. By 1822 (a year after Mexico became independent), American traders had established what we now call the Santa Fe Trail, which ran from what is now Kansas down to Santa Fe in New Mexico.

In 1846 Mexico and the United States went to war over Mexico's northern provinces. Mexico lost, and part of the result was that New Mexico became an American territory. New Mexico became a state in 1912, just ahead of Arizona, which had made up the other half of New Mexico territory when it first joined the United States!

ARIZONA: The Grand Canyon State

Geography and Industry

When you think of Arizona, what do you think of? The Grand Canyon? Lots and lots of desert, and rocks, and maybe a few mountains? Well, Arizona has all of those things, but it has so much more! There are forests and large rivers in Arizona, and the state has farms that produce lots of food.

The northern part of the state, where the Grand Canyon is, is part of the Colorado Plateau, and is very rugged and mountainous. It's also covered in several places, including part of the southern rim of the Grand Canyon, with evergreen forests, especially Ponderosa Pines. The Colorado River system (including the Little Colorado River) runs both through the Grand Canyon, which it has carved over millions of years, and through the north central and northwestern parts of the state.

WORDS TO KNOW

Pueblo

The word "pueblo" has a couple of different meanings. It comes from the type of adobe (mud brick) buildings built by several different cultures in the Southwest. It has also come to stand as a collective name for the cultures (the Anasazi, the Zuni, the Hopi, and so on) who built with it. Adobe is still used as a building material to this day in the region!

ALL ABOUT Arizona

CAPITAL: Phoenix

LARGEST CITY: Phoenix

POPULATION: 5,130,632 (2000 Census)

STATE BIRD: Cactus Wren

STATE TREE: Paloverde

STATE FLOWER: Saguaro Cactus Blossom

STATE MOTTO: *"Ditat Deus* (God Enriches)."

STATEHOOD: February 14, 1912

POSTAL ABBREVIATION: AZ

The southern part of the state is mostly extremely dry desert plains with a few mountains rising on either side of the Gila River valley. The Gila is a large river that runs east to west across the state and empties into the Colorado.

Like many of the western states, Arizona has a lot of beautiful scenery, so tourism is a major industry in the state. In addition to the Grand Canyon, there are other popular areas such as the Painted Desert, the Native American pueblo ruins at places like Canyon de Chelly in the northeastern part of the state, the Petrified Forest National Park, and the Mogollon Rim.

Just like in the other western states, cattle-ranching and crop-raising are very important industries in Arizona. The main crops raised are broccoli, cauliflower, cotton, lettuce, and sorghum.

History

Before the Spanish began exploring the region during the sixteenth century, there were many different tribes of Native Americans living in what is now Arizona. An early culture we know as the Hohokum ("hoh-HOH-kem") lived in pit houses dug into the earth and covered with thatched mud roofs. They were farmers who irrigated their fields with water from neighboring rivers. They flourished for nearly 1,000 years, from 500 A.D. to 1450 A.D.

The Spanish explorer Francisco Vasquez de Coronado visited Arizona, discovering the Grand Canyon in 1540. Although many Spanish soldiers came to the region over the next 100 years, they were exploring—looking for gold, not interested in settling the area. The first Spanish visitors to settle permanently in Arizona were Spanish priests who came as missionaries to convert the local Native Americans to Christianity. These friars established the first permanent settlements near Nogales and Tucson in 1692.

Mexico briefly controlled Arizona before losing it as part of the Mexican Cession to the United States in 1848. In 1853, the United States bought more territory from Mexico and added it to the New Mexico Territory. This land was south of the Gila River, and the United States hoped to build a railroad through it out to California. It later became part first of the Arizona Territory (1863), then of the state of Arizona.

During the forty-nine years that Arizona was a territory, it had quite a colorful history. Several tribes of the Apache nation maintained an on-again, off-again war with the U.S. government. Such great Apache leaders as Mangas Coloradas (whose name in Spanish means "Red Sleeves," referring to the color of his favorite shirt), Cochise, and Geronimo fought the U.S. Cavalry to a standstill for decades.

The Apache were skilled at the art of guerilla warfare. They struck in one place, and faded away like smoke. They would also raid a site and then slip across the border into Mexico, where they knew the soldiers weren't allowed to chase them. Even after they agreed to move to reservations, many young Apache braves would slip off the reservation, raid several settlers' farms, and then slip back on to the reservation before their absence had been noticed. The government's solution was to remove such warriors as the great Geronimo from Arizona and send them to a reservation in Oklahoma. (Geronimo was eventually sent all the way to Florida!)

Beginning in the 1870s, large copper mines sprang up in the hills around Tucson. In 1877, silver was discovered in Cochise's old stomping grounds in the Dragoon Mountains near Tombstone, which was a boom town east of Tucson. Miners flooded into the area, and so did gamblers, saloon-keepers, gun-fighters, and other people right out of a Western movie!

Arizona became a state in 1912, just a few months after neighboring New Mexico. From 1940 to 1960, Arizona's population increased by 100 percent, the fastest growth-rate in American history! To this day, people are moving to the state for its warm climate and mild winters.

WORDS TO KNOW

Guerilla

"Guerilla" is a Spanish word that refers to a type of warfare where the people fighting specialize in hit-and-run raids, rather than acquiring, occupying, and holding enemy territory.

Fun Facts

THE MOST FAMOUS GUNFIGHT

People such as the Earp brothers, led by the famous Wyatt Earp, came to Arizona looking to get rich quick. The Earps eventually got into a power struggle with another local family, the Clantons. This power struggle led to the most famous gunfight in western history: the gunfight at the OK Corral!

ALL ABOUT Nevada

CAPITAL: Carson City

LARGEST CITY: Las Vegas

POPULATION: 1,998,257 (2000 Census)

STATE BIRD: Mountain Bluebird

STATE TREE: Single-leaf Pinon

STATE FLOWER: Sagebrush

STATE MOTTO: "All for Our Country."

STATEHOOD: October 31, 1864

POSTAL ABBREVIATION: NV

NEVADA: The Silver State

Geography and Industry

Within its borders, Nevada has high mountains (the Sierra Nevada, which run along its border with California) and a couple of huge deserts (the Great Basin, which is located in the eastern and central portions of the state, and the Mojave, which runs across the southern tip). In the northern part of the state are some high plateaus, which have the state's available grazing land. Nevada is poor in water—it is the driest state in the Union—but wealthy in minerals.

Mining is a very important industry in Nevada. Nevada's mines produce more gold, mercury, and silver than those of any other state. There are copper and oil deposits in the state as well. What few crops that are grown in this harsh, dry climate include hay to feed the livestock bred in the north.

Nevada's climate varies widely between the state's different regions. In the mountains of the northwest, the winters are very cold. In the southern tip, near Las Vegas, the summer heat gets so hot that it takes your breath away!

Like many other western states, Nevada relies heavily on tourism as well as on its mineral wealth. Reno in the northwest and Las Vegas in the south are very popular tourist destinations, attracting millions of visitors per year. Lake Tahoe, which is close to Reno, is also one of the most popular skiing vacation destinations in the world. On the Colorado River, which forms part of Nevada's border with Arizona in the south, Hoover Dam was built during the 1930s. It is one of the largest dams in the United States and generates inexpensive hydroelectricity to power the bright lights of neighboring Las Vegas.

History

Before white settlement in the mid-nineteenth century, Nevada was relatively empty. Members of the Paiute and Ute tribes lived in the north and the Great Basin. From the 1820s through the 1840s, a number of fur traders and explorers like Peter Skene Ogden of Canada's North West Fur Company, the independent American trapper Jedidiah Smith, and U.S. Army Captain John C. Fremont visited the region and explored it extensively.

Also beginning in the 1840s, two wagon-train trails were blazed across Nevada. One trail crossed the Sierra Nevada in the north, and another passed through the small town of Las Vegas in the south, both connecting the American states in the east to the California gold fields on the Pacific coast.

At first very few settlers stopped in Nevada. Most of them just kept heading for California. The Comstock strike in northern Nevada in 1858 changed all of that. The Comstock Lode turned out to be the richest silver strike in American history, and it attracted so many people so quickly to work claims in the Sierra Nevada that what had been an empty part of the Utah Territory just a few short years before became the Nevada Territory in 1861, and the state of Nevada in 1864.

Hoover Dam

By the turn of the twentieth century, times were tough in Nevada, because silver prices were down and most of the gold mines in the state weren't producing as much as they had previously. During the early twentieth century, the U.S. government began to take a big part in developing the state's economy. First the government funded the building of Hoover Dam (which was finished in 1936) and then it decided to make Nevada the major site for its nuclear testing.

WORDS TO KNOW

Lode

A lode is a deposit of any sort of metal that is connected and continuous. These are sometimes also called veins.

Hoover Dam brought cheap electric power to neighboring Las Vegas. Thanks to this, and to Nevada's new laws that legalized gambling, Las Vegas began to attract tourists away from places in the east where gambling was legal, such as Atlantic City.

Another result of Hoover Dam's construction across the powerful Colorado River was the creation of Lake Mead. Boating, camping, water-skiing, and fishing in the waters of Lake Mead are all popular outdoor activities in southern Nevada.

Lastly, Hoover Dam has helped divert countless tons of water from the Colorado River and send it to irrigate much of the fertile (but arid) farmland of neighboring southern California. As a result, California is one of the biggest producers of fruits and vegetables in the world today!

CALIFORNIA: The Golden State

Geography and Industry

California is so big that it could practically be a country on its own. It's true! Even though it's not the largest state in the Union (Alaska and Texas are larger), it is the third-largest area-wise, and it does have the largest population of any state. What's more, if California were an independent country, this state's economy is so huge that it would be listed among the ten largest economies among the nations of the world!

California occupies 800 miles along the American Pacific coast, which is over half of America's western coastline. It is long and thin, measuring around 250 miles wide, and bordered on the east by the mighty Sierra Nevada Mountains in the northeast and the Colorado River in the southeast.

In many ways California is one huge valley. Bordered in the east by the Sierra Nevada, its west coast is covered by a long range of low-lying mountains known as the Coast Range. Running for hundreds of miles along the central part of the state in between these two mountain ranges is the Central

ALL ABOUT
California

CAPITAL: Sacramento

LARGEST CITY: Los Angeles

POPULATION: 33,871,648 (2000 Census)

STATE BIRD: California Valley Quail

STATE TREE: California Redwood

STATE FLOWER: Golden Poppy

STATE MOTTO: "Eureka (I Have Found It)."

STATEHOOD: September 9, 1850

POSTAL ABBREVIATION: CA

Valley. Two large river systems, the Sacramento and the San Joaquin, run through this valley and provide water for one of the most fertile areas in the world.

Although other states are known mostly as farming states, none produces more fruits and vegetables than California. California grows more almonds, broccoli, carrots, lettuce, onions, strawberries, and tomatoes than any other state. It also leads the country in dairy products. So more milk, cheese, and eggs come from California than from anywhere else in the nation! Cotton, grapes, flowers, and oranges are other important crops grown in California.

California doesn't just lead the country in food production, though. It has a lot of high-tech industry in the state, especially in the north, where part of the San Francisco Bay area is known as Silicon Valley because of all of the computer parts it produces (silicon is a mineral used in making computers). It is also a leading manufacturer of everything from appliances and car parts to airplane parts. During World War II, southern California's manufacturing industry blossomed because of defense contracts to build planes, tanks, jeeps, cars, and so on for the American forces fighting in the war.

History

Before the arrival of the Spanish in the mid-sixteenth century, there were many Native Americans living in California's mild climate. These groups weren't really tribes, but small family groups. These people were skilled basket weavers, and their art survives down to the present day. Most of them spoke dialects of Native American languages such as Chumash, Coastanoan, and Digueno.

The Spanish claimed all of the North American west coast, and explored it far north of what is now California during the sixteenth, seventeenth, and eigh-

Fun Facts

THE HIGH AND THE LOW OF IT

Did you know that both the highest and the lowest points in the continental United States are in California? Mount Whitney, which measures 14,494 feet, is less than ninety miles from Death Valley, which is the lowest point at 282 feet below sea level. Death Valley has also had the highest recorded temperature in the United States at 134 degrees Fahrenheit in 1913!

teenth centuries. They finally began to colonize north of Mexico, moving into what is now San Diego in the province they called Alta California (upper California) to differentiate it from the established province of Baja California (lower California) in the year 1769.

The Spanish set up a mission system that allowed the Catholic Church to hold the land of the local Native Americans "in trust," and cultivate it, using the Native Americans themselves as their labor. So these Mission Indians (as they came to be known) had their land taken from them, and then they were herded into the mission settlements and forced to work the very land that was stolen from them for no pay!

After Mexico declared independence from Spain, the Mexican government seized the mission lands and freed the Mission Indians from their slavery. But the Mexican period in Alta California did not last long. Even before Mexico lost California at the end of the Mexican-American War in 1848, Americans had begun to immigrate to California in droves.

During the Mexican War, a young army captain sent west to map the American possessions in the Rockies led his exploring expedition to northern California in order to see what good he could do for his country there. His name was John C. Fremont, and he succeeded in stirring up American settlers (as well as many Californians of Mexican descent), resulting in the Bear Flag Revolt. The Americans and many Californios (Californians of Mexican descent) threw out the occupying Mexican troops. A republic was formed just long enough to vote to join the United States. California became a free state (a state where slavery was outlawed) in 1850.

One of the reasons why there were enough Americans living in California for it to become a state in 1850 was that gold had been discovered in northern California at a place called Sutter's Fort. The people who crossed the continent intending to get rich quickly in California became known as Forty-Niners because the California Gold Rush began in 1849.

HAWAII: The Aloha State

Geography and Industry

Stretching over 1,000 miles from southeast to northwest in the central Pacific Ocean, the islands that make up the state of Hawaii were built up over centuries by volcanic activity on the ocean floor. There are still several active volcanoes in the Hawaiian Islands today. These mountains include Haleakala on the island of Maui, and Mauna Kea and Mauna Loa on the island of Hawaii. The largest islands in the group are Hawaii, Lanai, Kahoolawe, Kauai, Maui, Molokai, Niihau, and Oahu.

The "big" island of Hawaii is both the largest and the "youngest" of the islands in the group. Oahu has the most people living there, and is the most popular tourist destination, with Waikiki Beach, and Waimea Bay drawing thousands of visitors per year.

Tourism is Hawaii's chief industry, although specialty foods sugar cane and pineapples are grown there in abundance. There is so much to do in Hawaii: for starters, there's skiing on the mountains of the Big Island, snorkeling along the many coral reefs that have sprung up around the islands, surfing, whale-watching off of Maui, and watching "cowboys" rounding up Hawaii's other big food export, cattle!

Another popular Hawaiian recreational activity is fishing. Whether it is surf fishing from the beach, or sport fishing out on the blue waters surrounding the islands, fishing is not just a recreational industry—for some people, it's a way of life. In fact, fish and fishing are so important in Hawaii that it's the only state to have its own official state fish!

History

Hawaii was first settled by Polynesian settlers from the South Pacific around A.D. 400 For over a thousand years afterward, the natives of the individual islands fought each other, Oahu against Kauai and so on.

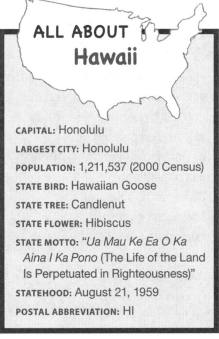

ALL ABOUT Hawaii

CAPITAL: Honolulu
LARGEST CITY: Honolulu
POPULATION: 1,211,537 (2000 Census)
STATE BIRD: Hawaiian Goose
STATE TREE: Candlenut
STATE FLOWER: Hibiscus
STATE MOTTO: *"Ua Mau Ke Ea O Ka Aina I Ka Pono* (The Life of the Land Is Perpetuated in Righteousness)"
STATEHOOD: August 21, 1959
POSTAL ABBREVIATION: HI

Fun Facts

PINEAPPLES— NOT A HAWAIIAN FRUIT?

Did you know that pineapples are not native to Hawaii? It's true! Pineapples evolved in the jungles of northeastern South America, in what is now Guyana. They were first imported to Hawaii in the late nineteenth century, and they quickly became a popular cash crop!

WORDS TO KNOW

Humuhumunukunukuapuaa

Hawaii is the only state in the Union with an official state fish, and its name is bigger than it is! The fish is also known as a triggerfish. However, it is better known by its name in the Hawaiian language: humuhumunukunukuapuaa ("hooh-mooh-hooh-mooh-nooh-kooh-nooh-kooh-ah-pooh-ah-ah").

The first Europeans to visit the islands were the crew of the British naval vessel the *HMS Discovery*, under the command of the famous explorer Captain James Cook, in 1778. Soon after Cook's expedition revealed Hawaii's existence to the outside world, American whalers began to visit Hawaii. They were followed by Christian missionaries in the early 1800s.

In 1810 King Kamehameha I ("kah-MAY-uh-MAY-uh") united the islands and established the Kingdom of Hawaii. His family ruled the islands until 1872, when his grandson, King Kamehameha V, died. The royal family tried for decades to resist the influence of American missionaries and businessmen (who came to Hawaii to make money from the booming sugar trade), with little success.

In 1893 a bloodless revolution deposed Queen Liliuokalani ("li-LEE-uh-oh-kah-LAH-nee"), the last monarch of the Kingdom of Hawaii. John L. Stephens, the American minister (ambassador) to Hawaii, was appointed the head of the new government, and declared Hawaii a U.S. protectorate (meaning that it became a protected territory of the United States).

Interestingly enough, American president Grover Cleveland refused to sign the order annexing Hawaii! He correctly believed that most native Hawaiians didn't support annexation, and he didn't want the United States to be a political bully.

The next U.S. president, William McKinley, supported American annexation of Hawaii, and he got his wish in 1898. Hawaii became a territory in 1900. Hawaii's fine port of Pearl Harbor became a major U.S. naval base over the next few decades. In fact, Pearl Harbor was so important to the U.S. military that when the Japanese decided to go to war with the United States in December of 1941, the first thing it did was bomb the harbor. The Japanese Navy launched a surprise attack against Pearl Harbor, sinking several of the battleships of the U.S. Pacific fleet and killing over 2,000 American civilians and military personnel.

Hawaii became the fiftieth state in 1959, less than eight months after Alaska became the forty-ninth state in January of that same year.

CHAPTER 19

THE NORTHWEST, DISTRICT OF COLUMBIA, AND PUERTO RICO

The Pacific Northwest runs from the foothills of the Rocky Mountains to the coast of the Pacific Ocean, and from northern California to the Canadian border, then onward to the Arctic and the massive state of Alaska.

The Pacific Northwest is a region of massive rivers and high mountains, and it has the only non-jungle rain forest in the United States. Although many people think of the Pacific Northwest as a place where the sun never shines and it never stops raining, there are parts of the region that are as dry as any desert.

OREGON: The Beaver State
Geography and Industry

Oregon has three major mountain ranges crossing it: the low-lying Coastal Range, which runs along the shore of the Pacific Ocean; the rugged Cascade Range (including the gorgeous Mount Hood and the picturesque Mount Batchelor), which goes north to south through the west-central part of the state; and the Blue and Wallowa Mountains, which run from northeastern Oregon into neighboring Washington and Idaho.

Nestled between the Coastal Range and the Cascades is the incredibly fertile Willamette River Valley. The eastern and central parts of the state are arid plateau land, which receives very little rainfall but under irrigation has become very productive farmland in many places. This part of Oregon is ideal grazing land, and the state has a huge cattle industry.

Oregon's major agricultural products include beans, broccoli, cherries, hay, onions, pears, peppermint, strawberries, and wheat. Oregon has also begun to produce wine locally during the past couple of decades, made from grapes grown in the state's arid central region.

ALL ABOUT Oregon

CAPITAL: Salem
LARGEST CITY: Portland
POPULATION: 3,421,399 (2000 Census)
STATE BIRD: Western Meadowlark
STATE TREE: Douglas Fir
STATE FLOWER: Oregon Grape
STATE MOTTO: "The Union"
STATEHOOD: February 14, 1859
POSTAL ABBREVIATION: OR

Oregon has been called a sportsperson's paradise for many good reasons, including skiing in the Cascades; fishing, kayaking, and boating on the ocean and in the state's many lakes, streams, and rivers; and hiking in and around Oregon's many mountain ranges.

Because there is so much to see and do in Oregon, tourism has become a major industry in the state. The state's beaches are some of the most beautiful in the world, and every inch of them is public land, which by law cannot be sold. In southeastern Oregon, the Sea Lion Caves are popular with tourists, as is Crater Lake, which is at the center of Crater Lake National Park.

History

Before the first Europeans began visiting the region during the sixteenth century, there were many different tribes of Native Americans living in what is now Oregon. The Nez Perce lived in eastern Oregon, in the Wallowa Valley. The Modoc lived in dry lava beds of southern Oregon. The Cayuse and Umatilla lived in eastern and northern Oregon. And the Chinook lived and traded along the Columbia River all the way from its mouth up to the present-day site of Portland, Oregon's largest city.

After Captain Robert Gray of Boston, Massachusetts, located the mouth of the Columbia (which he named after his ship, the *Columbia Rediviva*) in 1792, other ships began to visit the region. The Chinooks began to act as middlemen who traded furs from tribes living farther up the river for the trade goods (blankets, glass beads, guns, and so on) that these ships brought.

The first permanent settlement in what is now Oregon was the establishment in 1811 of the fur-trading post of Astoria on the present site of the city of Astoria, Oregon. The post

Fun Facts

CRATER LAKE

Nearly 7,000 years ago, an 11,000-foot-high mountain stood on the spot today occupied by Crater Lake. Around 4850 B.C., that mountain erupted with the force of several hundred nuclear warheads. When the mountain blew up, it left behind a smoking crater that filled with water over the course of several centuries. And that's how Crater Lake came to be.

WORDS TO KNOW

The Oregon Trail

Established in the early 1830s, the Oregon Trail began in Independence, Missouri, crossed the Great Plains, the Rocky Mountains, the Great Basin, and finally the Cascade Range, ending in the farmland of the Willamette Valley. Although it is no longer used today, there are places along the trail where the wagon ruts made over 150 years ago can still be seen!

was founded by members of the American Fur Company, and they named the post after the company's owner, New York's John Jacob Astor. During the War of 1812, the post was seized by the British, and for the next thirty years Americans competed with British subjects for control of the Oregon Country.

Oregon at the time ran from California in the south up the west coast nearly to Alaska in the north, and from the Continental Divide in the east to the Pacific Ocean in the west. Parts of the present-day states of Wyoming and Montana, as well as all of the states of Oregon, Washington, and Idaho, and the entire Canadian province of British Columbia were included in this vast territory.

In 1818, and again in 1842, Great Britain and the United States agreed to a joint occupation of the Oregon Country by their citizens, and to no active military units in the area. In the 1830s, American settlers began to cross the continent by wagon train, coming all the way to the Willamette Valley to settle and establish farms. These early settlers established the Oregon Trail, which thousands followed afterward.

In 1846 the United States and Great Britain split the Oregon Country along the Forty-Ninth Parallel. They did so peacefully, without a shot being fired. The American side became the Oregon Territory, and remained so until Oregon became a state in 1859.

Scared Silly

These two old miners are trying to tell you a joke. The answer is the name of a kind of town found in many western states. In fact, the state of Oregon has more than 1,000 of them! Figure out the miners' secret language so you can laugh along with them.

HINT: Look for a common word that is repeated over and over.

Wboohbooeboorbooeboo
cbooaboonboo yboooboouboo
fbooiboonboodboo   tboohbooeboo
sboopbooiboorbooibootboo
oboofboo   tboohbooeboo
oboolboodboo
wbooeboosbootboo?

Iboonboo aboo
gboohboooboosbootboo
tboooboowboonboo!

ALL ABOUT Washington

CAPITAL: Olympia

LARGEST CITY: Seattle

POPULATION: 5,894,121 (2000 Census)

STATE BIRD: Willow Goldfinch

STATE TREE: Western Hemlock

STATE FLOWER: Western Rhododendron

STATE MOTTO: "*Al-ki* (By and By)."

STATEHOOD: November 11, 1889

POSTAL ABBREVIATION: WA

WORDS TO KNOW

Geoduck

The word "geoduck" ("GOO-ee-duk") comes from a local Native American phrase that means "dig deep." A geoduck is not a bird; it's a huge species of clam that can be found only in and around Washington's Puget Sound. These clams have shells that only measure about six inches around, but they can weigh as much as twenty pounds!

WASHINGTON: The Evergreen State

Geography and Industry

Washington is a large western state that has the Columbia River running north to south through most of it. Then the river turns westward and runs along Washington's southern border with Oregon, all the way to the sea. Puget ("PYOO-jit") Sound, the largest saltwater inlet on the west coast, runs through western Washington and separates the large Olympic Peninsula from the rest of the state.

The jagged, picturesque Olympic Mountains rise on that peninsula, and within Olympic National Park lies almost all of the only rainforest in the continental United States. The east side of Puget Sound is bordered by the very tall Cascade Mountains. They reach their greatest height at the summit of Mount Rainier, which lies just southeast of the state's largest city of Seattle, and rises up to a little over 14,000 feet.

The Cascades block warm wet ocean air from reaching the state's interior (and are the cause for a lot of the rain that falls around Puget Sound). As a result, the Columbia River Basin, which stretches from the eastern Cascades to the foothills of the Rockies in the eastern part of the state, is pretty dry. Large rivers such as the Spokane, the Wenatchee, the Yakima, and the Snake all flow into the Columbia in this region.

Because the soil of the area is made up of large deposits of nutrient-rich volcanic dirt, water from these rivers used for irrigation of the dry land has turned Washington's desert area into a garden. Such crops as apples, pears, cherries, wheat, barley, hops, and grapes grow in such abundance here that they are a major export for the state.

In addition to all of the fruits and vegetables grown for sale in this state, there is a large livestock industry (including beef cattle and sheep, and especially poultry). On top of that, Washington's position on the northwest coast, near some of the north Pacific's richest fishing grounds, ensures that it produces a lot of seafood, including salmon, cod, halibut, and shellfish (such as clams, scallops and oysters). One particularly famous local clam is the geoduck.

Washington is famous for producing more than apples and clams, though. Nearly half of the state is covered in evergreen forests, and although it's not as essential as it once was, logging is still a big industry in Washington. Manufacturing is important to the state as well. The Boeing Company has been producing airplanes and airplane parts in the state for nearly a hundred years. Over the last two decades, Microsoft Corporation, based in Redmond, Washington, has become one of the most influential and innovative software manufacturers in the world.

Another popular industry in the state of Washington is the tourism industry. With national parks such as Olympic National Park, North Cascades National Park, and Mount Rainier National Park, and the active volcano Mount St. Helens in southwestern Washington, there are plenty of places to hike, boat, fish, hunt, and camp in the Evergreen State.

TRY THIS!

Apples!

More apples are grown in Washington State than in any other area in the world. In fact, the next time you go to the store, take a look at the apples that are displayed for sale. Wherever you live, there is a more than 90 percent chance that these apples will have a sticker that says "Grown in Washington"!

History

Before European exploration and settlement of the area, Washington was occupied by tribes who either spent most of their time on horseback or out in canoes fishing and hunting whales. The interior tribes such as the Yakama, Spokane, Palouse, Walla Walla, Colville, and Cayuse lived much as the Plains tribes did: moving from place to place and hunting buffalo nearly year-round. The coastal tribes, including the Duwamish, the Hoh, and the Makah, lived in long houses made from cedar planks, and hunted whales out on the open ocean in massive dugout canoes carved from the trunks of huge cedar trees.

During the sixteenth, seventeenth, and eighteenth centuries, Spanish sailors explored along Washington's coast, leaving their mark with place names such as the Strait of Juan de Fuca. In the late eighteenth century, Captain George Vancouver explored along Washington's coast looking for the mouth of the Columbia River (American sea captain Robert Gray had beaten him to it by just a few weeks).

The Only One

What makes the state of Washington's name unique?
To find out, fill in all the letters G and W, and the numbers 1 through 5.
Read the remaining white letters from left to right, and top to bottom!

WIGT1IGS23THGE3OWNGL
WY43SGTAWTGE5NWAGM
GE33D13AWFGT3EGR3WGA
2PGR3EGSGIGD2EGNT3!

American explorers Lewis and Clark visited the southern part of the state when they followed the Snake River out of Idaho and all the way to where it empties into the Columbia in 1805. After Lewis and Clark, the region was jointly occupied by citizens of the United States and Canadians (who were British subjects) for nearly forty years until the Oregon Treaty in 1846 split the region into the Canadian province of British Columbia and the American-run Oregon Territory.

When Oregon became a state in 1859, the rest of the territory became known as the Washington Territory. It included parts of what later became Idaho and Montana as well. In 1889, Washington became a state.

ALASKA: The Last Frontier

Geography and Industry

Alaska is beyond big, larger than large, more than massive. Alaska has so much land area in it that it would take 20 percent of the states that make up the forty-eight continental United States to equal the size of Alaska alone! When it comes to population, though, Alaska is on the other end of the spectrum. Only the states of Vermont and Wyoming have fewer people living within their borders.

Alaska is separated from the continental United States by western Canada, and is closer to Russian Siberia than to the rest of America. The northern part of the state is made up mostly of the Seward Peninsula, and lies above the Arctic Circle. This includes the North Slope, which is where most of Alaska's oil is produced. This region also contains Point Barrow.

The Yukon River runs out of the Yukon Territory in neighboring Canada, crosses Alaska from east to west, then empties into the Bering Sea, which borders Alaska on the west. Southwest of the Yukon River Valley lies the Alaska Peninsula, which stretches

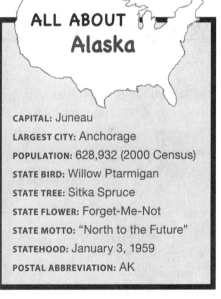

ALL ABOUT Alaska

CAPITAL: Juneau

LARGEST CITY: Anchorage

POPULATION: 628,932 (2000 Census)

STATE BIRD: Willow Ptarmigan

STATE TREE: Sitka Spruce

STATE FLOWER: Forget-Me-Not

STATE MOTTO: "North to the Future"

STATEHOOD: January 3, 1959

POSTAL ABBREVIATION: AK

Fun Facts

POINT BARROW

Point Barrow, which extends northward into the Arctic Ocean from Alaska's North Slope, is the northernmost point in the United States!

WORDS TO KNOW

Mount McKinley

Mount McKinley, which rises to a height of 20,320 feet, is the tallest mountain in America. Local Native American tribes called it "Denali," which means the Great One. (It is now commonly known by both names.) It was named for then-president William McKinley in 1897. The mountain sits at the center of Denali National Park.

out into the islands chain known as the Aleutians. These islands separate the Bering Sea from the northern Pacific, and are storm-ravaged, small, rocky, and barren. Few people live there these days.

Separating the Alaska Peninsula from the rest of southern Alaska is the massive Gulf of Alaska. The Kenai Peninsula pushes south of Anchorage (Alaska's largest city) and into the gulf in the direction of Kodiak Island.

Across the Gulf of Alaska from the Alaska Peninsula lies the so-called Alaskan Panhandle. It's made up mostly of small islands and a narrow coastal strip of land that rises quickly into the steep Coastal Range of mountains. The state capital of Juneau is in this region, which has a climate similar to that of western Washington state: lots of rain, not much snow (in Alaska, one of the snowiest states!).

To the north of Anchorage lies the Alaska Range of mountains, which are very snowy and very rugged. The Alaska Range's highest point is the summit of Mount McKinley.

Because it is so close to the fish-rich North Pacific, Alaska is home to a large year-round fishing fleet that catches millions of pounds of commercial fish per year. In 1968 oil was discovered on Alaska's North Slope, and petroleum extraction remains a very important industry in the state to this day. In fact, Alaska's oil reserves are the largest in North America. Alaska is also the only place in the United States where fur-trapping is still done to any noticeable extent.

History

Beginning in 1741 Russian fur traders explored much of southern Alaska, including the Aleutian Islands and the Alaskan Panhandle. They established their first permanent settlement on Kodiak Island in 1784.

Russia controlled Alaska for the next eighty years, and at various times tried to expand southward along the coast as far as Vancouver Island. In fact, in 1812 Russian settlers established a trading post in northern California at Fort Ross, near the Russian River (which they also named).

By the 1860s the Russian fur trade in Alaska had become so costly that there was no more profit to be made by continuing it, and the Russian Czar (king) sought to get something in return for it. He found a buyer in U.S. Secretary of State William Seward, who arranged for the United States to pay $7,200,000 for Alaska.

Big and Small

Alaska is one of the largest states while Rhode Island is one of the tiniest. Just how different in size are they? Figure out the following equations and you will learn how many times you could fit the state of Rhode Island into the state of Alaska!

The number of states:

_____

MULTIPLY by the number of states with four letters in their name:

_____

MULTIPLY by the number of states that start with the letter O:

_____

SUBTRACT the total number of letters in Idaho, Missouri, Pennsylvania:

_____

ANSWER:
The state of Rhode Island could fit into Alaska

_____ times!

Seward spent the rest of his career (and his life) defending this purchase. Alaska was known far and wide as either Seward's Icebox or Seward's Folly, because it seemed to be nothing more than an icy desert, virtually worthless.

Alaska did not even get a governor or official territorial government until after gold was discovered there in 1880. After that, things began to pick up, as other minerals were found and mined, including petroleum in 1968. Seward was proven to not just be right in the end, but to be brilliant, because Alaska has repaid its purchase price many times over since the United States acquired it. Alaska became the forty-ninth state in January of 1959.

PUERTO RICO

Geography and Industry

Puerto Rico isn't a state, but it's under the authority of the United States. Officially, it's a commonwealth, and its head of state (which in a state would be a governor) is the U.S. president. It does have a governor who is elected by Puerto Rico's voters.

Puerto Rico is an island in the eastern end of the West Indies. It is bordered on the south by the Caribbean Sea and on the north by the Atlantic Ocean. Located closer to the equator than the continental United States, the island is semitropical, with a long growing season and no discernable winter.

Puerto Rico is crossed by mountains such as the Cordillera Central. Its rivers are short and too shallow for river travel. The commonwealth of Puerto Rico includes several smaller off-shore islands, the largest of which is Vieques (VYA-kays).

ALL ABOUT Puerto Rico

CAPITAL: San Juan

LARGEST CITY: San Juan

POPULATION: 3,917,000 (2005 estimate)

FORM OF GOVERNMENT: Self-governing Commonwealth within the United States.

STATE BIRD: N/A

STATE TREE: N/A

STATE FLOWER: N/A

STATE MOTTO: N/A

STATEHOOD: N/A

POSTAL ABBREVIATION: PR

Puerto Rico's capital and largest city is San Juan. Other important cities include Caguas, Mayaguez, and Ponce.

Manufacturing of items such as clothing, electronics, and pharmaceuticals is Puerto Rico's main industry. Agriculture such as the raising of livestock, coffee, sugar cane, and tobacco are also very important to Puerto Rico's economy.

With its semitropical climate, lush scenery, and gorgeous white-sand beaches, Puerto Rico profits highly from year-round tourism. People from all over the world visit Puerto Rico for the beaches alone.

History

There were members of the Arawak tribe of native people living on Puerto Rico when Christopher Columbus visited it in 1493. In 1508, Juan Ponce de Leon led a force of conquistadors ashore on the island he named Puerto Rico (Spanish for "rich harbor") and conquered for Spain.

The Spaniards enslaved the local natives and forced them to work on the sugar plantations they built once they had conquered the island. As the Arawaks died out from overwork and disease, the Spaniards replaced them with black slaves brought from Africa.

Puerto Rico's capital city of San Juan quickly became a jewel in the crown of the Spanish Empire, with gorgeous buildings and a thriving economy. The rest of the island languished in a slow-moving sugar-based economic rut, which was made worse over the decades by repeated raids on the island by English, French, and Dutch buccaneers.

By the nineteenth century, Puerto Rico's native population had become dissatisfied with Spanish colonial rule, and there were several rebellions on the island. The Spanish brutally put down each one.

Fun Facts

PONCE DE LEON

Ponce de Leon conquered and named the island of Puerto Rico, and was the island's first governor. As a result of this expedition and his governorship, Ponce de Leon became a very wealthy man. And yet he isn't usually remembered for this accomplishment. He is remembered as the man who explored Florida looking for the Fountain of Youth and failed.

ALL ABOUT
District of Columbia

CAPITAL: Washington, D.C.

LARGEST CITY: Washington, D.C.

POPULATION: 572,059 (2000 Census)

STATE BIRD: N/A

STATE TREE: N/A

STATE FLOWER: N/A

STATE MOTTO: N/A

STATEHOOD: N/A

POSTAL ABBREVIATION: DC

The situation changed in 1898, when the United States defeated Spain in the short and nearly bloodless Spanish-American War. As part of the treaty that ended the war, Spain ceded control of Puerto Rico to the United States.

In 1917 Puerto Ricans received both U.S. citizenship and the right to vote in their local elections. In the years since, they have had the choice to become independent, to stay a self-ruling commonwealth of the United States, or to become a state. The citizens of the island have chosen to remain a commonwealth.

THE DISTRICT OF COLUMBIA

Geography and Industry

This federal region on the Potomac River between the states of Maryland and Virginia is not a state. It is a district controlled directly by the U.S. Congress, and its sole purpose is to serve as the seat of the U.S. government in the form of the nation's capital: the city of Washington. It was once a ten-mile perfect square, and contained the village of Georgetown and the county of Alexandria, all situated on land donated by both Maryland and Virginia. The land on the Virginia side of the Potomac River was later given back to the state of Virginia.

The District of Columbia only has one industry: the U.S. government, which employs most of the people who live in the district. Others work for the city of Washington, which is another large employer within the district.

History

President George Washington chose the site of the United States' new capital city in 1790. French architect Pierre L'Enfant

won a contest with his plans for laying out the new city. It was designed on his proposed model.

At first the district was officially a territory, just like many of the states were before they became states. Unlike with other territories, though, the district was never intended to become a state, and has never had a governor. Until 1961 Americans who lived in the District of Columbia weren't even allowed to vote in presidential elections!

Slavery was abolished in the district in 1850 as a result of the political compromise of the same year (the Compromise of 1850, of course!). The territorial type of government was discontinued in 1874, and the president appointed a council to run the district's government. This lasted until 1967, when a mayor-council system was put in place. From 1967 until 1973, the president appointed the mayor and council members. In 1973, they became elected officials.

Fun Facts

THE SITE OF THE DISTRICT OF COLUMBIA

Located right on the Potomac River not far from George Washington's estate of Mount Vernon, the District of Columbia's location was personally selected by our first president. Many people since have wondered why he chose to build the nation's capital on what was at the time a swamp!

PUZZLE ANSWERS

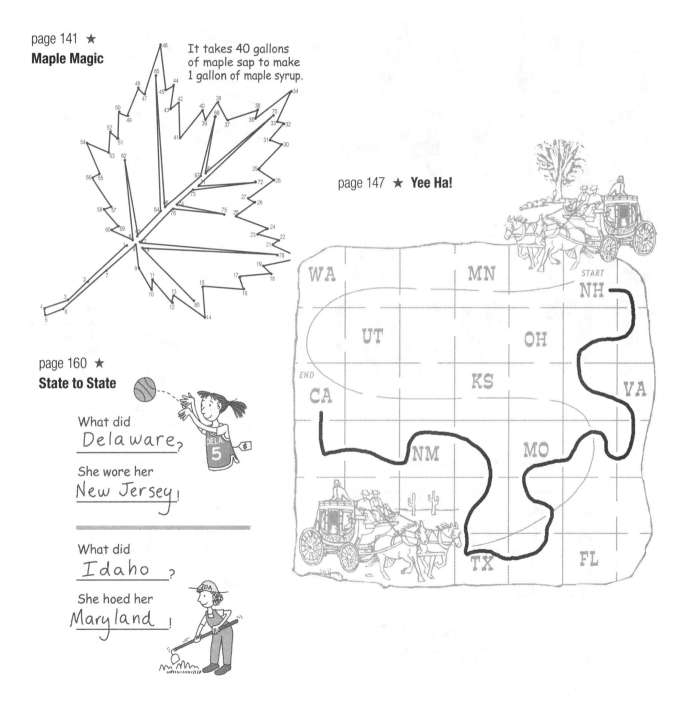

page 141 ★
Maple Magic

It takes 40 gallons of maple sap to make 1 gallon of maple syrup.

page 147 ★ **Yee Ha!**

page 160 ★
State to State

What did
Delaware?

She wore her
New Jersey!

What did
Idaho?

She hoed her
Maryland!

page 169 ★ **One to Grow On**

HAPPY BIRTH-
DAY
TO YOU

page 179 ★ **Pickles?**

page 184 ★ **Where are my glasses?**

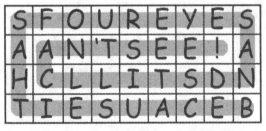

S	F	O	U	R	E	Y	E	S
A	A	N'T	S	E	E	!	A
H	C	L	L	I	T	S	D	N
T	I	E	S	U	A	C	E	B

**Because it has four
eyes and still can't see!**
(I's)

page 189 ★ **Get in Shape**

The state flag of Ohio
is triangular, with
two pointed tails.

page 192 ★ **Crossing Indiana**

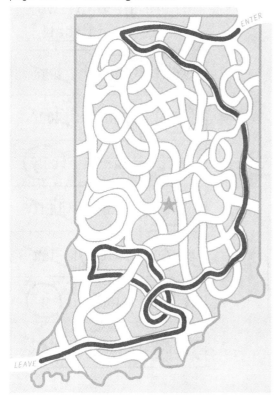

page 205 ★ **Rock 'n' Roll**

W 23rd	H F+2	A 1st	T R+2		S 19th	O before P	U 21st	T S+1	H J-2
D A+3	A E-4	K L-1	O after N	T V-2	A Z-25	N 14th			
R 18th	O M+2	C 3rd	K J+1		G F+1	R S-1	O Q-2	U T+1	P 16th
H 8th	A 1st	S 19th		F D+2	O M+2	U 21st	R P+2		
M L+1	E 5th	N 14th		W Z-3	H 8th	O Q-2			
D 4th	O M+2	N P-2	' T 20th		S 19th	I G+2	N 14th	G I-2	?

M after L	O Q-2	U V-1	N M+1	T 20th
R Q+1	U 21st	S before T	H 8th	M before N	O N+1	R after Q	E 5th	!

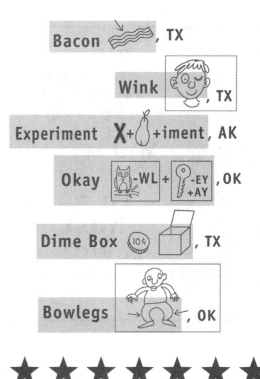

Bacon ⌇⌇, TX

Wink 😉, TX

Experiment X + 🍐 +iment, AK

Okay 🦉-WL + 🔑 -EY+AY, OK

Dime Box 🪙10¢ 📦, TX

page 214 ★ **You Live Where?**

Bowlegs → 🧍 ←, OK

page 221 ★ Life in LA

The

Jean Lafitte had a hideaway in Louisiana.

The brown

is the Louisiana state bird.

page 257 ★ Scared Silly

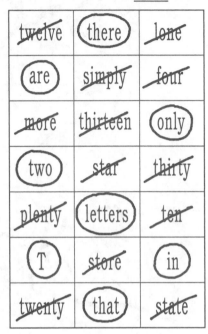

page 226 ★ Totally Texas

There are only two letters T in <u>that</u>!

~~twelve~~	(there)	~~lone~~
(are)	~~simply~~	~~four~~
~~more~~	~~thirteen~~	(only)
(two)	~~star~~	~~thirty~~
~~plenty~~	(letters)	~~ten~~
(T)	~~store~~	(in)
~~twenty~~	(that)	~~state~~

page 260 ★ **The Only One**

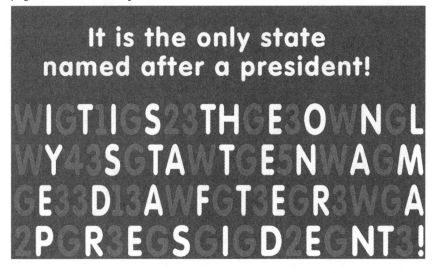

It is the only state
named after a president!

The number of states:

50

page 263 ★ **Big and Small**

MULTIPLY by the
number of states with
four letters in their name:

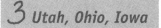

3 *Utah, Ohio, Iowa*

MULTIPLY by
number of states that
start with the letter O:

3 *Oregon, Oklahoma, Ohio*

SUBTRACT the
total number of letters in
Idaho, Missouri, Pennsylvania:

25

ANSWER:
The state of Rhode Island
could fit into Alaska

_425_ times!

Part 3

Way Cool
Science Experiments

INTRODUCTION

What does it take to be a great scientist? Think of the most famous scientists you know—Isaac Newton, Louis Pasteur, Albert Einstein, Thomas Edison, Pierre and Marie Curie, Stephen Hawking, and so on. What do all these people have in common? Well, for one thing, they're all very smart. In some cases they even taught themselves most of what they knew about their particular subject. In fact, Sir Isaac Newton had to invent a new branch of mathematics (calculus) just to solve the problems he was trying to do in physics. There is something else they all had in common that set them apart from the other smart people of their time—their ability to ask questions.

Just having a good brain isn't always enough. To be a great scientist, you need to be able to look at a problem that hundreds, maybe even thousands, of people have already looked at and been unable to solve, and ask the question in a new way. Then you take that question and come up with a new way to answer it. That is what made Newton and the others so famous. They coupled intelligence with a curiosity that said, "I want to know the answer to this." After coming up with the right questions, they discovered ways of answering those questions and ultimately became famous for their discoveries.

Could you be the next Thomas Edison and invent something the world has waited for, or the next Isaac Newton and answer a question no one has been able to answer? Absolutely! To do it requires something all kids have naturally and many grown-ups wish they still had—curiosity.

This section will help you to tap into that curiosity by introducing you to five major areas of science—Biology, Chemistry, Physics, the Earth and Sky, and the Human Body. You will be presented with several questions that will help you to begin thinking like a scientist. Perhaps you've asked some of these questions before; for example, why is the sky blue? Some of them will probably be new to you.

Since asking the right question is only the first step toward being a great scientist, this book will also guide you in completing the second step: the experiment. Following each question there will be an experiment that will help you discover for yourself some of the mystery and magic of science. There are three different types of experiments offered in this section—simple activities you can do quickly, larger and more complex experiments, and science fair projects.

Why did the young scientist bring art supplies to science-class?

She wanted to draw some-conclusions!

THE SCIENTIFIC METHOD

First, let's take a look at the starting point for all scientific experiments: the Scientific Method. It was made famous by an Italian man named Galileo in the sixteenth century. It is simple and will help you ask and answer many of the questions you have about science. There are five parts to the Scientific Method:

1. Observe some activity in the world around you.
2. Make up a possible explanation for that activity, called a hypothesis.
3. Use your hypothesis to make predictions about the activity.
4. Test those predictions.
5. Come to a conclusion about your hypothesis and its ability to predict the activity.

Scientists have used this method for hundreds of years to understand their world. Now it's your turn!

The fun of this section lies in the fact that you can start reading just about anywhere and follow the idea as far as you like. And if this book doesn't take the idea as far as you would-like to go, use your imagination and keep exploring the idea. You are invited to join this exciting journey into the world of experimental science. Welcome aboard—let's begin the journey!

Quote Fall

Can you figure out where to put each of the scrambled letters? They all fit in spaces under their own column. When you correctly fill in the grid, you will have a quote from the brilliant scientist Albert Einstein. His theories and experiments led to an entirely new way of thinking about time, space, matter, energy, and gravity!

(All puzzle answers are located at the end of the book.)

T	O		T	T		O					
T	H		N	G	O	I	I		N	O	
Q	H	E	S	S	M	P	P	R	N	A	T
T	U	E	I	I	I	O	N	S	T	G	T

CHAPTER 20

BIOLOGY

Life. We all have it. The world around us is full of it, from the birds in the air to-the fish in the sea and all the land animals in between. But how does life really work? If you can answer that question, you will gain insight into one of the most widely studied topics in the natural world.

TRY THIS WATER COLORS

Humans and other animals are very complex creatures. So let's first consider plants. Plants seem to be simple examples of the way life works. You plant them in the ground, water them, and let the sun shine on them. Pretty soon, they grow, they bloom, and then they die. But inside a plant, there are processes happening that we don't see—processes unlike anything else we encounter. Let's begin to understand these processes with what everyone knows is the most important resource a plant can get: water.

QUESTION

How does water get from the ground to the leaves of a plant?

MATERIALS

4 full glasses of water at room temperature
Red, blue, green, and yellow food coloring 3 white carnations from a florist Sharp knife

PROCEDURE

1. Mix one color into each of your four glasses. The stronger the color of the water, the more effective the experiment will be.

2. Place your first carnation into the glass of your choice. You may need to trim the stem if it's too long.

3. Place your second carnation into another glass.

4. Take your final carnation and, with an adult's help, slice the stem lengthwise so that it looks like two smaller stems, both of which remain attached to the flower.

5. Place one half of the stem into your third glass of colored water and the other half into the fourth and final glass.

6. Place the flowers out of the sunlight and wait a day or so. Then look at each of the flowers.

WHAT'S HAPPENING

Through a process called capillary action, water travels up through the stems of plants until it reaches the outermost parts of the flowers. You saw this when the flower of each carnation turned the color of the water it was sitting in. Even more interesting is that the split stem produced a flower with both colors in it. You could easily repeat this experiment with other flowers and other colors to see if they behave in the same way. Celery stalks with the leaves on also work well in this experiment.

FOLLOW-UP

When you water the plants in your yard, should you water the leaves or the ground around the bottom of the plant?[1]

_____

_____

_____

_____

_____

_____

_____

_____

(The answers to all Follow-Up Questions are at the end of the book, starting on page 401. The number of the superscript marks the answer in-the back.)

WORDS to KNOW

capillary action: the process that allows water and other nutrients to move up from the ground to all parts of a plant.

Why did the silly scientist keep his shirt on when he took a bath?

Because the label said "Wash and Wear."

Science Online

ZooNet is a good starting point for information about animals, zoos, and more. Visit *www.zoonet.org*.

TRY THIS
FALLING LEAVES

Some trees stay green the whole year round while others lose their leaves in the fall and winter and grow new leaves in the spring. If you've ever seen trees lose their leaves in the fall, you may have noticed that the leaves turn from green to yellow, red, or orange before eventually falling to the ground.

QUESTION

Where do the leaves get their colors?

MATERIALS

4–5 spinach leaves
1 drinking glass
Spoon
Nail polish remover—ask a parent for
     help in getting this
Coffee filter
Scissors
Tape
Pencil

PROCEDURE

1. Tear the leaves into small pieces.
2. Place the pieces into the bottom of the glass and mash them together with a spoon.

3. Add several teaspoons of nail polish remover to the leaf mush. Wait until the leaves settle at the bottom of the nail polish remover. If the remover does not cover all the leaves, add enough so that they are totally covered.
4. Cut a rectangle from the coffee filter. It should be slightly narrower than the glass.
5. Tape the rectangle to the pencil and, when the leaves are settled, place the pencil across the top of the glass so that the coffee filter rests in the nail polish remover without touching the leaves.
6. Let the glass sit for several hours.

Cool Quotes

Autumn is a second spring when every leaf is a flower.

—Albert Camus,
French novelist

WHAT'S HAPPENING

You should see many colors work their way up the coffee filter. The green you see comes from the chemical that makes leaves green—**chlorophyll.** But you should also see other colors, like red, yellow, and orange. These come from different chemicals that are also found in green leaves.

During the spring and summer, **photosynthesis** produces so much chlorophyll you can see only the green color in the leaves. But as the days get shorter, less chlorophyll is produced and the green fades away so that you can finally see the other colors. When the green is gone, the leaf is not far from falling to the ground.

FOLLOW-UP

When fall comes, watch the leaves change color. Can you tell what causes this to occur?[2]

_____

_____

_____

_____

_____

_____

WORDS to KNOW

chlorophyll: the chemical in plants that makes their leaves green.

photosynthesis: the process by which plants turn sunlight and water into chlorophyll.

Fun Facts

Chlorophyll absorbs red and blue light and reflects green light back to your eyes.

What do you call a scientist who carries a dictionary in her jeans pocket?

A smarty pants!

KIDS' LAB LESSONS

QUESTIONS   Do seeds need light to grow? Do plants need light to grow?

EXPERIMENT OVERVIEW   You've already seen what happens to some trees when they don't get enough light—they lose their leaves. But plants and trees are different. In this experiment, you'll get to explore whether or not seeds and plants need light to grow by placing some seeds and plants in the dark while others stay in the light. You will decide whether or not light makes a difference in their growth pattern. This experiment will take a few days since most processes with plants occur very slowly, but the results should be obvious and a little surprising.

SCIENCE CONCEPT   Most gardeners believe that light and water are the basic needs of any plant. You'll test that theory by letting some seeds grow in a dark setting while others grow in a light setting. You'll then take two healthy plants and place one in a dark closet for a few days while the other sits in the sunshine. By doing this you will be using one of the most important pieces of the Scientific Method—testing one change at a time. It's important that you treat the seeds and plants exactly the same except for where they are placed. By doing so, you will know whether light makes a difference.

MATERIALS
2 paper towels
2 small dishes
Pinto beans (available at a grocery store)
Water
2 small, identical, healthy potted plants

PROCEDURE

1. Fold the paper towels so that each fits onto a dish.
2. Place the folded paper towel on a dish and place several beans on each paper towel.
3. Pour just enough water onto the paper towel so that it is damp. Pour out any excess water from the dish.
4. Place one dish of beans in a closet where it will stay dark for several days.
5. Water the potted plants until their soil is just damp and place one of the plants beside the beans in the same dark location.
6. Place the second dish of beans in a well-lit place alongside the second plant.
7. After two days have passed, slightly dampen the two dishes containing the beans and water the potted plants. Make sure that you give each the same amount of water so you keep the experiment fair.
8. After a total of four days have passed, take the beans and plant out of the closet and place each by its sunlit partner.

QUESTIONS FOR THE SCIENTIST

• Which sample of beans grew better—the one in the dark or the one in the light?

_____

• Which sample of potted plant grew better—the one in the dark or the one in the light?_____

• If you were going to plant seeds, where would you put them—in a light place or in a dark place? _____

• Think about the amount of light where seeds and plants normally grow. Does this experiment confirm that those locations are the best places for growing?_____

_____

• Do some seeds require different amounts of light? Experiment with different kinds of seeds and amounts of sunlight to see what factors most affect germination and growth._____

Totally Tubular

Can you find your way through all the tiny tubes in this leaf from START to END?

END

START

TRY THIS HOLE-Y WALLS

Another amazing talent plants have is the ability to absorb water right through their skin. This process is called **osmosis**, and you can do an experiment that shows how it works.

QUESTION

Can liquid really pass through walls?

MATERIALS

2 wide glasses or measuring cups
Water
Tincture of iodine (available at a drugstore)
Cornstarch
A small, sealable plastic bag

PROCEDURE

1. Fill both glasses approximately three-quarters full of water.
2. In one glass, mix two teaspoons of iodine with the water.
3. In the other glass, mix one tablespoon of cornstarch with the water, and pour about half of it into the plastic bag.
4. Seal the plastic bag and place it into the iodine mixture. You may need to wash the bag with water to make sure there is no cornstarch on the outside when you place it in the iodine.

5. Allow the bag to sit in the iodine for an hour and observe the changes that occur during that time. Meanwhile, drop a few drops of iodine into the glass with cornstarch in it and observe what happens.

WORDS to KNOW

osmosis: a process in which liquids pass through the walls of-cells.

WHAT'S HAPPENING

The cornstarch mixture turns a dark color when iodine is present. This was proved when you dropped the iodine into the second glass. Iodine also turns color when in the presence of a starch. However, you didn't see the iodine mixture in the first glass ever turn color. Somehow, iodine has passed through the wall into the plastic bag, but the cornstarch was not able to pass into the iodine. Cornstarch molecules are large, compared to those of iodine. More important, iodine molecules are smaller than the holes in the plastic bag (yes, there *are* holes in those bags!), so they can pass through. However, the holes are too small to allow cornstarch molecules to pass so they are held inside the bag. Thus the iodine mixture remains its original color.

Science Online

Learn about gardening from experts at Better Homes and Gardens. Visit *www.bhg.com/gardening/*.

KIDS' LAB LESSONS

QUESTION   Can you blow up a balloon with a banana?

EXPERIMENT OVERVIEW   In this experiment, you will watch as a banana decomposes over time and inflates a balloon. The process is not something you can see, but the effects are unmistakable. As a follow-up, you can try other fruits to see if they produce the same results as they decompose.

SCIENCE CONCEPT   Eventually, plants die. A banana is the fruit produced by a banana tree, and anyone who has ever seen a banana ripen and turn brown before it could be eaten will know that as it ripens and dies, it undergoes dramatic changes. When a banana decomposes, **bacteria** flock to it. Bacteria are so small you can't see them. But not only are they there, they multiply and multiply by eating what's left of the banana. In this manner of processing food, they give off gas. Not a lot of gas, but with enough bacteria present, the gas will inflate the balloon. Your challenge, once you complete this experiment, is to try other fruits to see if they produce the same results.

MATERIALS
A very ripe banana
A bowl
A small-mouth plastic or glass bottle
A balloon

bacteria: tiny organisms that live in everything. Some can make you sick, but many of them help keep you healthy.

PROCEDURE

1. Peel the banana (make sure it is very ripe) and mash it in the bowl until the lumps are gone.
2. Carefully scoop the banana mush into the bottle. This might be a little tricky (and messy!), but with patience, it can be done. (You may also want to try using a plastic knife to scoop the banana mush into the bottle. This may be easier.)
3. Place the balloon over the mouth of the bottle.
4. Place the bottle in a warm, sunny spot and watch the bottle over the course of a few days.
5. Measure the distance around the balloon each day to track the progress of the banana's decay.

QUESTIONS FOR THE SCIENTIST

- What is causing the balloon to inflate? _____
- What is happening to the banana? _____
- How long did it take for the balloon to begin inflating? _____

FOLLOW-UP

Now that you have the procedure down, try mashing other ripe fruit (like apples, oranges, grapes, melons) and repeating the experiment. By comparing the growth rate of each fruit's balloon, you will be able to determine which fruit decays the fastest.

CLEAN-UP

Be sure to clean up this experiment near a sink or somewhere outside. The smell is likely to be unpleasant and strong. Carefully dispose of all your materials before starting over.

Scientific Transformation

Can you turn a banana into a balloon in four steps? Start with the word BANANA on line one. In each of the next steps you can move one letter, change one letter into another (or two of the same letters into two other letters that are the same), or add one letter. Keep track of your changes on the empty lines.

1. BANANA

2. _____

3. _____

4. _____

5. _____

Fun Facts

The largest worm ever found was 22 feet long.

ANIMALS

The animal kingdom includes more than 1 billion different sizes, shapes, and species. Some people spend their whole lives studying animals and barely even scratch the surface of all there is to learn. When you're a kid, though, some of the most interesting groups of creatures are found right in your backyard—the creepers, the crawlers, and the buzzers.

TRY THIS LIGHT FRIGHT

If you've ever been in your yard after a hard rain, or had the chance to dig up a large rock from your garden, chances are, you've run across a worm. Besides their being great for catching fish, most of us don't know a lot about worms. They may be a little odd to look at, and it may seem as though they don't serve much of a purpose, but worms are very important to the earth. They actually make soil better for growing.

QUESTION

Do worms prefer light or darkness?

MATERIALS

Shoe box	Earthworms, either from your
Scissors	yard or from a bait shop
Paper towels	Desk lamp

PROCEDURE

1. Cut off about one-third of the lid of the shoe box.
2. Thoroughly wet several pieces of paper towel and lay them on the bottom of the box.
3. Place the worms on the paper towels toward one end of the box. Try to space them evenly so they don't overlap one another. CAUTION: Make sure you handle the worms gently and with respect. A true scientist treats all creatures with care.
4. Place the lid on the box so the opening is on the same side as the worms.
5. Place the lamp above the box so that it sits about 1 to 2 feet higher than the top of the box.
6. Let the box sit for 15 to 30 minutes.
7. When you return, remove the lid and look at where the worms ended up.

WHAT'S HAPPENING

Worms tend to avoid light. That's why they like the dirt so much. When you shined the light into the box, most of them moved as far away from the light as they could get. In some cases, worms will even crawl under the paper towel to avoid the light. Worms can't see like we do, but they can sense light. When their **nervous system** senses the light, they immediately begin moving away from it.

FOLLOW-UP

With a hand-sized magnifying glass, look at the worm's circulatory system. After your experiment, return your worms to the garden where they will help your plants grow.

WORDS to KNOW

nervous system: the system our bodies use to tell us how things feel.

Science Online

Worm Digest has a large store of-information about worms, composting, and gardening. Visit-*www.wormdigest.org*.

KIDS' LAB LESSONS

If you've ever left fruit out on the counter a little too long, you've probably noticed the flies that seem to be attracted to it. Here is an interesting experiment to study about fruit flies.

QUESTION   What do flies like to eat?

EXPERIMENT OVERVIEW   You will be taking an overripe banana and leaving it to rot inside an open jar. Next to the jar with the banana will be a jar with nothing in it. In time, fruit flies will flock to the banana and help the decomposition process. Then, seemingly out of nowhere, small creatures called **maggots** will appear as well. Meanwhile, the empty jar will sit untouched. Once you have seen these results, you'll be ready to extend the experiment to try other possibilities.

SCIENCE CONCEPT   For many years, scientists believed that rotting fruit, like your banana, caused spontaneous generation. This means that life could spring up from nothing. Now we know that fruit flies eat the rotting fruit and use energy from the fruit to lay their eggs. Then we see the maggots. The fruit flies perform an important role. In a compost bin, leftover food is stored so that as it decomposes, it can be turned into nutrient-rich soil. The fruit flies help speed up that same process in your banana.

WORDS to KNOW

maggots: tiny wormlike creatures that grow into fruit flies.

Fun Facts
Fruit flies live about two weeks.

MATERIALS
1 ripe banana
2 glass jars large enough to hold a banana

PROCEDURE
1. Peel the banana and place it into one of the jars. Leave the other jar empty.
2. Put the jars in a place they won't be disturbed for two weeks—preferably outdoors during warm weather.
3. Twice a day, observe the banana and keep a log of what you see. Include descriptions like color, consistency, smell, and the presence of flies or other living creatures.
4. Compare the contents of the empty jar to those of the jar with the banana.
5. After two weeks, look over your notes to mark the changes that occurred during that time.

QUESTIONS FOR THE SCIENTIST
- When did flies first appear? _____

- How long did it take for the banana to appear inedible? _____

- Where did the maggots come from? _____

- Can you think of any other creature that aids in the decomposing of discarded food? _____

FOLLOW-UP
Here are some variations on this experiment that you can try:
- Try putting a lid or a screen on the jar and see if you get the same results.
- Try another fruit, like an apple, orange, or a peach.
- Try placing the jars in different locations (light, dark, warm, cold, etc.).

TRY THIS
ANIMAL CAMOUFLAGE

If you know someone who has been trained in the military, you might have seen them in uniforms called fatigues. Sometimes they are called **camouflage** because these uniforms make it difficult for others to see the wearers when they are in hiding. But some animals, like the chameleon, do this naturally and serve as models for how to do it right.

QUESTION

How do animals blend into their surroundings?

MATERIALS

2 large sheets of construction paper in each of-three different colors
Scissors
A partner

PROCEDURE

1. Cut one sheet of each color into 2-inch by-2-inch squares.

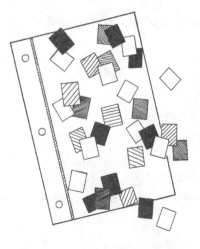

WORDS to KNOW

camouflage: how animals disguise themselves by blending into their surroundings.

2. Place all of the colored squares onto one of the large sheets while your partner closes his eyes.

3. When your partner opens his eyes, give him five seconds to grab as many colored squares as he can.

WHAT'S HAPPENING

Our eyes quickly notice sharp contrasts in color. You partner will usually pick out squares that are not the same color as the sheet they are lying on. When animals (and humans) use camouflage, they are taking advantage of the fact that when their colors match those around them (green frogs in grass, brown lizards on a tree branch) predators don't see any contrast, and the animals are somewhat hidden. If you placed a brown frog in the grass or a green lizard on a tree branch, that animal would stand out and would not be protected.

FOLLOW-UP

If you know someone who owns sunglasses called Blue Blockers, ask if you can try them on. When you do, what colors do you see most strongly? Do you know why this is?[3]

Eye Spy

Can you find the 10 creatures hiding in this picture?

KIDS' LAB LESSONS

QUESTION   Why are eggs shaped the way they are?

EXPERIMENT OVERVIEW   You will be exploring the shapes of eggs and the incredible strength they possess despite their fragile structure. By carefully preparing the eggs, you'll be able to place several books on top of four half-shells without cracking the shells. As a follow-up, you'll get to consider other versions of this test.

SCIENCE CONCEPT   Eggs are shaped the way they are for many reasons. A simple one is that the egg shape doesn't roll well. As a result, if a mother is sitting on her eggs and one gets away from her, it won't roll far before it comes to a stop. This allows the mother to quickly retrieve it. Try this before you begin the experiment. Gently roll an egg across the table or counter. Notice how its unique shape prevents it from rolling far like a ball would.

   Another reason for an egg's shape is that the dome shape gives it more strength than almost any other shape. Some people can place an egg in the palm of their hand and squeeze as hard as they can and not break the egg. The force of the hand is spread over the entire surface of the egg and nowhere is the force great enough to cause the egg to break. If you want to try this, you should either do it outside or in a large sink, for if you don't hold the egg just right, it will explode all over you!

MATERIALS
At least 4 raw eggs
Masking tape
Small scissors
Several books approximately the same size

PROCEDURE

1. Gently crack the eggs and break the shells as near to the middle (horizontally) as you can. If you don't get a good break, you'll need to try another egg.
2. Pour the raw eggs into a bowl and fry them up for your family.
3. Rinse and dry the empty half-shells.
4. Place one strip of tape around the open end of each shell, leaving the jagged edge exposed.
5. Use the scissors to trim off the jagged edges, taking care not to break the remaining shell.
6. You should now have four rounded egg bottoms and four pointed egg tops.
7. Select the rounded bottoms and place them in a rectangle on a table, approximately where the corners of your books will be.
8. Predict how many books your eggs will hold.
9. Gently add books until cracks first appear. This is the point when it becomes important that the egg supports are all about the same size. Note how many books caused the eggs to crack the first time.
10. Continue adding books until the eggs collapse.

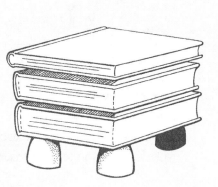

QUESTIONS FOR THE SCIENTIST

- Did your eggs hold more or less books than you predicted? _____
- Why do you think the eggs can hold so much weight when they can be broken so easily on the side of a mixing bowl? _____
- What changes could you make to this experiment so that, still using eggshells, even more books could be supported? _____

FOLLOW-UP   Try using the pointed ends of the eggs and repeating the experiment. Which end of the eggshell held more weight?

Think about the magicians who lie on beds of nails. How does this experiment explain the "trick"? Think about the use of snowshoes in lands where a large amount of snow falls. Do these walking aids have anything to do with your egg experiment?[4]

SCIENCE FAIR PROJECT: BIOLOGY

GRAVITY

You probably haven't ever seen a plant growing down toward the ground with its leaves reaching for the dirt and its roots facing the sun. Why not? Plants seem to know which way is up, and they grow so that their roots grow down into the soil, while their leaves and flowers grow up toward the sun. As a budding scientist noticing this, your next step is to wonder exactly how it is that plants know to grow the way they do. It's the perfect reason to design an experiment!

QUESTION

How do plants know to grow upward?

EXPERIMENT OVERVIEW

In this experiment, you'll start by testing the reaction of a potted plant to being tipped on its side. Once you've seen how a mature plant behaves, you'll grow beans and test them to see if they know which way is up.

SCIENCE CONCEPT

Find a hill in your town with trees growing on it, the steeper the better. Look closely at the direction the trunks are growing and you'll see that they grow straight up despite the fact that the hill slopes below them. Plants have a knack for sensing gravity and growing their roots down while the stems and leaves grow vertically upward. This is because of a chemical they have called auxin. Auxin makes plants grow longer and when gravity acts, the auxin tends to fall to the low side of a plant and its leaves. This makes the lower sides of the stem and leaves grow slightly longer, which turns the plant upward. Roots act differently, as they are a different part of the plant. On the root, the auxin causes slower growth. So, when auxin gathers on the lower side of the root, the upper side grows a little longer and the root turns downward. You'll get to observe both cases in this experiment.

MATERIALS

3 small, mature potted plants
Sunny location
Drinking glass
Water

Several pinto beans
Paper towel
Aluminum foil
Camera

PROCEDURE

MATURE PLANTS

1. Place all three potted plants in a sunny location, but tip one on its side toward the sun, tip another on its side away from the sun, and leave the third upright.

2. Water each plant as you would normally (you can turn them right-side-up to water them) and record their growth. This part of the experiment may take longer with some plants, so be patient. However, it shouldn't take too long for the tipped plants to try to right themselves.

SEEDS

1. Soak the beans in the glass filled with water overnight before starting.

2. Pour out the water and place the beans to one side of a paper towel, folded in-half.

3. Carefully, roll the beans up in the paper towel and wet it just so it's moist, but not dripping.

4. Fold a piece of aluminum foil around the paper towel so that the entire towel is covered and sealed.

5. Place the aluminum foil containing the beans into the glass with one end up and let the beans sit for one week.

6. After a week has passed, open the foil and carefully unroll the paper towel. Do not touch the beans as you will be using them again. You will be reusing both the foil and paper towel as well, so take care not to rip either.

7. Record the direction of growth of both the stem parts of the beans and the roots. They should be just beginning to grow and show that they have found "up" despite their orientation when you put them in the glass.

8. Take a picture of the beans to document their growth.

9. Moisten the beans as before, repack them in the paper towel and aluminum foil, and return them to the glass. But this time point the end that was originally up toward the bottom (turn the foil upside down).

10. After another week passes, open the foil and record the new growth. You should notice that after the original direction of growth, the beans adjusted to being placed upside down and continued their growth in the "right" direction. Take another picture for documentation.

QUESTIONS FOR THE SCIENTIST

• What did you observe about the growth of the potted plants?

• Was there a difference between the growth of the plant tipped toward the sun and the plant tipped away from the sun?

• How do you know that it was gravity and not the sun or another factor that made the plants grow the way they did?

• Did the beans grow in the direction you expected during the first week?

• After the second week, did the direction of the stems and roots change?

• Why do you think this change occurred?

• Can you tell that the beans started in one direction and then changed? How can you tell?

CONCLUSION

From the time they are just seeds, plants have the ability to know which way is up and immediately begin growing in that direction. Mature plants already have their root system in place, but will continually adjust the direction of stem and leaf growth in order to find up. Some plants that grow very tall will actually wind their way through and around obstacles in order to find their way up.

As a follow-up, you can plant your beans in soil by placing them on their sides and watch them adjust once more to the direction of gravity. Soon enough, the stems will pop through the soil and the roots will find their way to the bottom.

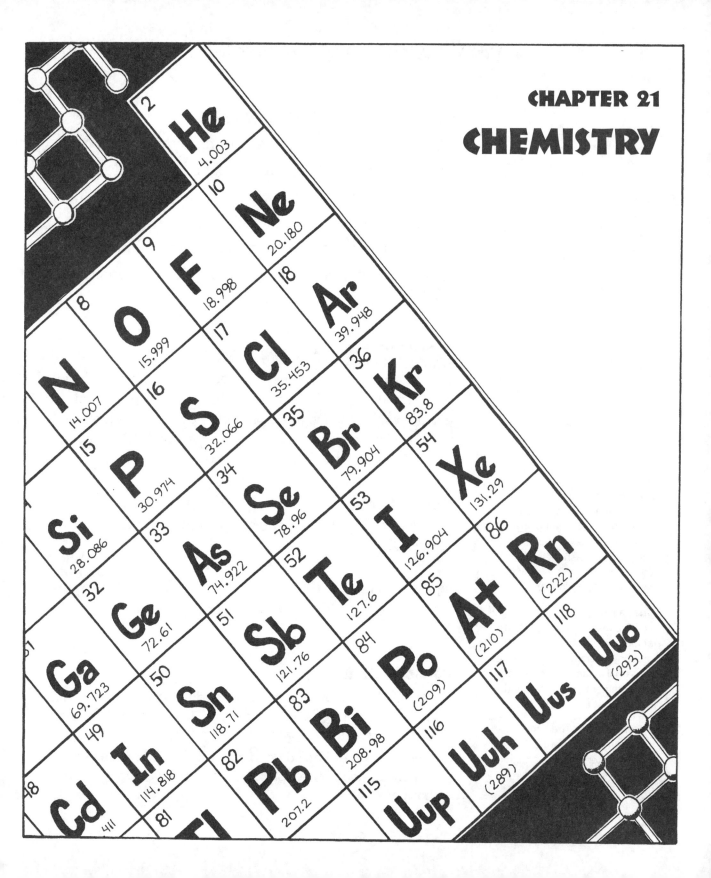

Fun Facts

When lakes freeze in the winter, they freeze from the top down. So as the top freezes, the water below is actually protected from the cold by the ice. This is how fish can survive.

WORDS to KNOW

solid: a state in which a material is hard and usually very dense. A solid will maintain its shape even outside a container.

liquid: a state in which a material is a fluid and is less dense than a solid, yet more dense than a gas. A liquid will assume the shape of its container, but won't expand in the container to do so.

gas: a high-energy state in which a material is a collection of molecules moving in random motion generally at high speeds. A gas will assume the shape of its container, but it will expand or compress in order to do so.

Second Law of Thermodynamics: heat always flows from a hotter object to a colder object.

CHEMICAL PROPERTIES

All materials you can see and many you can't are grouped by certain characteristics. Examples of these characteristics include density, pressure, temperature, volume, phase, and atomic makeup. In this chapter we'll look at questions relating to all-of-these, but we'll focus on phase, density, and-pressure.

TRY THIS BOILING ICE

Most materials with mass usually exist in three different phases: **solid**, **liquid**, or **gas**. Each of these phases has its own set of unique properties, and those properties describe the material in very special ways. Take water, for example. Do you know what it looks like in its solid, liquid, and gas forms?

QUESTION

Why does a pot of boiling water stop boiling when an ice cube is put in it?

MATERIALS

Pot of water   Several ice cubes
Stove

PROCEDURE

1. Set the pot of water on the stove and turn the burner on high until the water boils. You might need to ask for permission or some assistance for this step.
2. Once the water has come to a steady boil, place several ice cubes into the pot, keeping the water boiling. Observe what happens.

WHAT'S HAPPENING

The boiling should have stopped immediately. Why is this? It's because of the **Second Law of Thermodynamics.** According to this law, the heat coming from the burner will always flow to the coldest object in the pot—in this case, the ice. So the heat from the burner stops making the hot water boil and starts making the solid water melt.

FOLLOW-UP

When the ice finally melts, will the water start boiling right away?[1] Once the water boils again, notice the steam that rises from the pot. Where does it come from? It's just the same water in another state, a gas, and it's called water vapor. We see it when we take a shower in a cold room, and whenever we see clouds or fog in the sky.

Science Online

In 1869, a Russian chemist named Dmitri Mendeleev arranged all the known material in the universe into a chart that is now known as the Periodic Table of the Elements. Each element is defined by a certain arrangement of protons, electrons, and neutrons. The table is organized so that the elements are listed in order of their Atomic Number, the number of protons in the element.

Below you will find three links to interactive sites that show the Periodic Table.

Chemical Elements
www.chemicalelements.com
Chemicool
www.chemicool.com
Web Elements
www.webelements.com

Fun Facts

It takes nearly seven times more-energy to melt 1 kilogram of-ice than it does to boil 1-kilogram of water!

TRY THIS
FLOATING GRAPE

One of the many ways you can describe a material is by its density. Density is nothing more than the measure of how solid something is. For example, water is less solid than a chunk of concrete, and its density is less than that of concrete. Scientists use a formula involving mass (how much of the material there is) and volume (how much space the material takes up) to figure out an object's density. The less dense it is, the less tightly packed the particles are, and the more space it tends to take up.

Density is what makes balloons float up in the air, ice cubes float in your drink, and rocks sink to the bottom of a lake. But it can also be tricky! Here's a fun trick that is guaranteed to amaze your friends.

QUESTION

Can you make a grape float in the middle of a glass of water?

Cool Quotes

The whole of science is nothing more than a refinement of everyday thinking.

—Albert Einstein

MATERIALS

4 drinking glasses
Masking tape
Marker
1 larger glass or measuring cup
Water and sugar
Grapes
A spoon

PROCEDURE

NOTE: Before you do this for an audience, you should practice this by yourself. When you are ready to perform, you should have the glasses already prepared.

1. Using the masking tape and marker, label each glass as "#1," "#2," "#3," and "#4."

2. Fill the measuring cup with water and stir in enough sugar so that a grape will float at the surface of the water. If some sugar remains undissolved, allow it to fall to the bottom of the cup.

3. Fill Glass #1 full of water.

4. Place one grape into Glass #1 and observe what happens to it.

5. Fill Glass #2 with the sugar water solution you already prepared.

6. Place one grape into the sugar water solution. You should see it float at the surface.

7. Now fill Glass #3 half-full of the sugar water solution.

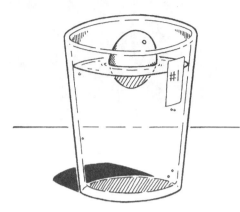

8. Slowly and carefully fill the rest of Glass #3 with plain water, taking care NOT to mix the heavier sugar water below it. You might want to place a spoon just inside the glass and pour the water so it falls onto the spoon before it hits the sugar water. This step may take a few tries to master, but when you are done, you should find that you can't tell the difference between the two liquids in Glass #3.

9. Place a grape gently into Glass #3 and observe what it does.

WHAT'S HAPPENING

The grape is denser than the water, so it sinks immediately to the bottom of the glass. The sugar water solution contains more matter in the same glass, so it is denser than the plain water. It is also denser than the grape, so the grape floats on top. The third glass is your "trick" glass. You know what is in it, but your unsuspecting audience does not. The grape sinks through the water, as it is denser than the water, but it floats on the surface of the sugar water solution since it is less dense than the

solution. If you prepare the solution far enough in advance, it will be almost impossible to detect the separation between the plain water and the sugar water.

FOLLOW-UP

With the final glass (#4), experiment to see if you can come up with a new sugar water solution that, when fully mixed, will cause the grape to float in the middle just like in Glass #3.

Fun Facts

The density of the sun is 1.41 times that of water. Here are the densities of the sun and all the planets in our Solar System as multiples of the density of water.

Sun:	1.41
Mercury:	5.43
Venus:	5.42
Earth:	5.52
Mars:	3.93
Jupiter:	1.33
Saturn:	0.69
Uranus:	1.32
Neptune:	1.64
Pluto:	2.06

KIDS' LAB LESSONS

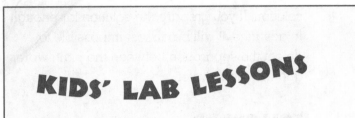

QUESTION   Can you make a liquid float?

EXPERIMENT OVERVIEW   You will be pouring liquids with different densities into the same container and producing a layered solution. Using colors, you will show how additional liquids poured into your solution find their way to the "right" layer. You will also "clean" some of the colored water and be invited to consider other possible color patterns.

SCIENCE CONCEPT   Ice cubes float in water because ice is less dense than water. In the same way, an oil spill tends to ride on the surface of the water because oil is also less dense than water. However, solid objects, or even thicker liquids, will sink in water because they are denser than the water. To compare the densities of two or more materials, you can set up a liquid test container with layers of liquids, each with different density. By noticing how the materials separate from one another, scientists can identify unknown materials. This makes it easier to clean up pollution in lakes and streams.

Fun Facts

The air we breathe is composed of several gases, but the two major ones are nitrogen and oxygen. The percentages are:

nitrogen (78%)
oxygen (21%)
other gases (1%)

MATERIALS

Red and blue food coloring
Measuring cup
1 cup corn syrup
Clear glass bottle—empty 24–32-ounce glass bottles
    work well
1 cup vegetable oil
½ cup water
½ cup liquid bleach (Be very careful with bleach. Always
    ask for an adult's help before using it.)

PROCEDURE

1. Mix red food coloring into a measuring cup filled with the corn syrup. Pour the syrup into the bottle.
2. Pour the oil into the bottle on top of the corn syrup. Do these liquids mix?
3. Mix blue food coloring into a measuring cup filled with the water. Pour the water into the bottle on top of the oil. Give it several minutes to settle. Where does the water go when you pour it into the bottle? Can you explain why it does this?
4. At this point, you should have three distinct layers in your bottle. The bottom layer will be red; the middle, a thinner layer of blue; and the top layer will be clear.
5. Now pour the bleach into the mixture and observe what happens to the blue water. Again, allow several minutes for the mixture to settle.

QUESTIONS FOR THE SCIENTIST

• What happened to the blue water?_____

• Can you describe where the bleach ended up?_____

• Why didn't the bleach mix with the syrup?_____

CONCLUSION   The first three liquids all have different densities and exist in layers in the bottle. When you added the bleach, it sank through the oil, because it is denser than oil. It is not as dense as corn syrup, so it did not sink through the bottom layer. This put it at the same layer as the blue water and it happens to mix easily with water. So the bleach and water were mixed and the bleach turned the blue water clear again!

FOLLOW-UP   It would be fun to make a mixture that has red, white, and blue bands, in that order. This would mean dyeing the oil (the top layer) either red or blue. Why isn't this possible in the setup you are using? _____

_____

TRY THIS

FLOATING WATER

Air is all around us. We breathe it, we use it to inflate the tires on our car, and we feel it when the wind blows. One of the surprising aspects of air is that we can't see it, we can't taste it, and only in certain cases can we feel, hear, or smell it. Yet it is a critical piece of our lives.

When air is in a container, it exerts pressure on its surroundings. This pressure is what creates wind and weather, it's what makes airplanes fly, it's what makes curve balls curve, and it's what keeps your car tires inflated and able to roll on the road. Simply put, air pressure is a part of everything we do.

Here's an easy magic trick to do that isn't really magic. Once you understand how air pressure works, you can amaze your friends once with the demonstration and then again when you explain how it works!

QUESTION

Can you make water float in the air?

MATERIALS

A small cup of water, clear plastic works best

A sink, bathtub, or tray to catch any water that falls while you practice this demonstration

A note card or other small piece of paper (the card must be large enough to fully cover the top of the cup)

PROCEDURE

1. Fill the cup about three-quarters full of water. The amount of water isn't that important, although you may find it more difficult to do this if the cup is full.

2. While the cup is held over the sink, slowly turn it over and observe how the water pours out of the cup.

3. Now refill the cup with water and place the card on top of the cup, making sure that it covers the entire top.

4. Press down gently but firmly on the card as you slowly rotate the cup upside down.

5. Keep your hand on the card for a few moments, then remove your hand. The card should stay in place and the water will appear to float inside the cup with nothing holding it up.

Cool Quotes

Imagination is more important than knowledge. Knowledge is limited. Imagination encircles the world.

—Albert Einstein

Egg-sactly!

Can you fill in the blanks to finish the following common sayings about eggs? Choose words from the Word List found in the bottom of the bottle.

WHAT'S HAPPENING

When you tipped the cup over the first time, the water ran out because gravity pulled it down toward the sink. The only way to prevent this from happening is to find some force that counteracts gravity. Enter air pressure.

When you add the card, you see the effects of air pressure. The air below the cup actually pushes up on the card, just like it pushes on everything around you. In this case, the upward force of air pressure is enough to cancel out the effect of gravity on the water and keep the water "floating" inside the cup.

Depending on the strength of the card you use, you may notice that eventually some water begins to leak out. As this happens, the seal begins to break and the card is no longer able to prevent gravity from winning the battle. Soon all the water will spill out.

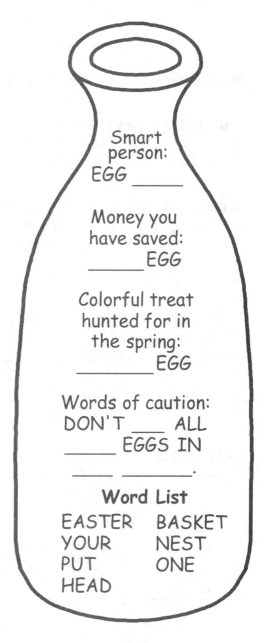

Smart person:
EGG _____

Money you have saved:
_____ EGG

Colorful treat hunted for in the spring:
_____ EGG

Words of caution:
DON'T ___ ALL _____ EGGS IN ____ _____.

Word List

EASTER   BASKET
YOUR   NEST
PUT   ONE
HEAD

KIDS' LAB LESSONS

QUESTION   Can you push an egg into a bottle without touching it?

EXPERIMENT OVERVIEW   Air has the ability to make objects move into and out of places where they otherwise would not fit. In this experiment, you will force a hard-boiled egg into a bottle without touching the egg.

SCIENCE CONCEPT   Air has an interesting behavior. It always flows from high pressure to low pressure. That is why when you get a hole in a tire on your bicycle the air leaks out. In this experiment, you'll be placing a hard-boiled egg between high pressure (the outside air) and low pressure (the air inside the bottle). Air wants so badly to get inside the bottle, it will push away anything in its way (the egg)! You'll use this principle to get the egg in.

   To make it work, you will have to lower the pressure inside the bottle so much that the outside air forces the egg into the bottle. You will do this by placing lit matches inside the bottle. The matches will burn until the oxygen inside the bottle has been consumed. At this point, there is less air (since some of it was consumed by the fire) inside the bottle than there previously was, which results in decreased air pressure. As the outer air pushes into the bottle, the egg slides in.

MATERIALS
Wide-mouth bottle (20–32-ounce juice bottles will work but make sure that the egg
   is just barely too big. If the opening is too small, the egg will probably get stuck.)
1 hard-boiled egg with the shell removed
3 matches
A very small piece of paper (1" × 1")

PROCEDURE

Insertion

1. Place the hard-boiled egg on the mouth of the bottle. It should sit comfortably without falling off. You may try to push the egg into the bottle to verify that it does not easily fit.
2. Remove the egg and place three lit matches into the bottle with the paper. Use matches only with adult supervision!
3. Quickly replace the egg on the mouth of the bottle, effectively sealing the top of the bottle.
4. Watch as the matches go out and the egg is pulled down into the bottle.

Removal

1. Turn the bottle upside down so the egg falls into the opening without coming out. Blow into the opening. (It is recommended to have an adult do this part.)
2. As the pressure inside the bottle increases, the egg should be pushed out of the bottle into your mouth.

QUESTIONS FOR THE SCIENTIST

- Why did the egg get pushed into the bottle? _____

_____

- What did the burning matches have to do with this experiment? _____

_____

- What are some other examples of air flowing from high pressure to low pressure?

_____

WORDS to KNOW

acid: materials that taste sour, like lemon. If strong enough, these can burn your skin.

base: materials that taste bitter, like ground coffee. If strong enough (for example, ammonia or bleach), these can also be dangerous.

Fun Facts

pH is what scientists use to measure the acidity of a substance. A pH value of 7.0 is called neutral, while a value higher than 7.0 indicates a base. pH values lower than 7.0 indicate acids. Here are some sample pH values for common foods:

Food	pH
Lemons	2.3
Strawberries	3.2
Tomatoes (whole)	4.6
Potatoes	6.1
Sweet corn	7.3
White eggs	8.0

CHEMICAL REACTIONS

Have you ever taken a bite of a lemon and had your mouth pucker up because it was so sour? Have you ever wondered why some foods taste the way they do? One reason is because of things called **acids** and **bases.** Lemons and other citrus fruits are filled with citric and ascorbic acids (vitamin C), which provide a wide range of health benefits. But they also make them taste sour. On the other hand, some foods we eat are called bases. They are on the other end of the acid scale and taste bitter. Bases include items such as baking soda (to make baked goods rise), antacid tablets (to help against indigestion and heartburn), and some soaps.

TRY THIS

RED CABBAGE INDICATOR

There are plenty of fancy ways to test to see if something is an acid or a base, but you can also do it simply in the comfort of your own home.

QUESTION

How can you figure out if something is an acid or a base?

MATERIALS

Cabbage **indicator**—the liquid from a jar of pickled red cabbage, available at the grocery store
Eyedropper

1 small plate for each of the materials you wish to test. Below
   are some samples:
   Lemon juice
   Orange juice
   Baking soda
   Vinegar
   Antacid tablet
   Tea bag—mix with water to make tea
   Ground coffee

WORDS to KNOW

indicator: a liquid (like the juice of a red cabbage) that tells you if something is an acid or a-base.

PROCEDURE

1. Pour some of the indicator into several small plates.

2. Drop a small amount of each test item onto a plate and watch what happens to the indicator.

Cool Quotes

The most exciting phrase to hear in science, the one that-heralds new discoveries, is not "Eureka!" (I found it), but- "That's funny...."

—Isaac Asimov, author and biochemist

WHAT'S HAPPENING

With some of the test samples, the indicator will turn a pink color. That is your clue that you've tested an acid. Other samples should have turned the indicator greenish blue. Those are the bases. Now that you know what to look for, can you find other acids and bases in your kitchen?

CAUTION: Some acids are very dangerous to humans. Be careful not to get any of the samples on your skin, and never try to eat or drink things that you are experimenting with.

TRY THIS
RAW EGG PEELER

Now that you know how to find acids, you are ready to see what an acid can do to a common kitchen item.

QUESTION

How can you peel a raw egg?

MATERIALS

Raw egg   Vinegar   Small glass

PROCEDURE

1. Place the egg into the glass.
2. Pour enough vinegar into the glass to cover the entire egg.
3. Let it sit for a few days.
4. You should return to find that the eggshell has disappeared and your raw egg has become see-through. You may need to rub the surface to remove the last parts of the shell.

WHAT'S HAPPENING

The acid in vinegar slowly ate away at the eggshell until none of it remained. When you returned to find the see-through egg, you were really seeing the thin membrane that holds the egg inside the shell. You may have noticed quite a bit of bubbling during the "peeling" process. Eggshells are made of calcium carbonate, which reacts with vinegar (an acid) and makes calcium acetate, carbon dioxide (the bubbles you see), and water.

Amazing Bubbles

Can you find your way from START to END without bursting any of the bubbles?

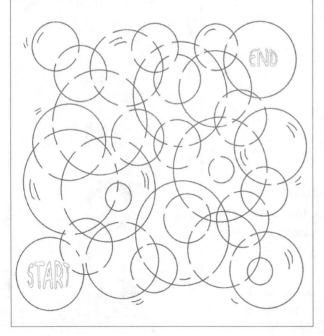

TRY THIS
FOAMING AT THE MOUTH

You put something in your mouth every day that has the ability to produce bubbles in a similar fashion to the previous experiment. However, this doesn't involve any acids, just toothpaste and a can of soda.

QUESTION
How can I make myself foam at the mouth?

MATERIALS

Baking soda toothpaste	**Carbonated soda** or water
Toothbrush	Sink

WORDS to KNOW

carbonated soda: a soft drink that has carbon dioxide gas in it, making it fizzy.

PROCEDURE

1. Brush your teeth with the toothpaste as you normally would.
2. Instead of spitting when you are done, open your mouth and take a sip of the carbonated soda or water. You should feel fizzing in your mouth.
3. Open your mouth and let the foam come rolling out!

CAUTION: This should be performed only under adult supervision. Also, make sure you have a place for the foam to flow into. Never try to swallow it or keep it in your mouth. You could get very sick from swallowing too much of this mixture.

WHAT'S HAPPENING

The ingredients of baking soda toothpaste are designed to make some bubbles, as you've probably noticed during your normal brushing routine. Adding the carbonated beverage, which has carbon dioxide gas, produces a reaction that will keep the bubbles coming and coming.

Fun Facts

New dental cleaning techniques involve using baking-soda as an abrasive in-place of scraping.

Baking soda toothpaste is an effective way of removing crayon marks from walls.

KIDS' LAB LESSONS

QUESTION   What makes things fizzy?

EXPERIMENT OVERVIEW   In this experiment, you will produce different combinations of mixtures that react to form fizzy **solutions.** You'll start with a baking soda/vinegar mixture, and then move on to make your own safe-to-drink, though not particularly tasty, lemon soda.

SCIENCE CONCEPT   Certain materials, when brought into contact with other materials, react in a way that forms bubbles. Acids and bases often combine to form carbon dioxide, which, as a gas, is what makes carbonated soda fizzy. You'll be experimenting with several common ingredients to determine which react in this way.

MATERIALS

Part I
½ cup vinegar
20-ounce glass bottle
2 tablespoons baking soda
¼ cup water

Part II
Food coloring
A pitcher of water
3 teaspoons baking soda
2 tablespoons sugar
2 tablespoons lemon juice

Part III
Large glass filled with water
Small (¼ pound at the largest) piece of dry ice (available at many grocery stores or fish markets—you may need an adult to buy and handle it for you)

solution: a mixture of two or more liquids.

PROCEDURE

Part I

1. Pour vinegar into the bottle.
2. Dissolve baking soda in water and pour the mixture into-the bottle.
3. Watch what happens.

Part II

1. With the food coloring, color the water in your pitcher any color you like. This is just for looks, but you will be able to drink your concoction when you are done, so pick a color you would like to drink.
2. Stir in baking soda and sugar. Mix until they dissolve.
3. Add lemon juice and watch your drink become carbonated!

Part III

1. Place the dry ice in the water and watch what happens. CAUTION: Dry ice is very cold and should be handled only with gloves with close adult supervision.

QUESTIONS FOR THE SCIENTIST

• What kinds of materials reacted to make bubbles? _____

• How did your soda taste? Can you think of any ingredients you could add to improve the taste? _____

• Would your lemon drink work with any other fruit's juice? Which fruits do you think would work? _____

• Could you use dry ice to make a carbonated soft drink? _____

What size T-shirt do you buy for a 200-pound egg?

Eggs-tra Large!

Science Online

For a fun look at how money is made and how much money is made, check out the U.S. Mint's Web site at *www.usmint.gov*.

TRY THIS CLEANING PENNIES

Some chemical reactions can take dirty objects and make them clean by removing the dirt. Detergents do this with the dirt on your clothes and your dishes, and the soap you use in the bath or shower does the same for your body. But what about metals? They are harder to clean.

QUESTION

How do you clean a penny?

MATERIALS

Vinegar
Glass jar
Dirty pennies
1 teaspoon salt

PROCEDURE

1. Pour vinegar into the jar until it is about half full.
2. Stir in salt until it dissolves.
3. Drop several dirty pennies into the vinegar.
4. After a few minutes, take out half of the pennies and lay them on a paper towel to-dry.

5. Remove the other pennies and rinse them with water before letting them dry.

6. Note the differences between the two groups of pennies after they have been out of the vinegar/salt solution for a while.

WHAT'S HAPPENING

The vinegar/salt solution is able to loosen the residue on the pennies, which is called copper oxide. With this residue removed, the pennies are shiny once more. When you rinse them off, the cleaning stops and they remain shiny. The unrinsed pennies still have some of the solution on them, and when oxygen in the air hits them, a new reaction occurs, turning the pennies a bluish-green color.

FOLLOW-UP

Try this same experiment with nickels, dimes, and quarters. Do you get the same results?[2]

_____

_____

_____

_____

_____

_____

_____

_____

Acid Bath

Oops! This young scientist tried to clean his friends' copper ID bracelets. But the acid was too strong and it removed part of each letter! Question: Can you add the missing lines to complete the letters and see to whom each bracelet belongs?

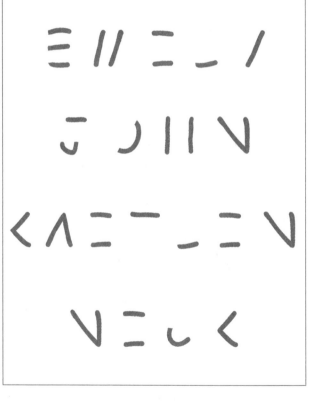

319

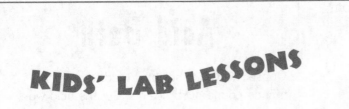

QUESTION   How are metal things made shiny?

EXPERIMENT OVERVIEW   Electroplating is the process of taking a metal and using it to coat something else. It is a complex process involving electricity and is difficult to perform in a home laboratory. This experiment is not electroplating in the true sense, but it does produce a transfer of copper from the pennies to the nails.

SCIENCE CONCEPT   It's possible to remove atoms of a material (like copper) and have them float around in a liquid without you seeing them. To retrieve them, you simply need to make them want to attach to the metal you want to coat. In this case, the vinegar/salt solution removes copper oxide atoms (the "dirt" on the pennies), and when they dissolve, they form copper atoms that want to attach to another metal. The nails attract the copper atoms floating in the water, and the atoms stick to them, coating them with copper.

MATERIALS
Vinegar/salt solution prepared as described in the
   "Cleaning Pennies" activity on page 40
Two clean nails or metal paper clips
Dirty pennies

electroplating: a process that uses one metal to coat another metal.

PROCEDURE

1. Prepare a solution of vinegar and salt as described in the previous activity.
2. Soak the dirty pennies in the vinegar/salt solution until they are clean.
3. Remove the pennies and set them aside.
4. Place your nails into the remaining solution and let them sit for a few hours.
5. When you are ready to remove the nails, remove them carefully and look closely to see if they have changed color. If they have not done so noticeably, return them to the solution. If you want to speed up the process, place more dirty pennies in the solution along with your nails.

QUESTIONS FOR THE SCIENTIST

- What is the coating on the nails? _____
- Why can't you see that coating in the solution before you place the nails in it?

_____

CONCLUSION

You are observing a pretty amazing process. The acid solution not only removes the dirt (which is a combination of copper and oxygen called copper oxide), but in doing so, leaves copper atoms floating in the solution. These atoms are so small you can't see them, but they will float in the acid solution until they find a negatively charged metal to stick to. When you place the nails in the acid, some of-their atoms are also removed and they are left with a negative charge. The copper atoms are attracted to the nails and stick to them, giving them a slight copper tint.

SCIENCE FAIR PROJECT: CHEMISTRY

BUILD A HOME BAROMETER

When you watch the evening news, the weather reporters often refer to the barometric pressure as an indicator of both current conditions and the predicted weather. In particular, they will tell you if the pressure is rising or falling. Generally, falling pressure, or the presence of a low pressure system, indicates bad weather, and rising pressure, or the presence of a high pressure system, indicates improving weather. When air warms up, pressure tends to increase, while cooling air is usually accompanied by lower pressure. You will also find this if you climb a mountain. At the higher elevations, the air is thinner, which means the pressure is lower, and the air is also usually cooler.

It's not hard to build your own barometer that will allow you to predict the weather from the comfort of your own home.

QUESTION

How does a barometer work?

EXPERIMENT OVERVIEW

You will be building your own home barometer, which will allow you to track the weather over several days and predict the weather to come. You will be using water levels in an empty 2-liter bottle to record the rise and fall of the atmospheric pressure. After you gather a few days' worth of data, you'll be able to compare your predictions to those of the local weather forecasters!

SCIENCE CONCEPT

Barometers are used to measure the air pressure outside at any given time. They can also be used to predict the weather. This requires tracking pressure values over time to determine if there is a trend toward increased pressure or toward lowered pressure.

By measuring the height of the water in your bottle due to the air pressure outside the bottle, you'll have a way to compare one day's value to another. Over time, you can use the changing heights to make your own predictions.

MATERIALS

Empty 2-liter plastic bottle (smaller bottles will work as well)   Marking pen
Fish tank   Paper
Water   Knife or scissors

PROCEDURE

1. Use a knife or scissors to cut the bottom off the plastic bottle so that it sits evenly on the table. You may need to ask for help from an adult for this step.

2. Fill the pan about half full of water.

3. With the bottom cut off of the bottle, the cap must be screwed on and, inverted, the neck of the bottle becomes the bottom when filling. Fill the bottle with enough water so that when inverted, the water level inside the bottle is above that of the pan. It will look a little like a funnel as it is filled. Then it will be inverted and placed into the pan of water. Place the bottle in the water so that it sits evenly on the bottom of the pan. Make a small mark on the bottle indicating the height of the water.

4. Take a strip of paper and make a scale with evenly marked intervals. There should be a zero point on your strip of paper, with several markings above and below that mark. You will use this to track the changing heights of the water. To accurately show the small increments that you will want to measure, make your scale fairly small, perhaps starting with markings every $1/8$ inch.

5. Attach your measuring scale to the side of the bottle, placing the zero point at the exact level of the water in the bottle.

6. Make one mark on your measuring scale at the beginning water level. Use your mark to indicate the date of your first measurement.

7. Wait 24 hours and measure again. Make another mark to represent your second measurement.

8. Continue measuring each day for one week. After the week has passed, take off the measuring scale, and look at your measurements.

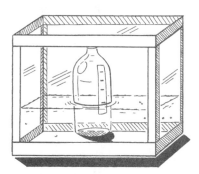

QUESTIONS FOR THE SCIENTIST

- Did the height of the water change over the week?

- Did the height go up or down?

- What kind of change in air pressure produces this kind of change in your water level?

- What kind of weather would you predict based on the change in heights?

- Did your local weather match this prediction?

Now that you have tried this experiment, you can repeat it by making more measuring scales and actually predicting the upcoming weather.

Congratulations! You are a **meteorologist!**

WORDS to KNOW

meteorologist: a person who studies and reports weather conditions.

CONCLUSION

If air pressure increases, the outside air will press down on the water in the pan and push it up into the bottle. This will produce an increase in height of the water. When weather forecasters use the term "inches of mercury," they are using a similar scale to measure the height of a different liquid due to the outside air pressure.

If the weather was pretty consistent during the course of the week, you may not have seen much change in your barometer. Don't be discouraged! Try it again, and give yourself more time. This experiment will work all year long.

MOTION

Playgrounds are fun. Whether you like swinging on a swing, climbing on the jungle gym, or riding the teeter-totter, there are plenty of fun things to do on a playground. Physics teachers love playgrounds, too, but not so much because the rides are fun. The rides you find at the playground can teach some of the most basic and important laws of physics that you can learn. What makes playgrounds so great is that you get to have lots of fun while learning!

TRY THIS SEESAW

QUESTION

How do you balance a seesaw?

MATERIALS

Pencil
Ruler with inch markings
10 pennies, minted after 1982 (because you need them to have the same metals inside)

PROCEDURE

1. Place the pencil on a hard surface such as a table.
2. Place the ruler on the pencil so that it balances at the 6-inch mark.
3. Place five pennies at one end of the ruler.
4. Take five more pennies and find the location on the other side of the ruler that will make the ruler balance.
5. Clear the ruler off.

How did the careless scientist start a war?

He invented the wheel and caused a revolution!

Science Online

Learn more about the world of-physical science. Visit *www. explorescience.com.*

6. Place six pennies at the 2-inch mark on the ruler.

7. Find the location on the other side of the ruler at which only three pennies will balance the original six.

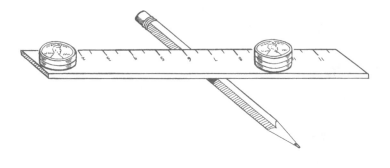

Fun Facts

Gravity on the moon is about one-sixth what it is on Earth. This means that objects fall six times faster on Earth than on the-moon!

WHAT'S HAPPENING

The pencil under the ruler turns the ruler into a **lever.** The pencil acts as the fulcrum, or the balance point. To balance the ruler, there needs to be the same kind of force on one side as there is on the other. The force is **gravity,** acting on the pennies. But there's a catch! The farther away from the fulcrum the pennies are, the more their gravity counts toward balancing the ruler. For example, three pennies located 4 inches from the fulcrum (think $3 \times 4 = 12$) will balance six pennies located only 2 inches from the fulcrum ($6 \times 2 = 12$). Can you think of other combinations that will balance those three pennies?[1]

FOLLOW-UP

The next time you want to ride the teeter-totter and find that your partner is much heavier than you, see if you can figure out where you both should sit. Will this work if you ride with one of your parents? If you know each other's weight, you should be able to come up with a seating arrangement that works.[2]

lever: a device used to lift very heavy objects.

gravity: the force that pulls us toward the center of the earth and keeps us on the ground.

TRY THIS WATER BALLOON TOSS

A fun game to play that people of all ages enjoy is the water balloon toss. From Mom and Dad's company picnic to the annual Fourth of July barbecue to kids' birthday parties, people love to see how far they can toss water balloons without breaking them. Of course, if they do break, you get wet, and that can be as fun as winning.

QUESTION

How do you keep the balloon from breaking?

MATERIALS

Several filled water balloons
A friend who doesn't mind getting wet

PROCEDURE

1. Pick up one balloon and stand facing your friend. Toss the balloon. After a successful catch, both of you take a step backward.
2. After your friend tosses the balloon back to you, each of you takes another step backward. Continue this process until the balloon breaks.
3. See how far apart you can get without breaking the balloon.

Fun Facts

A homemade water balloon launcher can send a water balloon over two football fields lengthwise.

What will you see if you drop a cup full of a hot drink?

You'll see gravi-tea (gravity) in action!

WHAT'S HAPPENING

A water balloon is simply water held by a rubber covering (the balloon). As long as nothing causes the rubber to burst, the balloon will stay intact. Pavement is hard and doesn't "give" when something collides with it, so water balloons tossed onto pavement will typically burst. Grass, on the other hand, is much softer than pavement, so balloons will often stay intact when they land on grass.

To win a water balloon contest, you apply what is known as the Impulse-Momentum Theorem—a fancy way of saying that if you give a little with your hands (move them backward as you catch the balloon), the force won't make the balloon burst.

FOLLOW-UP

Football players wear pads so that the collisions involved in tackling aren't as painful. Gymnasts and wrestlers perform on padded mats to cushion the impact. Skydivers bend their knees and sometimes run several steps when they reach the ground. Can you think of other people who use this idea of cushioning to soften a blow?[3]

_____

_____

_____

_____

_____

_____

_____

Cool Quotes

Every sentence I utter must be understood not as an affirmation, but as a question.

—Niels Bohr,
Danish physicist

KIDS' LAB LESSONS

QUESTION   Why do boats float?

EXPERIMENT OVERVIEW   Using pieces of modeling clay and other simple materials, you'll be exploring how size and shape affect a boat's ability to float. You'll also get to see just how much weight your boat can hold and which design works the best.

SCIENCE CONCEPT   According to the **Archimedes Principle,** boats float because water pushes up on them with a force equal to their weight. This is called buoyancy. You can take a material (clay for example), and form it into a shape that will sink. Or you can take the same amount of clay as you had before, and form it into a boat that floats. You, and boat designers around the world, have to determine what shape produces the most buoyancy. Once you do that, you're ready to begin loading your boat with cargo.

Science Online

For answers to your questions about how stuff works, check out HowStuffWorks.com. Visit *www. howstuffworks.com.*

MATERIALS

Tank of water (aquarium) or large
   mixing bowl
Modeling clay
Pennies
Paper clips

Archimedes Principle: an object displaces its own weight in water.

PROCEDURE

1. Roll a lump of clay about the size of your palm into a ball and drop it into the water.
2. Mold the clay into several different shapes until it floats. Then place pennies in your boat until it finally sinks. Keep track of how many pennies it held.
3. Test several successful shapes to see which holds the most pennies before sinking.

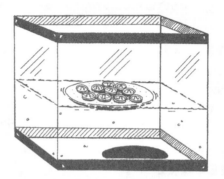

QUESTIONS FOR THE SCIENTIST

• Which clay boat held more weight? _____

• What characteristic of the winning boats helped them support the most weight?

_____

• Does this idea apply to large ships that cross oceans and carry thousands of tons of cargo? How do they stay afloat if they are made of metal? _____

_____

• Why don't people float like your boats did? _____

FOLLOW-UP   Another force that acts like buoyancy is air resistance. Air pushes back on falling objects in a manner similar to how water held up your boat. The project at the end of this section deals with how objects fall through the air and what effects air resistance has on their speed as they fall.

TRY THIS CORNERS

Most of what you've covered so far in this chapter has to do with gravity, but there's much more to the world of physics. Everywhere you look, objects are in motion—cars, birds, leaves, baseballs, children on a playground. Have you ever been in a car and felt pushed toward the door when the car turned? The car turns left and you are pushed to the right!

QUESTION

Why do you get pushed toward the door when the car turns?

MATERIALS

A car with an adult driving (everyone must be wearing a seatbelt!)

A road with several corners

Optional: Helium-filled balloon attached to a string

PROCEDURE

1. Have the adult make several turns at various (yet safe) speeds. Describe how you feel when the car turns and in which direction you feel pushed.

2. If you have a balloon, hold it by the string so it is free to move in the air.

3. Have the adult make several more turns and describe the motion of the balloon.

Fun Facts

Sir Isaac Newton discovered his Three Laws of Motion while in the country avoiding the spread of the plague in the 1600s in England.

WORDS to KNOW

inertia: a property of an object that makes it maintain its state of motion. That means that if it is moving, it will tend to stay moving. If it is at rest, it will stay at rest.

WHAT'S HAPPENING

You aren't actually being pushed toward the door. You possess something called **inertia**. It comes from being made of matter, and it is a little bit like your weight. Your inertia is moving in whatever direction you are, and according to a law discovered by Isaac Newton, called the Law of Inertia, it wants to keep moving in that direction. When the car turns, there's a problem. It's going in one direction and your inertia is going in another direction. The car is bigger than you are so it can make you change direction, but only by pushing on you. But this still isn't why you feel like you are being pushed toward the door. The door actually pushes on you, to make you turn! Inertia makes you feel like you're falling into the door.

FOLLOW-UP

The "door pushing on you" explanation still doesn't explain the motion of the balloon. Can you figure out why it went in the opposite direction you did?[4]

_____

_____

_____

_____

_____

_____

Around the Bend

Can you find the seven terms that have to do with the Laws of Motion? Instead of reading in a straight line, each word has one bend in it. Words can go in any direction. One word has been circled for you.

GRAVITY   FORCE
INERTIA   PHYSICS
REACTION   LEVER
ISAAC NEWTON   MOTION

```
W H Y G D L I D T H E
F A I R R E S I T U I
P N N A N V E R A Y S
H P E V I T Y H N Y A
Y S R I C I S T C C A
S R T I A O M S E C S
I C S T H F O R N E P
L A Y N O I T E C G R
R O U N D ? W T O E G
E T T O T T H E A O T
H E R N O I T C S L I
D E ! N H A H A H A !
```

TRY THIS BALLOON ROCKET

Once you have seen what causes objects to move in a certain direction, you are ready to think about how they get going in that direction in the first place. If you've ever seen a space shuttle take off, you probably noticed a huge cloud of gas and fire coming out of the back end as it lifted off. Why do rockets have to burn so much fuel to make the shuttle go?

QUESTION

How do rockets work?

MATERIALS

Latex balloon
Long string
Plastic straw
Tape

PROCEDURE

1. Blow up the balloon and hold the neck with your fingers so no air escapes.
2. Hold the balloon in front of you and let go of the neck. Observe the motion of the balloon.
3. Feed the string through the straw and attach both ends of the string to a wall or other solid support so that the straw is suspended above the floor of the room.
4. Blow up the balloon and hold the neck as before.
5. While holding the neck of the balloon, tape the balloon to the straw. Stand back and let go of the balloon. Observe the motion of the balloon.

Fun Facts

It would require a helium balloon more than thirteen feet in-diameter to make an 85-pound person float.

WHAT'S HAPPENING

To make something move, there must be a force on it. While nothing appears to push on your balloon, there really is something making it move—air! When the balloon releases its air, the air particles that escape encounter other air particles outside the balloon. Each group of air particles experiences forces from the other. That is why you can feel the air coming out of the balloon. But it's also what makes the balloon move. This is an example of another Law of Motion discovered by Isaac Newton, the one commonly known as Action/Reaction. It says that every action (the air escaping and pushing on the outside air) has an equal and opposite reaction (the outside air pushing back on the air in the balloon, and making the balloon move). Rockets work in the same way, but instead of using inflated balloons, they use huge engines burning very powerful fuel.

Silly Experiments . . .

Why did the scientist take the ruler to bed?

To see how long he slept!

•

Why did the scientist put sugar under her pillow?

To see if she had sweet dreams!

•

Why did the scientist sit on her watch?

To see what it was like to-be on time!

•

Why did the scientist keep a ruler in his laboratory?

To see if he could keep his-facts straight!

KIDS' LAB LESSONS

QUESTION   What makes a swing go?

EXPERIMENT OVERVIEW   In this experiment you will be setting up several swinglike devices, called **pendulums**, to test what makes them swing faster and slower. You will experiment with the length of the swing, the weight hanging off the pendulum, and the size of the swing to determine which affect the time it takes to complete one full swing.

SCIENCE CONCEPT   In the 1500s in Italy, Galileo was fascinated with the swinging chandeliers in the cathedral of Pisa. In his laboratory, he set up experiments to test the factors he thought would make the chandeliers swing faster. To make the experiments as similar as possible, he used the term **period** to describe the time it took to make one complete swing—from one side across to the other and back. The three easiest factors to test are how long the pendulum is, how much weight is on the pendulum, and how large the swing is. You will have to pick one factor at a time and, while keeping the other two constant, change the factor you chose to determine whether those changes had any effect on the period.

MATERIALS
Several identical items (for example, spoons, screws, washers, pencils)
1 long (36 inches or more) piece of string

Doorway
Thumbtacks
Stopwatch

PROCEDURE

Part I: Weight

1. Tie one item to your string.
2. Attach the other end of the string to the top of the doorway with a thumbtack.
3. Pull the string back and release it at the same time you start the stopwatch.
4. Count 10 complete swings and stop the watch when the tenth swing finishes. Record the time.
5. Attach another item to your string and repeat the experiment. (This picture shows how you can hang the string at different heights.)
6. Record your time and add another item. Repeat this process of adding items until you have four times recorded.

Part II: Size of Swing

1. Remove all but the first item and pull the swing back a small amount.
2. As before, count 10 complete swings and record your time.
3. Pull the swing back a little more than before and repeat the experiment. Record your time.
4. Repeat this process of pulling the swing a little farther back than before until you have four times recorded.

Part III: Length

1. Again, start with just one item and record the time for 10 swings.
2. Shorten the swing by about 4 inches.
3. Repeat the experiment, taking care to pull the swing back the same amount as before. Record your time.
4. Repeat this process of shortening the string by 4 inches until you have four times recorded.

QUESTIONS FOR THE SCIENTIST

- What factor(s) affected the period of the swing?_____

- Why do you think the other factors didn't have an effect on the period?_____

  _____

- When you swing on the playground, what do you have to do to keep from slowing down?_____

WORDS to KNOW

electricity: energy stored in positive and negative charges.

battery: a device that stores electrical energy.

Fun Facts

Some rocks are naturally magnetic. They are called lodestones and were first discovered in a region called Magnesia, near Greece.

ENERGY

Energy comes in many different forms. For example, the sun gives us energy in the form of sunlight and heat. When we eat food, we give our bodies energy so we can run and play. Cars, trains, and airplanes all have energy, too. Another form of energy is produced when we plug something into an electrical outlet in the wall.

CAUTION: Only an adult should ever plug an appliance into a wall outlet! This form of energy is called **electricity,** and it has been around for thousands of years, even though we've used it in our homes for only less than 200 years. One interesting use of electricity is to make it act like a magnet.

TRY THIS MAGNETIC ELECTRICITY

QUESTION
Can electricity confuse a compass?

MATERIALS
Small compass (used for navigation)
1 piece of insulated wire with bare wire on either end
1 **battery** (1.5 volts)

PROCEDURE

1. Lay the compass on a table so that it points to the north.
2. Place the wire across the top of the compass so that it lies in the same direction that the compass points. Leave the exposed ends of the wire outside the compass.
3. Touch each end of the wire to opposite ends of the battery. Observe what happens to the compass.

WHAT'S HAPPENING

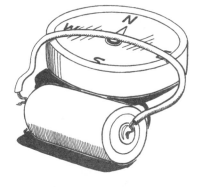

> ### Fun Facts
> The magnetic north pole (the location a compass points to) isn't located at the true North Pole. It's actually located at Ellef Ringnes Island in the Canadian arctic. It moves to the northwest approximately 15 kilometers each year.

Hans Christian Oersted discovered that electricity flowing through a wire, called a current, makes the wire act like a magnet. The magnet formed by the electricity attracts the compass, which is a very small magnet itself, and makes it point in a direction different from north.

FOLLOW-UP

Remove the wires from the battery and watch the compass return to its normal position. Now place the wire under the compass and touch the wires to the battery again. What do you see[5]?

> What did one magnet say to the other magnet?
>
> "I find you very attractive."

KIDS' LAB LESSONS

QUESTION How does an **electromagnet** work?

EXPERIMENT OVERVIEW In this experiment you will build your own electromagnet. By wrapping wire around a screwdriver, you will strengthen the magnetic field produced by the current flowing in the wire (which you explored in the previous experiment). Then you'll be able to measure the strength of your electromagnet by counting the number of paper clips you can hold.

SCIENCE CONCEPT Since one wire is known to produce a magnetic field, wrapping a wire into a series of loops or coils strengthens that effect. These coils are called **solenoids;** when they are used with a metallic core (like a screwdriver), they produce surprisingly strong magnetic fields. When an ordinary nail is exposed to those fields, it, too, becomes magnetized, as long as the field is there.

WORDS to KNOW

electromagnet: a magnet made by passing electrical current through a wire.

solenoid: a cylinder of wire formed into coils.

MATERIALS
Long piece of copper wire, preferably insulated
Screwdriver
Tape
AA, C, or D battery
Paper clips

PROCEDURE

1. Leaving about 3 inches of one end of the wire free, wrap the wire around the screwdriver 10 times.
2. Tape one end of the wire to the negative terminal (marked with a "−") of the battery.
3. Hold the handle of the screwdriver in one hand while you touch the free end of the wire to the positive terminal (marked with a "+") of the battery.
4. See how many paper clips you can pick up and hold with the screwdriver.
5. Remove the free wire from the battery and wind another 10 loops around the screwdriver.
6. Repeat the experiment and count the number of paper clips you can pick up.
7. Again, remove the free wire from the battery.
8. Wind any remaining wire around the screwdriver, leaving about 3 inches of wire free and repeat the experiment.

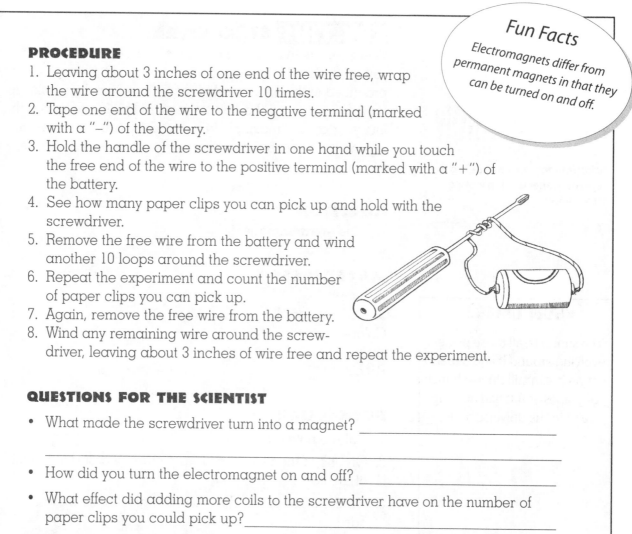

Fun Facts

Electromagnets differ from permanent magnets in that they can be turned on and off.

QUESTIONS FOR THE SCIENTIST

• What made the screwdriver turn into a magnet? _____

_____

• How did you turn the electromagnet on and off? _____

• What effect did adding more coils to the screwdriver have on the number of paper clips you could pick up? _____

• What advantages might there be to using a magnet that can be turned on and off? _____

FOLLOW-UP Practice lifting paper clips, moving them through the air, and then dropping them in another location. Can you think of anywhere someone would want to do this?[6] _____

_____

WORDS to KNOW

afterimage: what we see in our eyes even after we stop looking at an object.

Cool Quotes

The sun, with all those planets revolving around it and dependent on it, can still ripen a bunch of grapes as if it had nothing else in the universe to do.

—Galileo

TRY THIS BIRD CAGE

Energy exists in forms other than electricity. Look around—do you see colors? If so, you are receiving light energy that was produced in the sun, traveled more than 90 million miles to Earth, bounced off the objects you are looking at, and reflected into your eyes. Amazing! Light and color are examples of energy we see around us every day but we sometimes forget to notice.

QUESTION

What is an **afterimage**?

MATERIALS

Scissors
3" × 5" note card
Colored pens
Tape
Pencil

PROCEDURE

1. Cut the note card in half.
2. On one of the pieces, draw a picture of a bird in the middle of the card.
3. On the other piece, draw a cage, also in the middle of the card.
4. Tape each card, back to back, to the end of the pencil so you can see one picture on either side.
5. Rub the pencil very quickly between your palms until you have captured the bird in the cage.

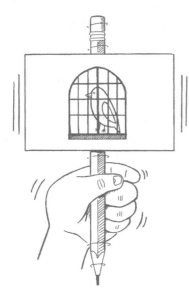

WHAT'S HAPPENING

Your eyes have the ability to see images even after they are gone. These are called after-images. When you spin the pencil fast enough, your eyes still see the cage while the bird comes into view, and it appears as though the bird is actually inside the cage. The same happens when the bird spins out of view. You still see it while the cage is visible, and the bird appears to be caught in the cage.

FOLLOW-UP

Try making other drawings for your afterimage viewer. Try flowers and a vase, a person on a swing, or even a face on the moon. You can use colors to make the images appear even more realistic.

Catchy Categories

An important part of the Scientific Method is putting things into categories. Take the words in the following list and group them into two categories. Complete each criss-cross grid with the words that fit the given category. HINT: We left you a L-I-S-T in each grid to help you get started.

WORD LIST:
fast
solid
slow
gravity
liquid
speed
gas
swing
balance
weight
inertia
mass
density
force
fall
size

Properties of Motion

Properties of Matter

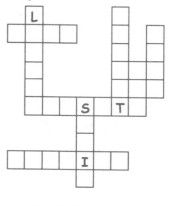

WORDS to KNOW

filter: a way to block certain colors of light from reaching your eyes.

Science Online

The EncycloZine has a collection of fascinating optical illusions. Visit *www.encyclozine.com.* From the main page, click on "Optical Illusions."

Where does a mad scientist go to college?

A looney-versity!

TRY THIS COLORS OF LIGHT

Color is a pretty interesting topic to study. In school, you probably learned to mix colors to make new colors. For example, green is made by mixing blue and yellow, and purple is made by mixing blue and red. In fact, every color can be made from the right combination of the three primary colors: red, yellow, and blue. But has anyone ever tried to convince you that red, blue, and yellow aren't the only primary colors? They aren't.

QUESTION

What are the primary colors of light?

MATERIALS

Cellophane or plastic squares large enough to cover the light end of the flashlight. You will need 1 each of red, blue, and green.
3 flashlights
Rubber bands
A white screen or wall

PROCEDURE

1. Secure one square of cellophane or plastic to the end of each flashlight with a rubber band.

2. Turn on each flashlight to make sure it produces the correct color of light.

3. Carefully shine the red and blue lights onto the screen so that the color circles overlap. What color is produced?

4. Shine the red and green lights onto the screen. What color is produced by this pair of colors?

5. Shine the blue and green lights onto the screen. What color is produced by this pair of colors?

6. Carefully shine all three lights onto the screen so that all three colors overlap in the middle. What color is produced by all three colors?

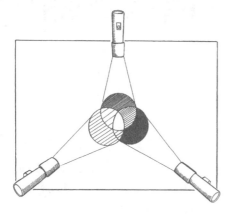

WHAT'S HAPPENING

Light behaves differently than paint does. Red, blue, and green can combine to form every color of light, so they are called primary. Secondary colors are formed when two primary colors are mixed. These were the first three colors you produced: magenta, yellow, and cyan (blue). When you shined all three colors onto the screen, you should have produced white light. If your cellophane covers weren't totally pure (most aren't), you may have seen an off-white color.

FOLLOW-UP

Try looking at the world through the red, blue, or green **filters**. You will probably notice that most of what you see is the color of the filter you are looking through. But you may also see some objects that look black. The light from these objects is being blocked by your filter, so you see no color.

Black and White

Can you find the figure that is the EXACT opposite of the three figures in the box below? Draw a line between each pair.

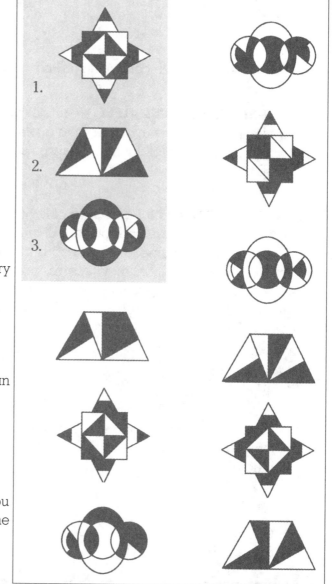

1.

2.

3.

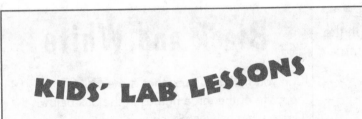

KIDS' LAB LESSONS

QUESTION   Which color is hotter: black or white?

EXPERIMENT OVERVIEW   In this experiment you'll be testing to see whether a black object heats up faster than a white object. You'll test the temperature of water inside a can of each color and also test the temperature of the air under a card of each color.

SCIENCE CONCEPT   Each color of light that we see reaches our eyes because it has reflected off another object. All the other colors of light that hit that object were absorbed. Some objects absorb more light than others. In fact, white objects must reflect all the light they receive, which means they don't absorb any. On the other hand, black objects reflect no light to our eyes, which means they absorb all the light they receive. This experiment will show which of these two ends up being warmer.

MATERIALS
2 thermometers
2 sheets of paper: 1 white and 1 black
2 tin cans: 1 painted white and 1 painted black (have an adult help you paint
   the cans)
Pitcher of water

PROCEDURE

1. Place the thermometers outside and lay one sheet of paper over each one.
2. Let them sit for 30 minutes.
3. Remove the papers and compare the temperature each thermometer shows.
4. Fill each can with water at the same temperature and place the corresponding sheet of paper on top to cover it (black on black, white on white).
5. Set both cans outside for 30 minutes. Remove the papers and compare the temperature of each can of water.

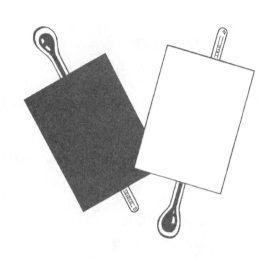

QUESTIONS FOR THE SCIENTIST

• Which thermometer measured a higher temperature in the first experiment?

_____

_____

• Which can of water was warmest? _____

_____

_____

• On a cold day, which color would be better to wear to school—black or white?

_____

_____

• If you lived in a very hot place, what color car would you buy if you wanted to stay as cool as possible? _____

_____

SCIENCE FAIR PROJECT: PHYSICS

GRAVITY

In the early days of science, it was generally accepted that heavier objects fell faster than light objects. In fact, Aristotle, a famous scientist during the fourth century B.C., tried to come up with a mathematical relationship between the weight of the object and how fast it fell. Nearly 2,000 years later, Galileo didn't think that was right. He tested several objects, without the technology we now have, and decided that it was the air that made certain objects fall more slowly than others, not their weight. What do you think?

QUESTION

Why do some objects fall faster than others?

EXPERIMENT OVERVIEW

In this experiment you'll be testing several objects to see what features determine how fast they fall. You'll be picking heavy and light objects, large and small objects, solid and hollow objects, and you'll drop them all. You will then be able to scientifically determine what makes one object fall faster than another.

SCIENCE CONCEPT

Long ago, people generally believed that the heavier something was, the faster it would fall through the air. The person most famous for holding this belief was named Aristotle. Today, we have plenty of examples that back that claim up. For example, if you were in a helicopter and you dropped a Ping-Pong ball and a bowling ball out of the door at the same time, the bowling ball would hit the ground first. But since Ping-Pong balls and bowling balls aren't the same size, try another example. Drop a Ping-Pong ball and a golf ball and the Ping-Pong ball still loses. So what's the big deal?

In the 1500s, a man named Galileo tried to show that it really didn't matter how much an object weighed—that it would usually fall at the same speed as any other object, as long as you didn't have to take air into account.

You've already looked at a few experiments about air and there are more to come, but for now, think about the effect air has on a falling object.

When you run down the street or open the window in your car, you feel the wind. If it's strong enough, it can make it hard to walk or run. Now imagine that you are falling through the air. The faster you go, the windier it feels and the harder it becomes to move. A heavier person wouldn't be affected as much as a light person would be. That is the idea of air resistance, and you'll explore it in this experiment.

MATERIALS

1 object you would call "light"—e.g., feather
1 object you would call "heavy"—e.g., rock
1 object you would call "small"—e.g., plastic figurine
1 object you would call "large"—e.g., basketball
1 object you would call "solid"—e.g.,
   croquet ball
1 object you would call "hollow"—e.g., Wiffle ball
4 other objects of your choice
1 sheet of paper
1 writing utensil
A platform or raised place from which you can drop these items. (The higher you
   can climb the better, but you must be sure that the area below is open and free of
   people. Dropping objects can be very dangerous.)
A partner who can tell you which object lands first

PROCEDURE

You will be recording results from each test. An example is shown below:

Test: Light (object name, e.g., feather) vs. Heavy (object name, e.g., rock)
Light object (feather)—small, white, weighs almost nothing, about 3 inches long, not
                    solid
Heavy object (rock)—medium sized, brown and black, weighs about
                    the same as a baseball, about 3 inches in
                    diameter, round, solid

Winner: The rock

1. In order, test the following pairs and record your results:
   Light—heavy
   Small—large
   Solid—hollow
   Other pairings from your collection of objects

2. When you have finished testing, look at the
   results and determine the factors that made
   objects fall the fastest.

QUESTIONS FOR THE SCIENTIST

- Of your entire collection, which object fell the fastest?

- Which characteristics of this object made it fall fast?

- Which characteristics had no effect on how fast it fell?

- Which object fell the slowest?

- Which pairing showed the most significant differences in how fast the objects fell?

- What could you do to eliminate air from this experiment so you could test Galileo's claim?

CONCLUSION

The shape of the object is a very important factor in how fast it falls. It's true that weight matters too—really light objects fall slowly no matter how they are shaped because once they start hitting the air, they immediately slow down. But the heavier the object, the more its shape matters. A simple test to verify this result is to drop a single sheet of notebook paper at the same time you drop a crumpled up piece of the same paper. Try it and you'll see the difference shape makes.

Modern science has shown us that if we take away air, objects will fall at the same speed no matter how big or small they are and no matter what shape they are. When the astronauts went to the moon, they dropped a feather and a hammer to see which would fall faster. On the moon, there is no air. (Astronauts wear special suits to help them breathe.) Can you guess what happened? The feather and hammer landed at the same time.

CHAPTER 23

THE PLANET EARTH

Do you ever have one of those days when you lay down in the grass, feel the warm sun all around you, look up at the clouds moving past, and wonder how it all happened? The earth is in many ways a miracle. Nowhere else in the entire universe has anyone discovered a place where life can exist. Sure there are other stars like our sun, and now scientists are discovering planets that orbit those stars. But so far, no one has found water, trees, grass, and a climate quite like ours here on Earth.

The planet Earth is a rare find in the universe, and it is in our care. If we don't take care of it, its wonder and beauty may soon be in danger. One of the growing concerns among people who are worried about the earth is the quality of our air and water. There are many ways to discover how precious these resources are.

TRY THIS ACID RAIN

QUESTION
What is acid rain?

MATERIALS
Empty glass jar
Water
Phenol red (available at pool
   supply stores)
A drinking straw

Why did the poor scientist experiment with baking bread?

Because he needed the-dough!

Fun Facts

Much of the acid rain in North America is caused by the burning of coal to produce electricity.

The rainiest day ever recorded was in 1952 in Cilaos, Reunion Island. In a 24-hour period, 73.63 inches of rain fell.

WORDS to KNOW

acid rain: rain that contains acids formed in the clouds. It can be dangerous to people, animals, and crops.

PROCEDURE

1. Fill the jar about half to three-quarters full of cool water.

2. Put approximately 20 drops of the phenol red into the water until it turns light red. You can practice this and adjust the amount you add, once you get the hang of the experiment.

3. Place the straw into the water and blow so that bubbles form in the water for about 20 seconds. CAUTION: Do not drink the water!

4. Check the color of the water. It should be a lighter red than it was before.

5. Repeat your 20 seconds of blowing a few more times. Before long, the water should be clear again.

WHAT'S HAPPENING

Phenol red reacts with acids to change color. (You have already learned a little bit about acids in an earlier chapter.) When you blew into the water, the carbon dioxide you blew out (which is not the same as the oxygen you breathe in) reacted with the tap water to form a very weak acid. The more you blew, the more the acid reacted with the phenol red and turned the water clear. Pool cleaners use phenol red to measure how acidic the water is. This tells them what kinds of chemicals to add to maintain the cleanliness of the water.

FOLLOW-UP

What does this have to do with acid rain? When we place too much carbon dioxide into

Wind Speed

How fast can you find 20 words that are hidden in the word ANEMOMETER (a device that measures wind speed)? Each word must be three letters or longer.

Extra Experiment: Use a separate piece of paper and see if you can come up with: 20-four-letter words, 5 five-letter words, and 4 six-letter words. If you are a SUPER scientist, you will even be able to make 1-seven-letter word!

_____   _____

_____   _____

_____   _____

_____   _____

_____   _____

_____   _____

_____   _____

_____   _____

_____   _____

_____   _____

the air, through burning coal, gasoline, or other fossil fuels, it can react with the water in the air (rainwater) to form an acid. When that rain falls to the ground, we get acid in our water and it can become unsafe. It pays to be careful with the gases we exhaust into the air!

KIDS' LAB LESSONS

Winds follow a pattern across the face of the earth, called the Coriolis effect. This pattern tends to produce winds that rotate in a counter-clockwise direction in the Northern **Hemisphere** and in a clockwise direction in the Southern Hemisphere.

QUESTION   How can you tell how fast the wind is blowing?

EXPERIMENT OVERVIEW   In this experiment you will build a simple **anemometer**, a device that measures wind speed. While you won't actually be able to come up with the true wind speed for this project, you'll be able to track different speeds on your own scale and identify which days were the windiest.

SCIENCE CONCEPT   Breezes constantly blow across the surface of the earth, and only rarely do they reach the point of being dangerous to people. An anemometer catches the wind in small cups that then rotate. The faster the cups rotate, the faster the wind is blowing.

hemisphere: half of the earth.

anemometer: a device that measures wind speed.

MATERIALS

Glue
Empty spool of thread
    or lump of modeling clay
Small block of wood
Pencil
Needle or thin nail
Stopwatch

1 large piece of sturdy
    cardboard
Scissors
Stapler
Foil muffin cups
1 bright sticker

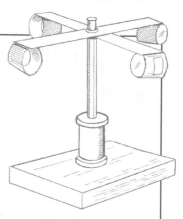

PROCEDURE

1. Glue the spool of thread to the block of wood and wedge the pencil,-eraser side up, into it.
2. Stick the needle into the eraser.
3. Cut two strips out of the piece of cardboard. They should be at least 16 inches long and 2 inches wide.
4. With the scissors, cut slits in the bottom of each strip so they fit together to make a cross. Start from the middle of the strip (about 8-inches from either side) and cut upward about 1 inch.
5. Glue or staple one muffin cup to each arm of the cross, making sure that each cup points in the same direction. This will ensure that every cup will catch the wind.
6. Place the sticker on one of the cups. Make sure it is clearly visible because you will be using it to measure wind speed.
7. Place the cross onto the needle so that it rotates freely. If you find that it doesn't rotate, use the needle to make a slightly larger hole until it spins easily.
8. Place the anemometer outdoors where it can catch the wind.
9. Over the course of several days record the wind speed at different times of day.

Fun Facts

Winds are measured on the Beaufort scale, which ranges from 0 (no wind) to 12 (hurricane speeds in excess of 75 mph).

The fastest wind recorded on-the ground was 231 mph in New Hampshire in-1934.

Instructions on Measuring Wind Speed   Use a stopwatch or a clock that will measure one minute. Count the number of times the cup with the sticker completes one revolution in a minute. Use that number as your wind speed. Each time you record a new measurement, compare it to the previous values.

QUESTIONS FOR THE SCIENTIST

• What was the fastest speed you recorded? _____

• What time of day was the windiest? The calmest? _____

• Are there places at your house that are windier than others? How could you test this? _____

• How do you suppose meteorologists measure the true wind speed?[1] _____

WORDS to KNOW

volcano: any part of the earth (especially mountains) that explodes when pressure below it gets too high.

molten: melted.

Science Online

The U.S. Geological Services Cascade Volcano Observatory (CVO) includes links to all of the world's known volcanoes. Visit *http://vulcan.wr.usgs.gov.*

TRY THIS MINI VOLCANO

QUESTION

What does an erupting **volcano** look like?

MATERIALS

Small plastic bottle
Baking soda
Wide tray or baking pan
Sand or dirt

½ cup vinegar
Measuring cup with a pouring lip
Red food coloring

PROCEDURE:

1. Fill the bottle one-quarter to half full of baking soda and place it in the middle of the tray.

2. Pile the sand around the bottle so that you can just see the opening. At this point it should look like a small volcano.

3. Pour the vinegar into the measuring cup.

4. Place several drops of food coloring into your vinegar and quickly pour it into the bottle top.

WHAT'S HAPPENING

You've already seen what kind of reaction occurs when baking soda and vinegar are combined. The red coloring makes this reaction appear to produce lava. In real volcanoes, you wouldn't find any vinegar, but you would find hot gases and liquid rocks under intense pressure. When the pressure builds up too much, the volcano explodes, and all the hot gases and rocks that have melted under the heat finally burst forth in the form of either hot ash or **molten** lava.

Head in the Clouds

Do you ever see the shapes of people or animals when you look at the clouds? Connect the numbered dots and then the lettered dots to see what familiar shape is floating overhead in this beautiful sky. HINT: To make a better cloud picture, connect the dots with curved lines instead of straight lines.

TRY THIS LAND WARMER

From the dirt in our gardens to the liquid metal core of our planet, the earth is a place where remarkable processes happen every day without our knowledge. One of the simplest processes is the manner in which sunlight warms our planet.

QUESTION

Which gets warm faster: land or water?

MATERIALS

2 small cups
Water
Dirt
2 thermometers

PROCEDURE

1. Fill one cup with water and the other with dirt.

2. Place both cups in the freezer for 10 minutes.

3. Remove both cups from the freezer and place a thermometer in each. Record the initial temperatures.

4. Place both cups in full sunlight for a period of 15 minutes.

5. After 15 minutes, record both temperatures.

Fun Facts

Earthquakes are measured on the Richter scale—a scale where every number represents an earthquake that is 10 times more powerful than the previous number. The largest earthquakes ever recorded occurred in Colombia in 1906 and in Japan in 1933. Both measured 8.9 on the Richter scale.

Where do scientists study-volcanoes?

In the lava-tory!

WHAT'S HAPPENING

Sunlight warms the land much faster than it does water. That is why your cup of dirt ended up warmer than the cup of water. This also explains why, on a hot day, a sandy beach can get extremely warm while the water in the lake remains cool.

FOLLOW-UP

When you dig in the sand on a beach, does the sand feel warm all the way down, or is it only the top level that gets hot?[2] Some animals dig into the earth to find cool places to make their nests. Can you find animals that do that?

_____

_____

_____

_____

_____

Cool Quotes

Space isn't remote at all. It's only an hour's drive away if your car could go straight up.

—Sir Fred Hoyle, British mathematician and astronomer

Up or Down?

What is a good way to remember the difference between a stalactite and a stalagmite? Use words from the word list to finish the following "science saying," and you'll never forget which is which!

Word List
MIGHTY
STALACTITE
STALAGMITE
TIGHT

A _____

hangs _____ to the ceiling.

A _____

grows _____ tall from

the floor.

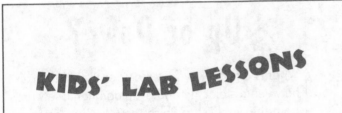

KIDS' LAB LESSONS

QUESTION   How do icicles grow?

EXPERIMENT OVERVIEW   In this experiment, you'll explore the formation of icicles by building **stalactites** and **stalagmites**—towers of rock-hard minerals usually found in caves deep in the earth. Surprisingly, the process by which they form is very similar to how icicles form. You'll be using a common drugstore product called Epsom salts and you'll get to watch the "icicles" grow right before your very eyes.

SCIENCE CONCEPT   Icicles can form only under special conditions. It must be cold enough for water to freeze, but there must also be a way for ice to melt so it drips. This is why icicles are commonly found along the edge of the roof of a house. The warmth of the house can cause snow on the roof to melt and drip to the edge of the house. As the water drips off the side, some of it freezes. Later, drops run down the frozen droplets and freeze when they reach the end. In this fashion, the icicle grows drop by drop.

In caves, stalactites and stalagmites grow in the same way. The only difference is that the water that drips doesn't freeze. Instead, each drop of water leaves behind a tiny amount of calcite, which hardens on the end of the stalactite. Eventually, enough calcite builds up and hardens that a stalactite forms. Stalagmites are formed when some of the calcite falls to the ground and gradually builds up from the floor. After a long time, the stalactites that grow from the ceiling meet up with the stalagmites growing up from the floor until they join and a **column** is formed.

WORDS to KNOW

stalactite: a long, thin piece of hanging mineral (like rock) that forms over long periods of time, often in caves.

stalagmite: a long, thin piece of mineral that grows up from the ground over long periods of time. (It is similar to a stalactite.)

column: what is formed when a stalactite meets a stalagmite and the two grow together.

MATERIALS

Large glass that you can use-for mixing
Water
Small spoon
Box of Epsom salts (available at a local drugstore)

2 small glasses
Thick string or a piece of cloth that will absorb water easily
Wax paper

PROCEDURE

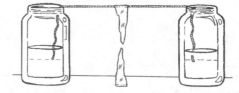

1. Fill the large glass with water and stir in the Epsom salts until you cannot dissolve any more (some of the salt remains and won't dissolve).
2. Fill each small glass with half of the solution you have prepared and place the jars on a piece of wax paper.
3. Place an end of the string in each glass and let the middle of the string hang between the glasses.
4. Watch your stalactite and stalagmite grow over the next few days.

QUESTIONS FOR THE SCIENTIST

• Which of your cones is the stalactite and which is the stalagmite? _____

• How fast did your stalactite grow (how many inches per day)?_____
• Did the process speed up at all during your experiment? _____

• If you live where it's cold enough for icicles, how do you suppose they form?
_____

• How could you prevent icicles from forming on your house? _____

_____

FOLLOW-UP

Do you think this experiment will work with other substances? Try baking soda, table salt, sugar, and so on. Considering the fact that Epsom salts is found in drugstores, can you find other uses for it?[3]

THE SKY ABOVE US

If you have ever looked up at the sky on a clear night, you have seen more stars than you can count. It gives you some sense of how large our universe is and might even make you feel like Earth is pretty small. Looking at the sky is one of the oldest activities known to man. Just about every ancient civilization had its own myths about what the stars mean. The passing of days, months, and years has long been tracked by the rising and setting of the sun, the phases of the moon, and the changing of the seasons.

The sky is blue and sunsets are red because of the way air breaks sunlight into colors. That fact alone is pretty fascinating. But for many of us, it's hard to imagine that air is made up of anything. You can't see it, you can't taste it, and you can only feel it when it moves. It makes you wonder whether air is really there like everyone says it is.

Science Online

These links below will take you into the world of astronomy and will help you learn more about the planets and stars:

Visit *Astronomy* magazine at *www.astronomy.com*

Visit *Sky and Telescope* magazine at *www.skyandtelescope.com*

Visit the Star Gazer home page at *www.jackstargazer.com*

Visit The Astronomy Café at *http://itss.raytheon.com/cafe/qadir/qanda.html*

TRY THIS SPACE OF AIR

QUESTION
Does air take up space?

MATERIALS
Balloon (minimum 9 inches)
Glass bottle with a small mouth
Pot of boiling water
Pot of ice water

Funnel
Masking tape
Water

PROCEDURE

1. Place the mouth of the balloon over the mouth of the bottle. It should hang limply at the side of the bottle.

2. Make sure the balloon makes a good seal around the top of the bottle and gently place the bottle into the pot of boiling water. Be careful not to stand too close to the boiling water. Observe the changes in the balloon.

3. Remove the bottle from the hot water, remove the balloon, then replace it over the mouth of the bottle. The bottle now contains very hot air.

4. Place the bottle into the pot of ice water and observe the changes in the balloon.

5. Remove the bottle from the water and let it sit at room temperature for 10 minutes.

6. Remove the balloon from the top of the bottle.

7. Place the funnel in the mouth of the bottle and tape the mouth of the bottle to the funnel so that no air can escape.

8. Pour water into the funnel and watch what it does.

WHAT'S HAPPENING

Air definitely takes up space! When you first put the balloon on the bottle, you "captured" the air that was in the bottle. It didn't inflate the balloon because it fit nicely into the bottle. When you heated it up, however, the air expanded and took up even more room. The only place it could go was into the balloon, so the balloon inflated. When you removed the bottle from the hot water and placed it into the ice water, the air was compressed. Not only did it *not* inflate the balloon, it pulled the balloon down into the bottle. When you returned the bottle to its original temperature, the balloon should have returned to its original size, shape, and location.

The funnel experiment shows that air takes up room and can't easily be squeezed. When you sealed the top of the bottle, you gave the air nowhere to go. So when you poured the water into the funnel, it wasn't heavy enough to compress the air in the bottle and it remained in the funnel, apparently defying gravity.

FOLLOW-UP

Can you think of other examples of air expanding or contracting that you might encounter?[4]

_____

_____

_____

_____

KIDS' LAB LESSONS

QUESTION   How can you use the sun to tell time?

EXPERIMENT OVERVIEW   In this experiment you'll get to build your own **sundial.** With it, you can keep time the way ancient civilizations did. As the sun rises and sets, it makes shadows of different lengths and angles. You'll use the location of the sun's shadow on your sundial to tell you exactly what time it is.

SCIENCE CONCEPT   The sun doesn't actually move around the earth; it only seems that way. Instead, the earth rotates on its axis, so at any one time about half the people on Earth can see the sun and the other half cannot. This is how we get night and day. What a sundial does is track the location of the shadow that the sun makes, and it uses that location to determine the time of day. You have to know a few things in order for your sundial to work. For example, you need to know where true north is, and you need to know where the sun's shadow will be at certain times of day. Once you have set up your sundial, you should find it to be pretty accurate!

WORDS to KNOW

sundial: an ancient time-telling device.

MATERIALS
Sturdy paper plate
Unsharpened pencil
Modeling clay
Compass
Marking pen

PROCEDURE

1. Poke a hole in the middle of the paper plate large enough for the pencil to fit through.
2. Stick the pencil through the plate. Make sure the bottom of the plate is facing up.
3. Place the end of the pencil in a lump of clay below the plate to anchor it down.
4. Use the compass to locate true north and place your sundial in an open space with the pencil pointing slightly to the north. (This method works for anyone who lives in the Northern Hemisphere. If you live in the Southern Hemisphere, you will point the pencil to the south.)
5. At 8:00 in the morning, mark on the sundial the location of the pencil's shadow. Label it "8:00 A.M." Repeat this step every two hours until sunset. Your sundial is ready!

QUESTIONS FOR THE SCIENTIST

- Are the markings evenly spaced? _____

- Do you think it matters what time of the year you build or use your sundial? What happens when the days get longer or shorter?_____

- At what time of day does the shadow of the sun point true north? Is it this way all year round?_____

FOLLOW-UP   Research some of the civilizations that used sundials and think about these questions:

- What were some of the variations they built?
- Were any of them like yours?
- Why do you think people stopped using sundials?

Look around your town to see of you can find any sundials. Check the accuracy of any you find.

Fun Facts

The earth is actually farther from the sun in the summer (94.6 million miles in June) than in the winter (91.4 million miles in-December).

The earth is tilted at an angle of 23° from vertical. This is why we have seasons.

tilt of the earth: the angle the north and south poles of the earth make with a vertical line.

TRY THIS SEASONS IN THE SUN

Another way of measuring time is to mark the changing seasons. From the heat of summer, to cool crisp days in autumn when the leaves fall, to the snows of winter, to the first blooms of spring, seasons show us that time is passing and that we are indeed making our way around the sun. It's a journey that takes a full year to complete. Many people believe that the reason why it is warm in the summer and cold in the winter is because the earth is so much closer to the sun in the summer than in the winter. However, this isn't so.

QUESTION

Why do we have seasons?

MATERIALS

Marking pen
Medium or large Styrofoam ball, available at a craft supply store
Desk lamp without a shade
Pencil or long knitting needle

PROCEDURE

1. Mark the top and bottom of the ball with the letters *N* (on top) and *S* (on the bottom). These marks indicate the north and south poles.

2. Draw a circle around the middle of the ball to indicate the equator of the earth.

3. Place the lamp in the middle of your room.

4. Push the pencil through the N and S markings on the ball and tilt the top of the ball slightly toward the lamp.

5. Turn the light on and notice what parts of the ball are illuminated. This represents the beginning of summer in the Northern Hemisphere (location I).

6. Notice which wall of the room the ball is tilted toward. You will want to keep the ball tilted toward the same wall throughout the experiment. Move to a position 90° away from your starting position (location II). Again, notice what parts of the ball are illuminated. This represents the first day of fall in the Northern Hemisphere.

7. Now move another 90° around the lamp and again notice what parts of the ball are illuminated (location III). This is the beginning of winter in the Northern Hemisphere.

8. Finally, move another 90° around the lamp and note the illuminated parts of the ball (location IV). This is the first day of spring in the Northern Hemisphere.

WHAT'S HAPPENING

We have seasons with longer and shorter days not because the earth is any closer to the sun, but because of the **tilt of the earth.** When the north is tilted toward the sun, the Northern Hemisphere has summer. Days are longer and warmer and you can see this effect if you rotate the ball and notice how long the northern parts of the earth are illuminated. In the Southern Hemisphere, however, little sun reaches the ball. Days are shorter and colder and this is when they have winter. Six months later (location III), the north has winter and the south has summer. You can see how the tilt of the earth gives the south much more sunlight and how the north gets little. In spring and fall, days are about the same length all over the earth. You can see this in locations II and IV.

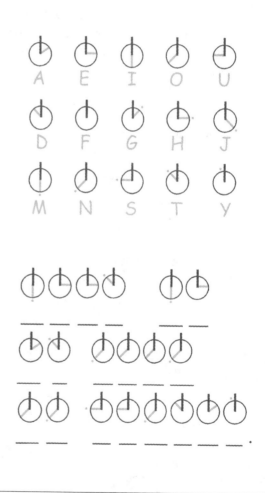

Sneaky Scientists

Two scientists want to arrange a secret meeting to discuss a new solar energy experiment. Use the sundial decoder to figure out the message that one scientist sent to the other. Write the secret message on the lines provided.

KIDS' LAB LESSONS

If you look into the sky a little beyond the sun, you'll see thousands of stars. Some of the stars appear to be connected with other stars, as if they formed a particular shape. In fact, ancient civilizations believed that the shapes formed by stars meant something, and they made up stories about the shapes. The shapes are called **constellations.** Can you find some of the more common ones?[5]

QUESTION   Why do we see only part of the moon?

EXPERIMENT OVERVIEW   In this experiment, you'll set up a model of the sun, the moon, and the earth and track the **phases of the moon** through drawings and a hands-on activity.

SCIENCE CONCEPT   Surprisingly, the same half of the moon always faces Earth. We can never see the "dark side of the moon" except from a spaceship. The only reason we can see the moon is because light from the sun reflects off its surface and back to our eyes.

As the moon orbits the earth (a journey that takes about 29 days), half of it always faces the sun. However, it isn't always the same half! So as the moon travels around the earth, we see any amount from 0 percent of the side that faces us to 100 percent of that side. These percentages are called the phases of the moon.

Formally, the phases are labeled as new moon (we can't see it), first quarter (we see the right half), full moon (we see the entire face), and third quarter (we see the left

WORDS to KNOW

constellation: any arrangement of stars in the sky into a familiar shape or pattern.

phases of the moon: the different portions of the moon that we can see during its orbit around the earth.

half). Every once in a while, the moon during its "new" phase crosses the line between the sun and the earth and-we experience a solar eclipse. Not as rare are lunar eclipses, when, during the moon's "full" phase, the earth passes between the sun and the moon and casts a shadow on-the-moon.

MATERIALS

Current newspaper
Paper plate
Marking pen
Desk lamp as bright as possible, without a shade
Small ball, a little larger than your hand
Clean sheet of paper
Time (This experiment will take up to a month to complete, but only requires a few minutes each day.)

PROCEDURE

1. Check in your local paper to find the date of the new moon. Start your experiment on this day.
2. On the paper plate, draw marks around the outer edge representing 28 days. You might want to draw lines that cut your plate in quarters and make seven marks per quarter of the circle. You will use this as your guide for locating the ball when you begin your experiment. Start at 0/28 and begin numbering in a counter-clockwise direction.

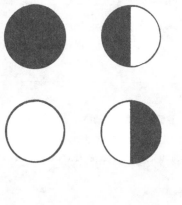

3. Set your lamp on the side of your room against one wall. Make sure this is a location you can easily keep the lamp or place it each day for your test.
4. Turn off the light in your room and turn on the lamp.

(continued on next page)

(continued from previous page)

5. Set the plate on the floor in the middle of your room and stand on it. Point Day 0/28 toward the lamp.

6. Face in the direction of the day you are recording (beginning at Day 0 and counting upward for 28 days) and hold your ball at arm's length.

7. Take a close look at the illumination of the ball. For Day 0, there should be no illumination, as this corresponds to the new-moon.

8. Record the ball's illumination on your sheet of paper in a table that allows you to-track the phases of the moon over the course of one month.

9. Repeat this step each day for 28 days. When you finish, you should have 29 drawings (Day 0 through Day 28) showing the phases of the moon.

10. Periodically, check your results with the actual moon outside at night.

QUESTIONS FOR THE SCIENTIST

- Did your drawings match the actual phases of the moon?_____

_____

- What effect did the fact that the moon's orbit is actually a little longer than 28-days have on the accuracy of your data? _____

_____

- What does the fact that solar and lunar eclipses are rare tell you about the orbit of the moon? Think about how this would look in your experiment. _____

_____

FOLLOW-UP Research the history of man's attempts to fly to the moon. What objects were left on the moon by those who visited? For a powerful look at a failed moon voyage that almost cost three astronauts their lives, rent the movie *Apollo 13*.

Fun Facts

The moon actually looks a reddish color during a lunar eclipse due to sunlight passing through the earth's atmosphere and being bent toward the moon—in effect, a "sunset" during an eclipse.

Giant Science Kriss-Kross

How can you find the answers to these science questions? If you've looked through all the chapters in this book, you will have no problem! Fill each answer into the numbered grid. The words in the shaded row will answer this riddle: **What is the best part about being a scientist?** We left you a few A-T-O-M-S to get you started. Need more help? Check out the Experiment Overviews.

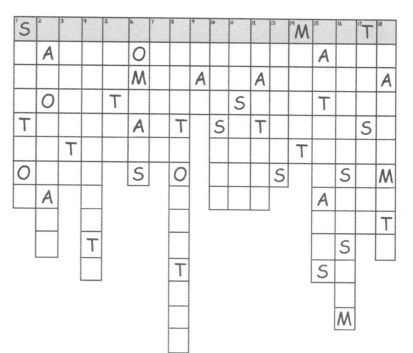

Clues:

1. A mixture of two or more liquids.
2. Animals use _____ to blend into their surroundings.
3. When you heat air in a bottle, you can _____ _ a balloon.
4. Scientists use this form of energy to light up their-laboratories. You use it at home, too!
5. Isaac _____ is the scientist who defined the laws of gravity.
6. A _____ points toward the magnetic north.
7. The sun gives us _____ in the form of heat and light.
8. A process that uses one metal to coat another metal.
9. An _____ is a picture that shows you the inside of your body.
10. Barometers are devices used to measure air _____.

11. Albert _____ is a scientist whose theories and experiments led to new ways of thinking about time, space, matter, energy, and gravity!
12. One of the Laws of Motion says that every action has an equal but opposite _____.
13. _____ only form when it is cold enough for water to freeze, but at the same time there is a way for water to drip.
14. Electricity flowing through a wire turns the wire into an electro_____.
15. A seismologist is a scientist who uses a Ricter Scale to measure the strength of _____ .
16. The _____ _____ (2 words) controls all the actions and reactions of the body.
17. An astronomer is a scientist who uses a _____ to look at the stars and planets.
18. A _____ grows up from the ground.

SCIENCE FAIR PROJECT: EARTH SCIENCE

RIVERS

Think about the last time you looked at a river—really looked at it. Was it straight, or did it bend and curve, and maybe even wind its way through town? The more you look at rivers, the more you might wonder why they aren't straight. They start in the mountains and run to the sea. It sounds like a simple path, one that they should have carved out early in their lives and never deviated from. However, the paths of rivers have surprised and intrigued people for thousands of years.

When a time of flooding comes to an area, the path of the river becomes a topic for even more discussion. It's almost like a river has a mind of its own!

QUESTION

Why aren't rivers straight?

EXPERIMENT OVERVIEW

In this experiment, you'll first get to build a mountain. To do that, you're going to need some mountain supplies and a pretty open space for the water to flow out. You're also going to need plenty of water, so plan ahead. You'll have two options to choose from, in terms of the "rain" that falls: steady or occasional. Each pattern will result in a different set of rivers, so you might even want to try both.

SCIENCE CONCEPT

When water flows down a mountain, it finds the quickest path to the bottom, even if that path isn't straight. Trees, rocks, and hills cause it to change direction and the speed it travels. When water moves slowly, it tends to dig away at its boundaries (the riverbank), and sometimes will cut out a piece of the bank, which makes the river a little wider at that point. Every time the river changes, the water flow changes and that causes even more variation in the path of the river. So over time, a river can carve out all kinds of interesting paths to the sea. But that's not all. When a new piece of the river is carved out, the current carries rocks and dirt farther downstream. Where this material lands, the river gets shallower. That is why the mouths of rivers, especially where they empty into the ocean, tend to be really wide, open, and flat, with water that moves slowly into the ocean.

MATERIALS

A large mountain of rocks, dirt, sand, mud, and so forth, at least 3 feet high
An open place where the rivers can flow and deposit the mud they accumulate as they flow down the mountain
Plenty of water, either through a hose, a sprinkler, or a watering can
Camera

PROCEDURE

1. Make sure the mountain is not the same all over. There should be obstacles all over it that will encourage the water to flow in interesting paths.

2. Predict where the rivers will form.

3. Choose a method of watering:

   Steady rain—Use a sprinkler on top of the mountain, or very near the edge of it to produce rainfall that will be steady throughout the experiment. A helpful assistant could simply hold a hose above the mountain or spray the water onto the top of the mountain. You may need to experiment to find what works best.

   Occasional rain—Use a watering can, a pitcher of water, or a short interval of rain from a hose. If you choose this method, you will need to return every hour or so to add more water. This allows the mountain to absorb some of the water and will result in a different set of rivers.

4. Begin watering the mountain.

5. If you are using a steady rain, take a picture before you begin, and then take a picture every 5 to 10 minutes until the rivers are no longer changing. Your goal is to observe the changes in the mountain over time. It's better to have too many photos than to have too few.

   If you choose the occasional rain method, take a picture before you begin and then during each rainfall. Apply the water for as long as you have chosen and then let the mountain sit until the next session. Repeat applications until the rivers stop changing. This method will likely take quite a bit longer than the other, but might give a more accurate depiction of true rainfall.

6. Keep a record of your method and the photos you took.

7. When you get the photos developed, you should have a record of the progress of the rivers you produced. If you find that the photos don't show enough change, use every other picture.

QUESTIONS FOR THE SCIENTIST

- Did the rivers form in the places you predicted?

- How much material was carried off the mountain to the surrounding area?

- Did you see any smaller rivers merge into larger rivers?

- Was there one river that changed its path more than the rest? If so, what were some of the characteristics of that river that made it change so much?

CONCLUSION

Each time you repeat this experiment, you will get a different result. That's part of the fun of science! Now that you've produced your own rivers, see if you can visit a local river and identify places where it veered over time, where it moves faster or slower than other places, and any obstacles that might affect the flow of water. Also, see if you can trace the source of the river, although it might be many miles away in the mountains.

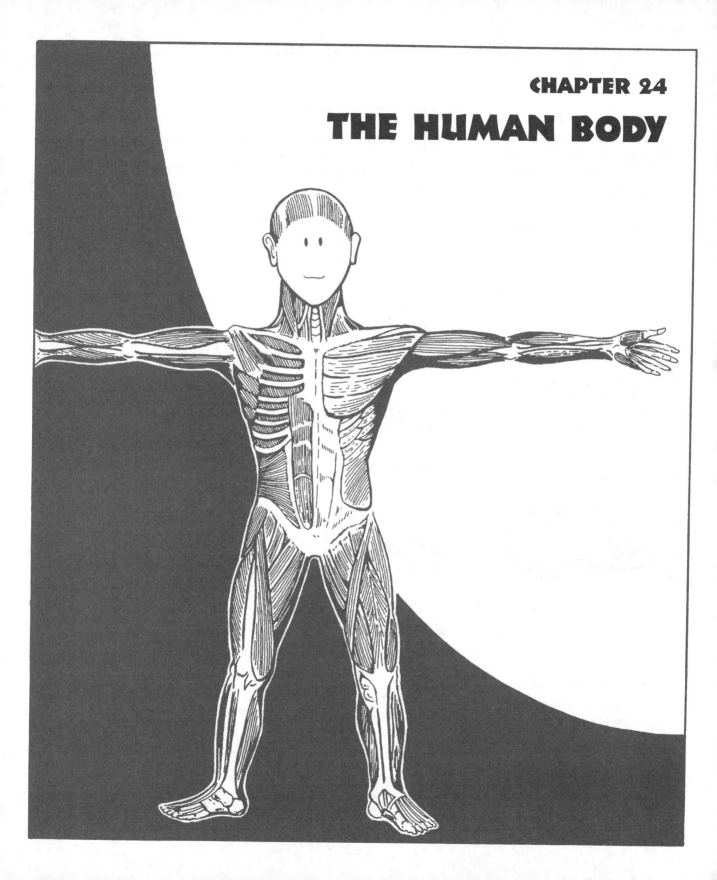

Science Online

For more fun activities involving your five senses, check out Neuroscience for Kids. Visit *http://faculty.washington.edu/chudler/chsense.html*

What did the clever scientist invent that was full of holes but could still-hold water?

A sponge!

THE FIVE SENSES

Our body is an amazing creation. In this chapter, you'll discover some of its many abilities that qualify it as a machine you won't find anywhere else in the universe. For now, though, let's focus on the ways we interact with the world around us. We have five senses: touch, taste, hearing, sight, and smell. Each of these senses allows us to understand the world in a different way and gives us a unique perspective on what we encounter each day.

TRY THIS HOT AND COLD

QUESTION
What makes us feel hot and cold?

MATERIALS
3 bowls of water: 1 warm, 1 cold, and 1 at room temperature.

PROCEDURE
1. Arrange the bowls of water in front of you from left to right as follows: warm, room temperature, cold.
2. Place your left hand in the bowl of warm water and your right hand in the bowl of cold water for 30 seconds.
3. Remove your hands from the water and place both into the middle bowl (room temperature).

Fun Facts

Insects use their antennae for up to four of their senses: touch, smell, taste, and hearing.

WHAT'S HAPPENING

Hot and cold are just a way of comparing what we are used to with what we are feeling. Your left hand was used to warm water, so when you placed it into the bowl with water at room temperature, it felt quite cold. On the other side, your right hand was used to cold water, so when you placed it into room-temperature water, it felt warm. Both hands were in the same water, but since they were used to different temperatures, one felt cold and the other felt warm.

FOLLOW-UP

Next time you take a bath or a shower, think about how the bathroom air feels when you get out. Ask someone who is dry to tell you how the air feels and see if you can explain why you perceive the air differently. Another place to try this is at a swimming pool. Try to explain how warm or cold the air and water feel when you are dry and when you are wet. Heat flows naturally from warm objects to cool objects and makes us feel warm or cold as a result.

Did you hear about the scientist who invented a gas that could burn through anything ?

Wow, that's terrific!

No, it's terrible—now he's trying to invent something to keep it in!

TRY THIS TASTELESS MEDICINE

QUESTION
Why can't I taste medicine when I plug my nose?

MATERIALS
Blindfold
Nose plug or your hand
Equal-sized pieces of apple, potato, onion, and jicama
Assistant

PROCEDURE
1. Place the blindfold over your eyes and plug your nose.
2. Have your assistant place one item into your mouth at a time, and try to guess what it is based only on how it tastes.

How many scientists does it take to make a stink bomb?

A phew!

Cool Quotes

Smell is a potent wizard that transports us across thousands of miles and all the years we have lived.

—Helen Keller

What's Going On?

Can you figure out these small picture clues? When you think of a word to go with each picture, fit it in the grid going up and down. Then you will need to add some extra letters to the shaded row. When you're finished, you will have the name of a group of important body functions. We gave you the Es to help you complete this experiment!

WHAT'S HAPPENING

Your sense of smell is a major
food items taste. When your no
you lose your normal ability to
from their textures, you probabl
detect the difference between th
tasted. When you unplug your no
flavors should come back, althoug
gest ones might overwhelm the otl

FOLLOW-UP

Have you ever had a really bad cold?
might remember that your food tasted
bland. When your nose is stuffed up, y
lose the sense of taste that you are acc
tomed to. As soon as your cold cleared up, you
were able to taste things again!

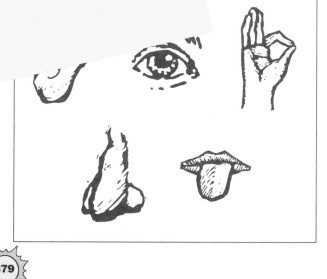

KIDS' LAB LESSONS

QUESTION   How can I taste different flavors?

EXPERIMENT OVERVIEW   In this experiment you will place different food items on different locations of your tongue to determine which taste buds can sense which flavors. You'll test sweet, sour, bitter, and salty.

SCIENCE CONCEPT   Our tongue has thousands of tiny taste buds on it. Each one reacts to a certain kind of taste. Taste buds that respond to the same taste are grouped together in certain locations on your tongue. Therefore, you will always taste salty foods in certain places, sweet foods in other places, and sour and bitter foods in still other places, no matter what food you are eating.

WORDS to KNOW

taste buds: little organs all over our tongues that interpret or pick up the sense of what flavors are in our food and liquids.

MATERIALS
Cotton swabs
Small bowls containing the following:
    Lemon juice
    Water
    Sugar
    Table salt
    Instant coffee
A diagram of the tongue, shown
    on page 103
Marking pen

Fun Facts

A typical human has around 116 taste buds per square centimeter at the tip of the tongue, compared to an average of 25 taste buds per square centimeter near the back of the tongue.

PROCEDURE

1. Dip a cotton swab in the lemon juice and spread it around your mouth.
2. Mark on the diagram where on your tongue you sensed this sour taste.
3. Dip a second cotton swab in water and then into the sugar. Spread enough around in your mouth so that you can tell where your tongue senses this sweet taste.
4. Repeat this same procedure with the salt and the instant coffee (a bitter taste).
5. Record on the picture the locations where you sensed each taste.
6. Check your picture to make sure that you have covered each part of the tongue. If you missed one, repeat the experiment to find the taste sensed by that part of the tongue.

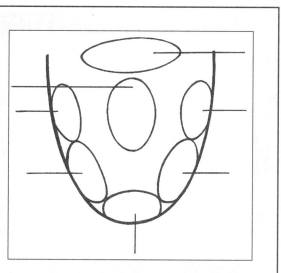

QUESTIONS FOR THE SCIENTIST

- Which parts of the tongue responded to sour? _____

- Which parts of the tongue responded to sweet? _____

- Which parts of the tongue responded to salty? _____

- Which parts of the tongue responded to bitter? _____

- Does your diagram of the tongue explain the location of sores after eating too much sugar? _____

_____

FOLLOW-UP

Try other foods that you know to be in one of these four categories. When you eat them, try to see if you can taste them on the part of your tongue that you marked in this experiment. Try plugging your nose and testing for these four tastes. Does your nose affect your ability to recognize tastes?[1]

TRY THIS CYAN, BLACK, AND YELLOW

Have you ever looked at a picture that had really bright colors only to find that when you looked away, you saw even more colors, though different from the ones in the picture? If so, you've experienced another side of afterimages. You learned a little about these earlier in the book (see page 64), but there's more to the story. Your eyes have the ability not only to "see" two images at a time, as you discovered in the "Bird Cage" experiment, but they can also block certain colors and keep them from being seen.

WORDS to KNOW

complementary color: a color that is the opposite of another color.

QUESTION

What colors can you see in an afterimage?

MATERIALS

Several sheets of paper

Marking pens, including blue, red, green, black, yellow, and cyan (like turquoise or teal)

Color picture of the American flag

PROCEDURE

1. On your first three sheets of paper, draw large circles. On sheet one filling the circle in red. On sheet two make it blue, and on sheet three make it green.

2. In order, focus your eyes on each of the circles (one at a time) for about 30 seconds.

3. After focusing on each of the circles, either look at a blank sheet of white paper or simply close your eyes. Describe the colors you see.

4. Next, focus your eyes on the picture of the American flag, again for about 30 seconds.

5. Look away and describe the new colors of the flag you see as an afterimage.

6. Try to draw an afterimage American flag. Make the stripes black and cyan, while the stars should also be black, but set on a yellow background. Use the picture of the actual flag as a guide.

7. When you are done, focus intently on your flag, then look away. Do you see the true colors of the flag?

WHAT'S HAPPENING

Your eyes use cones to detect colors. When you focus your eyes on a certain color, like green, your cones work extra hard to help you see that color. Then, when you look away, the cones for that color relax and temporarily don't work as well. Therefore you see everything but the original color. The term for what you see is **complementary color.** Can you tell which colors you see as afterimages of red, green, and blue?[2]

When you viewed the American flag, your cones focused on red, white, and blue. When you relaxed your eyes by looking away, the afterimage you saw was of the complementary colors of red, white, and blue. Those colors are cyan, black, and yellow.

FOLLOW-UP

Figure out which eye is your dominant one. Try the following test:

• Hold up a tube to your eye—which eye do you close and which do you use to sight through the tube? _____

I Can't Believe My Eyes!

Do your eyes always see things in just one way? No! Optical illusions are a kind of puzzle designed to fool your eyes (and your brain). See if you can tell the difference between illusion and reality in the following puzzles.

Do you see a 13 or a B in the center of the figures above?

What do you see where the white lines cross?

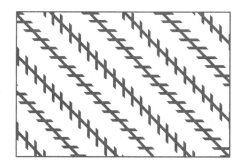

Are the long black lines parallel (even) with each other, or are they crooked?

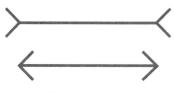

Which line is longer?

KIDS' LAB LESSONS

QUESTION   How does my eye work?

EXPERIMENT OVERVIEW   In this experiment you'll build a model that shows you what kinds of **images** your eyes form. You can determine the size of the image and will see how to extend this concept to building a **pinhole camera**.

SCIENCE CONCEPT   Your eye is a complex device designed to gather light, focus it onto your retina, and send signals to your brain about what you are seeing. The lens of your eye takes light rays from all around you and focuses them to a single spot on the back of your eye. There, the rods and cones turn that image into something your brain can understand. As complex as your eye is, you can build a model of your eye that produces an image that is quite similar to what your eye produces.

WORDS to KNOW

image: what we see when we look at something. The image is formed in our head and transferred to our brain.

pinhole camera: a device which allows you to look at an object indirectly.

lens: an optical device that bends light rays and makes it possible for us to see.

MATERIALS
Safety pin
Paper cup
Rubber band
Wax paper
Bare light bulb, turned on

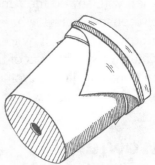

PROCEDURE
1. Poke a small hole with the pin in the bottom of the cup. If you want to make it bigger later on, you can. For now, keep it pretty small.

2. Use the rubber band to secure a square of wax paper across the top of the cup. This will be your screen.
3. Point the bottom of the cup at the light bulb from a distance of 2 to 3 feet.
4. Slowly move toward the light while keeping a close eye on the wax paper.
5. When you get close enough, you will see an image of the light bulb on the wax paper, but it will be upside down.

QUESTIONS FOR THE SCIENTIST

- How close did you get to the light before you could see the light bulb's image on the wax paper? _____

- How does this distance change if you make the hole in the bottom of the cup slightly bigger? _____

- Why is the image upside down? _____

- How is this similar to the way a camera works? _____

FOLLOW-UP

Now that you have built this model of your eye, you are ready to build a pinhole camera, which operates on many of the same principles.

You will need a ruler, an empty can of Pringles potato chips, a knife (with help from an adult), a thumbtack, tape, and aluminum foil.

1. Measure 2 to 3 inches from the bottom of the can and have an adult cut the tube into two smaller tubes.
2. Use the thumbtack to poke a small hole in the bottom of the smaller tube and place the plastic lid of the original can on top.
3. Place the larger tube on top of the smaller tube so that the lid lies between them. Tape these together to re-form the original tube.
4. Wrap aluminum foil around the whole tube. This needs to keep as much light out as possible so make sure you cover the entire can.
5. Hold the open end close to your eye and look into the tube. You should see inverted images projected on the screen (the plastic lid).

WORDS to KNOW

machine: a device that performs a specific task.

lungs: the sacks in our chest that fill up with air when we breathe.

Fun Facts

Swimmer Amy van Dyken won four gold medals at the 1996 Olympic Games in Atlanta despite having only 65 percent of the lung capacity of an average person due to asthma.

Why did the scientist take his nose apart?

He wanted to see what made it run!

HUMAN MACHINE

Human beings have produced some remarkable **machines** in the past hundred years or so. The airplane, the automobile, and the computer are just a few examples of machines invented by ordinary people that have forever changed our lives. But if you want to see a machine that is more complex, more beautiful, and more unique than any of these, look in the mirror. Our bodies are capable of things that no machine will ever be able to accomplish, no matter how powerful computers get. As we wrap this book up, let's take a look at some of the wonderful things human bodies can do.

TRY THIS DEEP BREATH

QUESTION

How much air can my **lungs** hold?

MATERIALS

Large, empty 1-gallon glass jar
32-ounce (quart) glass jar
Water
Large flat container, for example, an aquarium
Permanent marker
3 flat stones or other flat items
Sink or location that can get wet
18 to 24 inches of rubber tubing
1 sheet of paper
1 writing utensil

PROCEDURE

1. Fill the large jar by repeatedly filling the 32-ounce jar with water and emptying it into the large jar.

2. After each quart of water is added, make a mark on the jar indicating the height of one quart.

3. Fill the aquarium about three-quarters full of water and place the stones in a circle on the bottom.

4. Place the aquarium in the sink. Carefully turn the large jar over and place it on the stones on the bottom of the aquarium. Don't worry if some water spills out.

5. Make a note of the initial water level in the jar. This will be your starting point.

6. Place one end of the rubber tubing into the aquarium and under the mouth of the jar. Let the other end hang over the side of the aquarium.

Cool Quotes

The simplest schoolboy is now familiar with truths for which Archimedes would have sacrificed his life.

—Ernest Renan, French philosopher and theologian

7. Take a deep breath and blow into the free end of the rubber tubing.

8. Measure the resulting mark of the water in the jar.

9. Subtract the original mark to find your lung capacity in quarts.

WHAT'S HAPPENING

When you blow air out of your lungs and into the jar, it replaces some of the water. The water level will rise in the aquarium. You can measure how much air was added to the jar to see how much air your lungs held. Try this experiment again and see if you can improve your results.

The silly scientist discovered something that has a bottom at the top—what is it?

Your legs!

Fun Facts

The typical human reaction time in an experiment like the one you performed is around 0.20-seconds.

Science Online

Visit a human body online at *www.pa.k12.ri.us/Curric/Science/Human1.htm*

TRY THIS ACTION-REACTION

Every time someone gets into a car to drive, they must make decisions that will keep them safe. Some of them can be made slowly, for example, whether or not to roll the window down, while others must be made very quickly, such as swerving to avoid a collision with another car.

QUESTION

What is my reaction time?

MATERIALS

Dollar bill or note card
Friend
Ruler

PROCEDURE

1. Hold the dollar bill vertically lengthwise with one hand while placing your other hand's thumb and forefinger near the bottom of it.
2. Drop the bill and catch it with your other hand. You should be able to do this easily.
3. Now have your friend do the dropping. You should not know when the bill is to be dropped.

Cool Quotes

Every science begins as philosophy and ends as art.

—Will Durant

WHAT'S HAPPENING

When you dropped the bill, your brain was able to send a signal to your other hand telling it to start catching it. When your friend dropped the bill, you didn't have that head start, so you got a more accurate reading for your reaction time. The lower on the bill you were able to catch it, the faster your reaction time. If you weren't able to catch it at all, you aren't alone. Try dropping a ruler instead.[3]

FOLLOW-UP

This reaction time test is one of many you could do. See if you can come up with your own test.

_____

_____

_____

_____

_____

_____

I See!

If you are conducting experiments you must use your powers of observation—that means you must look very carefully at your information so as not to miss an important detail! Practice your powers by finding the 10 differences between these two pictures.

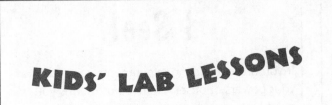

KIDS' LAB LESSONS

QUESTION   What is my **pulse**?

EXPERIMENT OVERVIEW   In this experiment you'll be measuring your pulse (heart rate) after several different activities. You'll also learn how to use different time intervals to measure your heart rate and where the best places are to find your heartbeat.

pulse/heart rate: how many times per minute your heart beats.

SCIENCE CONCEPT   Each time your heart beats it delivers oxygen-rich blood to your body, which allows it to function properly. When you are resting, your heart rate slows down, as your body doesn't need as much blood as it does when you exercise. People who are in good physical condition are able to engage in strenuous activities while keeping their heart rate low. On your body, the strongest beats can usually be felt over your heart, in your neck just below your jaw, on the inside of your wrists, and on your thumbs.

MATERIALS   Stopwatch

PROCEDURE
1. Sit quietly for a few minutes before beginning this test.
2. When you are ready, place your first two fingers either on your neck or on the inside of your wrist and locate your pulse.
3. Once you find your pulse, start the watch and for 60 seconds, count the number of beats you feel. That is your pulse.

4. Try the experiment again, but this time count for only 30 seconds. When you are done, multiply your count by two. Compare your pulses.
5. Repeat by counting for 15 seconds and multiplying your count by four, then counting for 10 seconds and multiplying by six.
6. Once you have determined your resting pulse, go somewhere that you can exercise vigorously for at least one minute. Exercise of this sort might include a fast jog, running stairs, skipping rope, or doing pushups. When you are done, you should be breathing hard. CAUTION: Do not exert yourself beyond what you are comfortable with. Pick an activity you can do safely.
7. Choose the length of the test you wish to perform and find your pulse again.
8. Compare your resting pulse with your pulse after exercise.

QUESTIONS FOR THE SCIENTIST

- What was your resting pulse? _____
- Which result(s) did you use to come up with this number? _____
- What was your pulse after exercise? _____
- What are the advantages to timing for a full minute to find your pulse? _____
- What are the advantages to timing over a shorter period of time (like 10 seconds), especially when you have just finished exercising? _____
- The American Heart Association has determined that the maximum heart rate should be 220 minus a person's age. Was your highest rate below that number?

_____

FOLLOW-UP

Regular exercise can reduce both your resting heart rate and your heart rate after exercise. For a long-term study of your own heart rate, try exercising for 15 to 20 minutes daily for one month. Once a week, recheck your heart rates before and after exercise to see if they go down. If you plan on drastically changing your exercise patterns, check with your parents or your doctor to make sure the change is appropriate for you.

WORDS to KNOW

balance: your ability to stay standing without falling over.

Fun Facts

One of the most natural and effective cures for motion sickness is ginger. Some people eat gingersnap cookies, while others drink ginger ale.

What kind of scientist studies shopping?

A buy-ologist!

TRY THIS BLIND BALANCE

One of the most fun things to do as a kid is to spin around really fast and get dizzy. Our sense of **balance** comes from our ears and the liquid inside them that sometimes gets sloshed around. When it calms down, the dizziness generally goes away. Balance is a difficult condition to understand. So is the question of why some people get dizzy riding in the back seat of a car or on a boat while others can ride the wildest roller coasters or perform as gymnasts or figure skaters and never get the slightest bit dizzy.

QUESTION

Is it harder to balance with your eyes closed?

MATERIALS

None

PROCEDURE

1. Stand on both feet in the middle of the room.
2. Try to balance for 30 seconds.
3. Close both eyes and try to balance for 30 seconds. Compare the difficulty of the two tasks.
4. Stand on one leg and balance for 15 seconds. Do not touch anything for support.
5. Close your eyes, stand on one leg, and try to balance for 15 seconds.

WHAT'S HAPPENING

Much of your sense of balance comes from your ability to see your surroundings. When you lose the ability to measure your balance with respect to the room (by closing your eyes) you have a harder time keeping your balance. People who get seasick on a boat have a similar problem. They look out at the land and water and it's all moving. Since there is no fixed point that they can look at, they lose their balance (and sometimes much more).

FOLLOW-UP

Try standing very close to a wall and repeating the experiment with one leg and both legs. This time, lightly touch the wall. Try not to use it for balance, just to remind you that it's there. Does it help you stay balanced?[4]

_____

_____

_____

Boy, Do You Look Familiar!

Do parents and their children look exactly alike? No, but often people can pick family members out of a group. Study the following faces and see if you can do it, too. Draw a line matching each pair of relatives.

393

KIDS' LAB LESSONS

WORDS to KNOW

center of gravity: your body's balance point.

QUESTION   Where is my **center of gravity**?

EXPERIMENT OVERVIEW   In this experiment you'll perform several physical tasks along with other people to determine the differences between the center of gravity of a man and a woman, as well as the differences between kids and adults.

SCIENCE CONCEPT   Every object has a center of gravity. It is the part of the object that must be supported to keep from falling over. Adult men and women have different centers of gravity, as you will see. Kids, due to the fact that they have not yet physically developed like adults have, don't always show those same differences.

MATERIALS   Adults and kids of both sexes   Coffee cup
                 Wall   Stool

PROCEDURE   Have each participant try these tasks. See who can complete them.

Test 1
1. Stand next to a wall so that one side of your body, including your foot, is touching the wall.
2. Try to lift your other foot off the ground and stay standing.

Test 2
1. Place the coffee cup 8 to 10 inches in front of your feet while standing in the middle of a room.
2. Bend over and pick up the cup.
3. Now move so that you are standing with your back and feet to a wall.

4. Place the cup 8 to 10 inches in front of you and try to bend over and pick it up.
5. Try to describe why this second task is so difficult. Repeat the original test in the middle of the room if you wish.

Test 3

1. Kneel on the floor and place the coffee cup the length of your forearm in front of your knees.
2. Place your hands behind your back and try to knock the cup over with your nose.

Test 4

1. Stand with your feet together, about 2 feet in front of a wall.
2. Have someone place a stool between your feet and the wall.
3. Lean toward the wall until your forehead is touching it. Keep your back straight while you do this.
4. Pick up the stool and hold it to your chest.
5. From this position, try to straighten your back and stand up.

QUESTIONS FOR THE SCIENTIST

- In Test 1, why do you fall immediately when you lift your outside leg?
- Try this same test in the middle of the room. Why don't you fall?
- Why are you able to pick up the cup while standing in the middle of the room, but you can't reach it with your back against the wall?

- Is there a difference in performance between men and women, or between adults and kids, for the first two tests?
- Is there a difference in performance between men and women, or between adults and kids, for the last two tests?
- Thinking about the idea of center of gravity, why do you suppose women have an easier time with the last two tests than men do?
- Kids tend to do better on these final tasks than adult men do. Can you think of a reason why this might be?

FOLLOW-UP

Think up other interesting tests you can perform to test for center of gravity.[5] Also, think of jobs or sports that require good balance and a knowledge of center of gravity. Do you engage in an activity that requires you to keep your balance? If so, think about where your center of gravity is during that activity.

SCIENCE FAIR PROJECT: HUMAN BODY

GENETICS

Perhaps people have told you that you "look just like your mother" or that you "have your father's eyes." If you have siblings, you may see no resemblance, while others say, "I can tell you are related." What is it about our looks that says so much about who we are and where we came from? The answer lies in our genes—the blueprint for how we are made. Each of us inherits our genes from our biological parents. But some traits or characteristics are more common, or dominant, in our families, while others are recessive, or less likely to occur. We can't easily look inside our genetic code to see what traits we inherited from which parent, but we can use a survey and probability to predict the patterns.

QUESTION

Why are my eyes green?

EXPERIMENT OVERVIEW

In this experiment you and your parents will complete a survey that asks about certain inherited traits, or traits that you have no control over. Then you'll pick two of them to complete a probability study using a tool called a Punnett square.

SCIENCE CONCEPT

Traits like hair or eye color, attached ear lobes, hitchhiker's thumb, and the ability to roll your tongue are called dominant or recessive. Each of us has two genes for each trait in us—one we inherited from our mother and one from our father. As you might expect, a person who has two dominant genes or two recessive genes will have that trait. However, a person with one of each will display the trait of the dominant gene even though they possess the recessive gene as well. Here's an example.

Suppose you own two black rabbits and they produce a baby rabbit. In rabbits, black fur is a dominant gene (shown as a capital letter) and brown is a recessive gene (shown as a lowercase letter). Let's suppose in this case that your two rabbits each have a black and a brown fur gene. Can you explain why they both have black fur? When they have a baby, the baby will inherit one of the many combinations of fur genes from its parents—either two blacks, a brown and a black, or two browns. In the first two cases, the baby will also have black fur. There is actually a 75 percent chance that this will happen. But there is a 25 percent chance that the baby will inherit both parents' brown fur genes and will be born with brown fur. That is, two black rabbits can produce a brown rabbit.

The Punnett square below shows how this could happen.

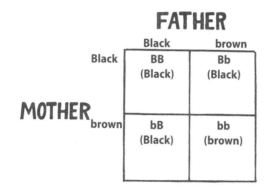

So if both of your parents have brown eyes but yours are green, that is a perfectly reasonable possibility.

MATERIALS

Survey (at the end of the chapter)
You and your biological parents. If this isn't possible, find someone who has access to his or her biological parents and ask him to help you.
Punnett square
2 coins

PROCEDURE

1. Complete the survey; then ask each of your parents to complete it as well. If you can think of other traits to include, add them.

2. Talk with your parents about the results. Discuss how many of the traits of each parent you have.

3. Pick two of the traits for the second part of the experiment. One should be a trait that both parents have in common but you do not have, if possible. Otherwise, just pick a trait that you all have in common. The second should be a trait that your parents differ on.

4. For each trait you select, build a Punnett square that could produce your family's results. A sample is shown below. Mother has green eyes, father has brown eyes, child has green eyes. In this case, the brown gene is dominant over the green gene. This could occur in either of the combinations on the right.

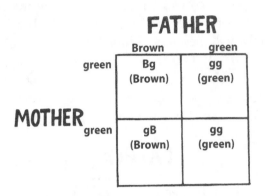

FATHER

	Brown	green
green	Bg (Brown)	gg (green)
green	gB (Brown)	gg (green)

MOTHER

5. Count the number of smaller squares that could produce your results. For the example above, there are two.

6. Divide this number by four, the total number of squares, to determine the probability, or chance, of this result occurring. For this example, the probability is 50 percent.

7. On a piece of paper, decide which gene will be represented by heads and which will be tails for each coin you will be flipping. It might be easier to use different coins to represent each parent.

8. Toss both coins 20 times for each trait. Count the number of times you get a result that matches your own results (in our example, the result we're looking for is that the child has green eyes) and divide that number by 20. This is your experimental probability.

9. Compare your experimental probability with your theoretical probability and present your findings.

QUESTIONS FOR THE SCIENTIST

- Are there any traits that your parents share but that you do not possess? What are they?

- Are there traits that all three of you share?

- Do you think these traits are carried by dominant or recessive genes?

- How close were your experimental results to the values you calculated from the Punnett square?

- What does it mean if your results don't match your predictions?

- Does the Punnett square mean that if a mother and father have four children each child will fit into one of the squares? Why or why not?

CONCLUSION

Genetics is one of the most fascinating and scary topics in biological research today. From cloning to disease prevention, doctors are searching for ways to improve our lives by understanding what it is we are made of. So far, there is no guaranteed way to predict the traits of one's children, and that's probably a good thing. However, an understanding of your past helps you prepare for your future and that's one of the many reasons why children who are adopted try to find their birth parents. No matter who we are, it's reassuring to know that we didn't happen by chance, and that there is a plan, however complex it may be, for our being who we are.

SURVEY

1. Can you roll your tongue? Stick out your tongue. Try to curl it into a u. Write "yes" or "no."
You_____
Mother_____
Father_____

2. Are you right or left thumbed? Put your hands together, interlocking your fingers. Which thumb is on top? Write "right" or "left."
You_____
Mother_____
Father_____

3. Do you have dimples? Smile at a friend. Do they see any dimples? Write "yes" or "no."
You_____

Mother_____

Father_____

4. Are your earlobes attached or unattached? Write "attached" or "unattached."
You_____
Mother_____
Father_____

5. Do you have "hitchhiker's thumb" (curved thumb when you stick it straight out)? Write "yes" or "no."
You_____
Mother_____
Father_____

NOTES

Chapter 20

1. *Water Colors (page 280)*—You should usually water the ground around your plants, not just the leaves. While some water is absorbed through leaves, the plant will get its water more easily by the process you saw in the experiment—through its roots in the ground.

2. *Falling Leaves (page 282)*—The leaves change color when the days begin to get shorter. With less light, the trees are not able to produce as much chlorophyll, and this begins the process of falling leaves.

Chapter 21

1. *Boiling Ice (page 302)*—When the ice melts into liquid water, it is still very cold. In fact, it's 0°C (32°F), just like the ice was. Water can boil only when it is all at 100°C (212°F), so before it can start boiling again, all the melted ice must be warmed up to 100°C. Once all the water in the pot is at that temperature, it will begin boiling once more.

2. *Cleaning Pennies (page 318)*—The other coins listed are not coated with copper. The cleaning reaction works only with a weak acid (like the vinegar/salt solution) and copper. You won't get the same results with the other coins.

Chapter 22

1. *Seesaw (page 326)*—Two pennies 6 inches away will balance, as would one penny located 12 inches away. Unfortunately, on this ruler, the farthest you can get away from the fulcrum is 6 inches. Another combination that would work would be eight pennies located 1½ inches from the fulcrum (because 8 × 1½ = 12).

2. *Teeter-Totter (page 327)*—The heavier person needs to sit closer to the middle (the fulcrum) so his or her weight doesn't count as much. With your parents, the weight difference might be big, especially if you are young. Your parent might have to sit almost at the middle to make the teeter-totter balance, but it can be done.

3. *Cushioning the Blow (page 329)*—Some examples: boxers wear padded gloves; bicycles have padded seats; tennis shoes have padded soles; air bags in cars soften the impact in an accident; and catchers in baseball use a soft, oversized mitt to catch pitches.

4. *Corners (page 332)*—Helium is lighter than air, so unlike most objects, it doesn't fall to the ground. Instead, it rises upward, toward the sky. When the car turns, everything in the car wants to keep moving in a straight line except the balloon. It wants to follow the turn. For more fun, watch what a balloon does when

you speed up and slow down in a car. You'll soon see why balloons in a car can be a safety hazard.

5. *Magnetic Electricity (page 338)*—The electromagnet formed by the electricity works only when the battery is attached. When you disconnect it, the compass returns to normal. However, when you place the wire under the compass, the magnet formed by the electricity is flipped so it points in the opposite direction. Thus, the compass also points in the opposite direction.

6. *Electromagnet (page 340)*—One of the most common places you'll find electromagnets of this kind is a wrecking yard. There they use a crane with an electromagnet turned on to lift large vehicles into the air, and when they are ready to drop them into their new location, they simply turn the magnet off and the vehicle drops.

Chapter 23

1. *Wind Speed (page 353)*—First, you need to measure the radius of your anemometer (the distance from one of the cups to the center of your device) in inches. Then you multiply that number by 6.28 to find the circumference, or the distance a cup will travel in one complete circle. Now, count the number of circles, or revolutions, the marked cup makes in one minute. Multiply this number times your circumference and you'll have a speed in inches per minute. To convert this speed to miles per hour, simply divide this final result by 1,056 and you'll have your speed in miles per hour.

   Example:

   Your radius is approximately 8 inches. This makes a circumference of $8 \times 6.28 = 50.24$ inches. If you count 40 revolutions in one minute, then the cup travels a total of 40×50.24 inches $= 2,010$ inches in one minute. Divide this result by 1,056 and you get a speed of 1.9 miles per hour.

2. *Land Warmer (page 358)*—Only the top layer of sand gets warm on a typical beach. The sun cannot reach the lower levels of sand, so it isn't able to heat those levels. For the same reason, the top layer of water in a pool or even a small lake is often warmer than deeper water.

3. *Icicles (page 360)*—Epsom salts is often used to help heal bruises and sprains. It is also used in the production of high fructose corn syrup, something you'll find in most soft drinks. One of its most popular uses is in bathtubs for people who want to soak and relax. If you have problems with raccoons, you can sprinkle it around your garbage cans and it will drive the raccoons off without harming them. As an added benefit, it is great food for your plants, too!

4. *Space of Air (page 362)*—In the summer, balls can become very bouncy when left in the sun, but in the winter they become a little flat if left in the cold. Also, if you keep juice in your refrigerator in a pitcher with a cap or tight lid, take it out and let it sit on the counter for a few minutes with the lid still closed. When you finally open the lid, you'll hear the air escape. For another fun experiment, blow up a small balloon and place it in the freezer. You'll be able to see the effects of air compressing as it cools.

5. *Constellations (page 368)*—Look toward the north for what appears to be a large cup with a handle. This is called the Big Dipper, but it is actually part of a larger constellation called Ursa Major—the Great Bear. Look on a star chart to see the shape of the bear. Using the two stars at the far right of the dipper, trace a straight line upward until you encounter another star. It isn't the brightest star in the sky, but it's an important one. It's the North Star (Polaris) and it indicates the direction of due north.

   The North Star is actually part of a constellation called the Little Dipper, or Ursa Minor. Some people say that the Little Dipper pours its contents into the Big Dipper.

   Other interesting constellations to find include Orion, the hunter (recognizable by his "belt," which is made up of three stars in a row), which is visible throughout the winter months; Cassiopeia, the queen (a *W*-shaped collection of five stars found in the northern skies); Gemini, the twins (winter); Pegasus, the winged horse (autumn); and Leo, the lion (spring). See how many you can find on your own!

Chapter 24

1. *Taste Buds (page 380)*—As you saw earlier, your sense of smell has a major impact on your ability to taste. When your nose is plugged, your taste buds aren't able to send the proper signals to your brain to tell it what kind of flavor they are tasting.

2. *Cyan, Black, and Yellow (page 382)*—The complement of red is cyan, for green it's magenta, and for blue it's yellow. The complement of white (all colors) is black (no colors). That is why a flag of yellow, black, and cyan should produce an afterimage of a flag that is red, white, and blue.

3. *Reaction Time (page 388)*—

If the ruler fell . . .	your reaction time is . . .
4 inches	0.14 seconds
8 inches	0.20 seconds
12 inches	0.25 seconds

4. *Balance (page 392)*—Just having the wall close by serves as a reminder that something is fixed and not moving. You should find it easier to stay standing, especially on one leg, when you lightly touch the wall.

5. *Center of Gravity (page 394)*—Take a yardstick and place your two forefingers under it to support it. It doesn't matter where you put them. Now, slowly move your fingers toward one another, keeping the yardstick balanced. They will meet at the location of the yardstick's center of gravity (usually the middle). You can hang something on one end to change the center of gravity and try it again—you will always find it using this method.

PUZZLE ANSWERS

page 278 • Quote Fall

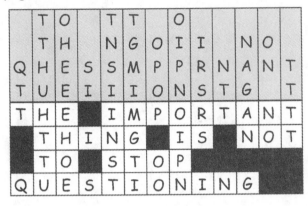

	T O		T T		O					
	T H		N G	O	I	I		N O		
Q	H E	S S	M P	P	R	N	A N		T
T U	E I	I I	I O	N	S	T	G		T
T H E		I M	P O	R	T	A N	T
	T H	I N	G		I S			N O	T
	T O		S T	O P
Q U E	S T	I O	N I	N G

page 290 • Scientific Transformation

1. BANANA
2. BANNAA   move second N close to first N
3. BALLAA   change N to L
4. BALLOO   change A to O
5. BALLOON   add N

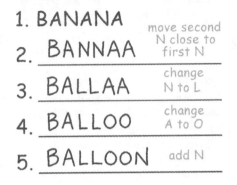

page 286 • Totally Tubular

END

START

page 295 • Eye Spy

Goose	Owl
Snake	Mouse
Bunny	Snail
Giraffe	Spider
Moth	Hummingbird

PUZZLE ANSWERS

page 309 • **Egg-sactly!**

Smart person:
EGG <u>HEAD</u>

Money you have saved:
<u>NEST</u> EGG

Colorful treat hunted for in the spring:
<u>EASTER</u> EGG

Words of caution:
DON'T <u>PUT</u> ALL <u>YOUR</u> EGGS IN <u>ONE</u> <u>BASKET</u>.

Word List

EASTER   BASKET
YOUR   NEST
PUT   ONE
HEAD

page 319 • **Acid Bath**

EMILY
JOHN
NICK
KAITLIN

page 314• **Amazing Bubbles**

page 333 • **Around the Bend**

WHYGDLIDTHE
FAIRRESITUI
PNNANVERAYS
HPEVITYHNYA
YSRICISTCCA
SRTIAOMSECS
ICSTHFORNEP
LAYNOITECGR
ROUND?WTOEG
ETTOTTHEAOT
HERNOITCSLI
DE!NHAHAHA!

PUZZLE ANSWERS

page 343 • Catchy Categories

Properties of Motion

Properties of Matter

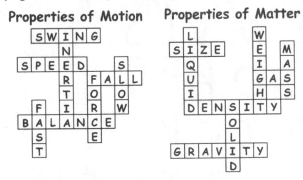

page 345 • Black and White

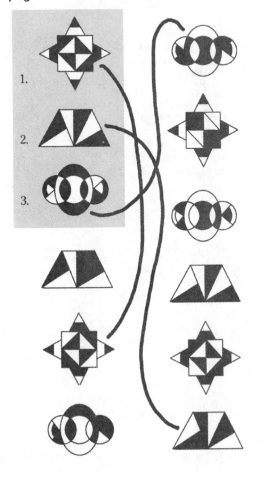

page 353 • Wind Speed

Here are some possible answers:

Three-Letter Words:	Four-Letter Words:	Five-Letter Words:
ant	ram	moan	enter
are	ran	more	manor
arm	rat	name	meant
art	tan	near	meter
ate	tar	neat	tenor
ear	tea	note	
eat	ten	rant	Six-Letter Words:
era	toe	rate	remote
man	ton	rent	rename
mat		roam	moment
men	Four-Letter Words:	rote	meteor
met	amen	tame	
mom	ammo	team	Seven-Letter Word:
net	atom	tear	memento
not	earn	teen	
oar	mane	term	
oat	mare	tone	
one	mate	torn	
ore	mean	tram	
	meat	tree	
	meet		

page 357 • Head in the Clouds

PUZZLE ANSWERS

page 359 • **Up or Down?**

A <u>STALACTITE</u>

hangs <u>TIGHT</u> to the ceiling.

A <u>STALAGMITE</u>

grows <u>MIGHTY</u> tall from

the floor.

page 367 • **Sneaky Scientists**

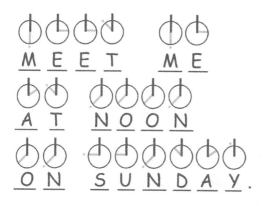

M E E T   M E

A T   N O O N

O N   S U N D A Y .

page 371 • **Giant Science Kriss-Kross**

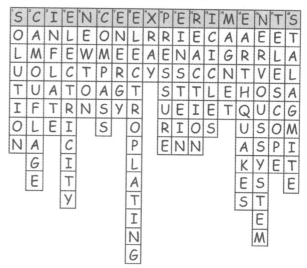

page 379 • **What's Going On?**

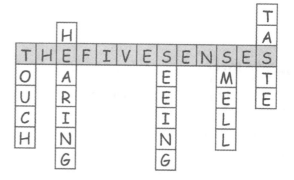

PUZZLE ANSWERS

page 383 • I Can't Believe My Eyes!

13 or B?
You see a number 13 or a capital letter B depending on which way you read, left to right, or top to bottom. Visually, the letters and numbers are so similar that the figure in the middle trick your eyes, and can be read either way.

Crooked Lines or Straight?
The long black lines are parallel to each other. Take a ruler and measure to see that this is true. The short lines that go in different directions fool your eyes into thinking that the long lines are crooked.

Longer or Shorter?
Both lines are the same length. Measure them to see that this is true. The short, slanting lines at the end of the longer lines fools you eyes into thinking the top line is longer.

Where the Lines Cross
You should see flashing grey dots where the white lines cross. What's really interesting is that if you look directly at a gray spot, it disappears!

page 389 • I See!

Differences in the two pictures happen in these places:

1. Flower in girl's hat
2. Lines on girl's socks
3. Leaves on plant in flowerpot
4. Lines on flowerpot
5. Label on watering can
6. Number of checks on calendar
7. Days of week on calendar
8. Spelling of LIGHT on boy's paper
9. Eraser on boy's pencil
10. Hair above boy's ear

page 393 • Boy, Do You Look Familiar!